HARRY C. TREXLER LIBRARY

PARENTS FUND
1988 - 1989

MUHLENBERG
COLLEGE

THE ECONOMIC
STRUCTURE AND FAILURE
OF YUGOSLAVIA

THE ECONOMIC STRUCTURE AND FAILURE OF YUGOSLAVIA

James H. Gapinski

Westport, Connecticut
London

Library of Congress Cataloging-in-Publication Data

Gapinski, James H.
　　The economic structure and failure of Yugoslavia / James H.
　Gapinski.
　　　　p.　cm.
　　Includes bibliographical references (p.　　) and index.
　　ISBN 0-275-94600-2 (alk. paper)
　　　1. Yugoslavia—Economic conditions—1945-　2. Yugoslavia—Economic
　policy—1945-　I. Title.
　HC407.G357　1993
　338.9497—dc20　　　93-19091

British Library Cataloguing in Publication Data is available.

Library of Congress Catalog Card Number: 93-19091
ISBN: 0-275-94600-2

First published in 1993

Praeger Publishers, 88 Post Road West, Westport, CT 06881
An imprint of Greenwood Publishing Group, Inc.

Printed in the United States of America

The paper used in this book complies with the
Permanent Paper Standard issued by the National
Information Standards Organization (Z39.48-1984).

10 9 8 7 6 5 4 3 2 1

To Helen and Henry for love,
support, and friendship

Contents

Figures and Tables

TABLES

Preface

This volume is the product of a long journey through time and space. By at least one reckoning, it began in November of 1985 when representatives from Ekonomski Institut Zagreb and Florida State University met in Tallahassee and agreed to sponsor a project to model the Yugoslav macroeconomic system. It ended, with regard to substantive matters at any rate, in January of 1993 as Sarajevo remained under siege and as Czechoslovakia split in two. From the headquarter cities the journey ventured to Amsterdam, crisscrossed Yugoslavia to Dubrovnik, veered to London, headed to New York, and even stretched to a tranquil place known as St. George. During the lengthy passage the various travelers, writing jointly or separately, composed numerous books and journal articles, a doctoral dissertation, a chapter of a second dissertation, and a master's thesis that was judged in a competitive review to be the University's finest. Much was experienced, much was learned, new friends were made, old friends grew older, frustration yielded to satisfaction, and this volume came into being.

By their very nature, extended journeys call upon the services of many. This one was no exception. Data collection, regression running, and other statistical exercises were commendably facilitated by Zoran Anušić and Andrea Mervar, who proved to be much more than research assistants as they offered valuable insights on an almost continual basis. Donald Cooper, Michelle Liddon, and Beverly McNeil chronicled the major events that took place in Yugoslavia during the country's final days and in the aftermath of disintegration. Broadening the inquiry, Michelle then prepared a briefing document on the happenings elsewhere in Eastern Europe.

Comments from colleagues often spell the difference between doubt and conviction, between confusion and understanding, or simply between wrong and right. In this regard thanks go to Ljubiša Adamović, Zvonimir Baletić, Dinko Dubravčić, Stefan Norrbin, and Dragomir Vojnić. Thanks also go to William Laird, Chairman of the Economics Department, for making extra resources available during the critical phases of the volume's development. Special acknowledgment must be given to Borislav Škegro, without whose help nothing would have been accomplished. From revising the national accounts to specifying the model to solving the system, Boro was both a master and a companion. It was unfortunate that war dragged his attention away to other, more pressing concerns, among them the economic performance of a new nation called Croatia.

If the production side of publishing a book is to be something less than an ordeal, it must draw upon the energies of people who hold to high standards and who respect detail. It did. Carol Felton, Karen Hollen, and a talented individual who prefers to remain anonymous deftly processed the words and tables, while Peter Krafft handled the artwork with his customary ease. At Praeger Publishers James Dunton, the editor-in-chief, expedited the decision process and graciously extended the corporate welcome. Copyediting fell to Charles Eberline, who responded to the challenge with care and consistency. Catherine Lyons, the production editor, tenaciously kept everything moving in the same direction to assure prompt completion of the production work.

Fundamental motivation for doing what one does often comes from the family circle and from the generations that lie at different distances beyond the circle. Certainly, heartfelt tributes go to Gerri, Suzie, and Missy; to Nancy; and to Sally and Henry. Tribute also goes to Helen and Henry, but for them it takes the form of a dedication.

1

A Sketch of Facts

It was the best of times, it was the worst of times, it was the age of wisdom, it was the age of foolishness, it was the epoch of belief, it was the epoch of incredulity, it was the season of Light, it was the season of Darkness, it was the spring of hope, it was the winter of despair, we had everything before us, we had nothing before us, we were all going direct to Heaven, we were all going direct the other way.

Charles Dickens
A Tale of Two Cities

Although Dickens composed this passage to describe events that took place some 200 years ago, it applies with equal force to the events surrounding contemporary Yugoslavia. For roughly three decades following World War II, this country of six republics and two autonomous provinces, this country of multiple ethnicities, multiple languages, and multiple religions, this country of 24 million persons, this country whose labor force approximated the population of Michigan and whose size approximated the area of Wyoming enjoyed economic success that some observers characterized as miraculous. Then came the 1980s, when economic success turned into economic failure. The winter of despair set in, and soon thereafter Yugoslavia ceased to exist. The date was June 1991.

Could the failure have been prevented? That question motivates the present volume, whose methodological base is a model of the Yugoslav economic structure that prevailed at the time when remedial action would have been taken. The next few pages sketch historical and

economic facts in the life of the country. Chapter 2 turns to theory
and to the relationship between theory and practice in the case of
Yugoslavia. Chapters 3 and 4 study economic structure, whereas
Chapters 5 and 6 simulate remedial scenarios. Chapter 7 draws
conclusions from a comprehensive program of restructuring, from the
regional makeup of the country, and from the profound changes that
have swept across Eastern Europe.

1.1 A HISTORY THROUGH TITO

Yugoslavia, the Land of the South Slavs, came into being in
December of 1918 by virtue of the Versailles peace arrangement.[1] At
its inception the country was called the Kingdom of the Serbs, Croats,
and Slovenes, a fragmented name that, though changed in 1929 to the
Kingdom of Yugoslavia, was quite appropriate because even from the
start the alliance among the different peoples was an uneasy one.
Croatia and Slovenia had been living under Austro-Hungarian rule.
Serbia, on the other hand, had been ruled by the Turks and exhibited
a contrasting disposition. Moreover, Serbia's first preference was for
the creation of a Greater Serbia, although it eventually did agree to
the "Yugoslav idea." Still, ethnic tensions filled the air until World
War II, when Yugoslavia fell to the Axis powers.
   During the war itself the sparring between the Croats and Serbs
turned ugly. Croatia saw the rise of the fascist Ustashi, the Serbs had
their Chetniks, and as the tragedy of events unfolded, thousands died
in the exchange of gunfire.
   War's end brought a new beginning. Yugoslavia was recast in the
Communist image from the Soviet mold of Stalin, and hence the state
owned the means of production, resources were allocated by detailed
central plans, and the Party stood without political opposition. In
November 1945 the country became known as the Federal People's
Republic of Yugoslavia, a name that would change in April 1963 to
the Socialist Federal Republic of Yugoslavia. With Josip Broz Tito at
the helm, it began to steer its own course. Significant among its early
initiatives was the 1946 Constitution, which, as Figure 1.1 shows,
divided the territory into the six republics Bosnia-Herzegovina,
Croatia, Macedonia, Montenegro, Serbia, and Slovenia. It also
identified two autonomous provinces within Serbia: Kosovo and
Vojvodina. Furthermore, and almost prophetically, it explicitly gave
republics the right to secede.
   Although Yugoslavia was deeply rooted in Stalinism, its relations
with the Soviet Union soured as the months went by. Stalin had
designs on the country, but the country had other ideas. Before

Figure 1.1
Yugoslavia, Its Republics and Autonomous Provinces, and the Capital Cities

long, Stalin's patience wore thin, and in 1948 Yugoslavia was expelled from the Cominform. By 1950 all trade with Eastern Europe had come to a halt.

The split with the Soviets forced the Yugoslavs to reject Stalinism, which they called "etatisam" or "statism," and to search for a new philosophy that would distinguish them from their neighbors. That philosophy turned out to be self-management, wherein capital was owned by society as a whole rather than by the state. In addition, workers managed the socially owned firms consonant with legislated dictates. In a sense, workers acted as partners in the firms, and as such they participated in the decision process.

Self-management doctrine took shape slowly from about 1950, and two of its more important delineators arose somewhat late in the evolutionary cycle. One was the economic reform (or reforms) of 1965; the other, the Constitution of 1974. The goals of reform were to increase the presence of the market in business activity, to decrease the presence of the state in income redistribution, and to streamline foreign trade while strengthening its domestic impact. The means to the first end involved relative prices: They were revised dramatically. Tax reductions were the instrument for achieving the second objective, whereas dinar devaluation and reduced customs duties were directed at the third. But besides these undertakings, the reform made banks accountable to all of their depositors instead of to the state alone. In other words, the banking system gained more independence from the political apparatus, a move intended to improve the operation of the investment mechanism. Along this same line, peasant farmers were allowed to buy equipment and to use bank credits to finance those purchases. Rounding out the reform package was the issuance of a new dinar, one unit being equivalent to 100 old dinars. That is, the decimal point was shifted two places leftward.

The 1974 Constitution, the country's fourth, was voluminous.[2] It proved to be the world's longest constitution, and in keeping with its length, it sought to cover everything from the principles of economic and political systems to the rights of parents in family planning. As regards economics, it strengthened the role of workers in the conduct of firms by ratifying BOALs as the central legal entity of the economy. Each BOAL—Basic Organization of Associated Labor—acted as an independent work unit, groups of which constituted a firm. Furthermore, banks were made responsible to the BOALs. On the political scene, the Constitution eliminated direct elections and reduced the size of the collective Presidency from 23 members to 9, 1 from each republic and province plus ex officio the president of the League of the Communists of Yugoslavia. Leadership of this collective was installed in a position called the president, which rotated from member to member.

On May 4, 1980, Tito died at the age of 87. Following an established line of succession, his position as president of the Republic was passed on to the president of the Presidency, and thus the head-of-state functions continued. Nevertheless, it may be argued that with Tito's death the cohesive force that bound the separate Yugoslav peoples together disappeared (Rusinow, 1977, p. 280; Stanković, 1981, p. 1). In the vacuum that resulted, the deteriorating economic fortunes of the 1980s intensified the general level of tension, and in due course the old animosities again became newsprint material.

1.2 THE FINAL MONTHS AND BEYOND

The final months of Yugoslavia were tumultuous ones.[3] During May 1988 two dozen people went to trial in Bosnia-Herzegovina for the Agrokomerc financial scandal, which destroyed at least one government career and left political chaos in its wake.[4] Also in May the Yugoslav prime minister publicly cast aside demands by Croatia and Slovenia that he resign over a failing economy and instead blamed the poor performance on an antiquated economic system. A few weeks later radical changes were proposed countrywide to foster a market economy based on the profit motive. Significantly, the paradigm being envisioned for Yugoslavia was neither a Soviet-style command apparatus nor the so-called Third Way of self-management; instead, it was capitalism with its axiom that capital be privately owned.

Meanwhile, the province of Kosovo was causing problems in the south. Its ethnic Albanians demanded a greater degree of autonomy, and at the same time the Serbs and Montenegrins there felt persecuted by that majority in a manner reminiscent of the mutual persecution felt by the Croats and Serbs during World War II. Soon protests erupted to press for the removal of Kosovo officials and to decry the acute economic conditions. In response, the Serbian government offered assurance that the Kosovo demonstrations would be brought to an end.

Economic woe likewise set the tone for 1989. Early in that year it precipitated a wave of political resignations across Montenegro, but without much effect. In March the annual inflation rate reached 368 percent, in April it stood at 441 percent, and by midyear it topped 700 percent. Yugoslav currency had eroded to the point where money brokers at the Austrian border were measuring the dinar in cubic meters, and the once-proud and cherished Tito bill of 5,000 dinars was being exchanged in "brick" lots rather than in individual units. By September Slovenia had had enough. In an action that could be interpreted as a retreat behind a provision of the 1946 Yugoslav Constitution, it amended its own constitution to allow secession. Continuing that nationalistic spirit, it championed more autonomy for all republics. As these developments were occurring, annual inflation roared to 1,188 percent, and in November it catapulted to almost 1,900 percent, prompting on December 18 an announcement of a new currency. This "super" dinar moved the decimal point *four* places to the left, twice as far as the decimal relocation implemented by the reform of 1965. Now the Tito was worth less than a dinar.

The year 1990 began dismally as annual inflation raced past 3,000 percent. Violence and death dominated events in Kosovo, and in the north Slovenia's Communist Party severed its ties with the national party, paving the way for free multiparty elections. Held in April, those elections dealt the Slovene Communists a decisive blow while ushering in Demos, a coalition slate, and contributing to the sentiment that "democracy was winning in Yugoslavia." Following Slovenia's lead, Croatia too held elections in April, and again the Communists suffered a solid defeat as the Croatian Democratic Union took power. However, the new government's treatment of the Serb minority in the republic only heightened ethnic friction, and in August armed conflict broke out at Knin in southern Croatia. Aggravating the situation even more, the Serbs in Croatia declared the predominantly Serbian areas of the republic to be autonomous. Predictably, the Croatian government dismissed their October proclamation.

December of 1990 gave witness to two major happenings. Early in the month Serbia took its turn at free elections, but this time the ruling Socialist Party, a reconstituted form of the Communist Party, was soundly endorsed by the voters. Apparently, the people of Serbia were content with the status quo. Expressing this view derisively, Vuk Drašković, leader of the main political opposition, said in defeat:

> On December 9, Serbia voted to decide between Bolshevism and democracy, the past and the future, darkness and light, ruin and salvation, disgrace and honor. Official results show that the citizens voted for bondage, Bolshevism, the past, darkness and disgrace.

As December drew to a close, Serbia initiated an action that absolutely infuriated Slovenia and Croatia. Specifically, its government approved in secret and without legal basis a measure requiring Serbian-controlled banks to issue a massive amount of unbacked currency. In other words, the banks were instructed to run the printing presses, and imagining the consequences that they themselves would have to suffer, Slovenia and Croatia branded the Serbian deed as outright robbery.[5]

The first half of 1991 was heavy with talk as leaders of the various republics frequently met to discuss the country's future. Federation versus confederation versus secession was a chief theme, but little was settled by talk. On June 25, a Tuesday, Slovenia and Croatia resorted to decisive action and declared their independence, a move that spelled the end of Yugoslavia as the modern world knew it.[6] Immediately, the Serbian-led Yugoslav army swept into Slovenia to secure the border posts. Croatia came next a few days later. There the war was intense, and charges of Ustashi and Chetnik brutality again rang out. Furthermore, charges that Belgrade intended to create a Greater Serbia could be heard anew. It was the two world wars all over again. Abroad, the European Community shaped its position and in December agreed to accept the independence of any Yugoslav republic that asked to be recognized. By the middle of January 1992 it had officially recognized Slovenia and Croatia. Proceeding down a now more familiar path, Bosnia-Herzegovina and Macedonia also pressed the Community for recognition, and during the initial days of April Bosnia's request was granted. Only hours later the United States formally recognized Bosnia along with Croatia and Slovenia. These happenings left Serbia (with its autonomous provinces) and Montenegro as the remnants of the Yugoslav federation.

Fascinating sidebars accompanied the domino effect of independence. New flags flew, new currencies appeared, and even the family of athletes took notice. For instance, in July 1992 the International Olympic Committee ruled that Bosnia-Herzegovina could compete at the Barcelona Summer Olympics under its own flag, and Croatia met the US Dream Team in basketball under a banner that replaced the Yugoslav red star by a red-and-white checkered shield, the crest of the old Croat kingdom. Another sidebar regards the suspension of data, but it is more appropriately handled in the next section.

1.3 AN ECONOMIC RECORD

As has already been suggested, when economic fortunes take wing, ethnic animosities fade into muted memory, and regional—synonymously, nationalistic—differences recede into tolerable annoyances. By the same token, when those fortunes plummet, ethnic and nationalistic tensions can build until a combustible mixture is created. This hypothesis easily fits the facts of Yugoslavia, and since its root lies in economics, a close look at some of the economic statistics presented in Table 1.1 might be warranted.

From the prereform period 1952-64 to the post-Constitution half decade 1974-79, social product tripled to 319.4 billion dinars per year. Productivity, which is output per worker, similarly tripled between the two epochs. Investment and consumption followed the Rule of Three as well, the former registering 105.7 billion dinars per year in the half decade, while the latter posted 171.5 billion. Not surprisingly, such abundance meant good news for the household's standard of living. Consumption per capita rose from 3,173 dinars annually to 7,902, and disposable income per capita soared from 3,359 dinars yearly to 9,367. Correspondingly, the real wage almost doubled from 18,448 dinars per worker annually to 33,712. The best of times indeed had trickled down to the households.

Table 1.1
Statistics on the Yugoslav Economic Experience from 1952 to 1988

Series	1952 -64	1965 -73	1974 -79	1980 -88	1984 -88
	Mean Levels				
Social Product	102,699	208,307	319,368	392,486	398,541
Employment	7,375	7,913	8,125	8,229	8,247
Productivity	13,789	26,292	39,278	47,696	48,330
Unemployment	1.8	3.7	7.2	10.5	11.4
Investment	31,351	63,268	105,660	92,017	80,551
Consumption	57,755	115,065	171,456	195,908	195,761
Consumption per Capita	3,173	5,678	7,902	8,538	8,413
Disposable Income	61,181	139,457	203,198	209,217	205,297
Disp. Income per Capita	3,359	6,880	9,367	9,121	8,822
Real Wage	18,448	30,447	33,712	31,787	30,927
Exports	15,262	43,970	64,588	78,196	81,104
Imports	18,559	51,270	87,345	82,452	77,392
Net Exports	-3,297	-7,300	-22,758	-4,256	3,712
	Mean Growth Rates				
Social Product	8.9	5.4	6.3	0.7	0.6
Employment	1.0	0.1	0.5	0.2	0.6
Productivity	7.9	5.3	5.8	0.5	0.8
Investment	11.7	3.6	8.9	-5.7	-4.2
Consumption	7.2	5.4	5.8	0.0	0.5
Consumption per Capita	6.0	4.4	4.8	-0.6	-0.2
Disposable Income	7.9	6.5	4.6	-1.1	-0.2

Table 1.1 (continued)

Series	1952 -64	1965 -73	1974 -79	1980 -88	1984 -88
Disp. Income per Capita	6.7	5.5	3.6	-1.8	-0.8
Real Wage	3.8	5.1	1.0	-2.3	-1.1
Money Wage	10.3	19.0	18.5	70.5	102.3
Social Product Deflator	7.0	13.4	18.1	75.4	106.9
CPI	6.4	15.5	18.1	74.7	106.1
Exchange Rate	0.0	26.7	2.7	79.8	103.7
Exports	12.2	9.2	3.0	2.8	5.8
Imports	10.7	9.8	6.8	-2.1	3.8

Source: The data bank developed at Ekonomski Institut Zagreb in conjunction with research jointly funded by that institution and Florida State University. Included among its authorities are the publications *Statistički Godišnjak Jugoslavije* and *Bilten Narodne Banke Jugoslavije*.

Notes: Measurement units for the level entries differ across series. Social product, investment, consumption, disposable income, exports, imports, and net exports are all expressed in millions of 1972 dinars. Employment is denominated in thousands of persons; productivity, in 1972 dinars per worker; and unemployment, in percentages. Moreover, both per capita variables and the real wage are gauged by 1972 dinars. As regards the growth rates, all are percentages. For them, however, the first epoch begins in 1953, not 1952, due to the loss of the initial observation. The exchange rate refers to dinars per US dollar.

Perhaps these achievements can be seen more clearly in terms of growth rates. During the years 1952-64 social product grew at a phenomenal rate of 8.9 percent per annum, a rate whose vigor, if not magnitude, persisted into the next two epochs. Productivity grew first at 7.9 percent annually and then sequentially at 5.3 percent and 5.8 percent. According to the accounts given by Maddison (1987, p. 650) and Griliches (1988, p. 10), such a sustained pace was truly remarkable. Investment and consumption repeated the pattern of strong growth as they generated respective rates of 8.9 percent and 5.8 percent in the 1974-79 period. Consumption per capita averaged a growth rate of 5.0 percent over the three epochs; yet its success was surpassed by the 5.2 percent average for disposable income per capita.

Of course, not all statistics through 1979 were favorable. For instance, the unemployment rate quadrupled from 1.8 percent to 7.2 percent, the consumer price index (CPI) inflation rate almost tripled to 18.1 percent yearly in the same time frame, and imports continually outstripped exports. Still, it must be said that Yugoslavia enjoyed enviable economic fortune through the 1970s.

Then the worst of times took hold. From 1980 to 1988 social product, whose annual growth rates had been averaging over 5.0 percent, stagnated. Productivity too slowed to a near halt, while investment actually fell at an average annual rate of 5.7 percent. Moreover, the standard-of-living measures all declined: consumption per capita at 0.6 percent per year, disposable income per capita at 1.8 percent, and the real wage at 2.3 percent. What did increase were unemployment and prices. Unemployment hit double digits, 10.5 percent, as annual CPI inflation quadrupled from 18.1 percent to 74.7 percent. Helping to keep Yugoslav products competitive in foreign markets, the dinar depreciated by 79.8 percent.

The second half of the 1980-88 epoch, the period 1984-88, was even harsher for unemployment, inflation, and dinar depreciation. But compared with what was to come, it represented only the initial snow of winter; the blizzard struck in 1989. As Table 1.2 indicates, unemployment crept upward to 13.1 percent despite the tradition of employment tenure, a trademark of worker self-management under the soft-budget constraint promoted by a government that was seen as a benevolent uncle.[7] Simultaneously, annual inflation headed into four-digit numbers, reaching 2,719 percent in December. Dinar depreciation followed suit.

January of 1990 opened the door to more of the same or even worse. Unemployment rose to 13.3 percent while inflation jumped to 3,282 percent, calling to mind the classic cases of hyperinflation studied by Cagan (1956, pp. 25-27). Dinar depreciation continued along a parallel path, but now the economic decay spread to output. Although

Table 1.2
Economic Conditions Expressed as Rates or as Rates of Change for Yugoslavia's Final Months

Month or Mean	Index of Industrial Production			Unemployment	CPI	Money	Exchange Rate
	Total	Equipment	Consumables				
1989							
Jan	3.9	3.0	6.9	12.5	276.3	229.5	347.1
Feb	0.9	4.0	-1.9	12.5	328.6	234.5	428.6
Mar	2.9	9.4	1.9	12.5	367.9	233.1	536.4
Apr	3.9	11.8	1.0	12.5	440.8	287.3	633.3
May	3.9	9.5	2.9	12.4	544.8	318.1	642.9
Jun	2.9	8.4	0.9	12.3	593.8	387.0	600.0
Jul	0.0	6.5	-1.9	12.5	759.7	499.6	825.0
Aug	1.0	11.6	3.9	12.6	871.4	578.4	1,000.0
Sep	-1.9	-2.0	1.9	12.7	1,187.5	736.5	900.0
Oct	1.0	-1.0	6.0	12.9	1,529.2	956.6	1,200.0
Nov	2.0	-4.1	6.1	13.1	1,892.1	1,227.8	2,100.0
Dec	-8.3	-20.7	-5.7	13.1	2,719.2	1,933.2	1,800.0
Mean	1.0	3.0	1.8	12.6	959.3	635.1	917.8
1990							
Jan	-4.7	-11.8	-2.8	13.3	3,282.4	2,275.8	1,909.5
Feb	-7.4	-14.4	-3.8	13.3	3,079.2	2,298.3	1,557.6
Mar	-9.3	-17.1	-7.5	13.4	2,732.2	2,365.9	1,205.6
Apr	-13.2	-22.1	-11.7	13.4	2,269.3	2,122.4	958.4
May	-15.0	-26.0	-13.2	13.4	1,867.8	2,016.9	725.2
Jun	-15.9	-26.2	-12.3	13.4	1,411.7	1,743.7	601.9
Jul	-8.7	-10.1	-2.9	13.6	1,044.5	1,302.0	349.9
Aug	-11.3	-23.6	-7.5	13.8	811.4	1,093.5	228.3

Table 1.2 (continued)

Month or Mean	Index of Industrial Production			Unemploy-ment	CPI	Money	Exchange Rate
	Total	Equipment	Consumables				
Sep	−12.5	−24.5	−8.6	14.0	551.2	853.6	228.6
Oct	−6.7	−17.5	−1.9	14.3	367.6	548.1	112.7
Nov	−10.6	−21.3	−5.8	14.5	241.8	350.7	4.2
Dec	−16.2	−25.0	−8.0	14.6	122.9	148.4	6.6
Mean	−11.0	−20.0	−7.1	13.8	1,481.8	1,426.6	657.4
1991							
Jan	−17.6	−34.4	−13.2	14.9	69.9	110.5	13.5
Feb	−21.0	−32.6	−15.8	15.0	68.0	105.5	15.4
Mar	−22.4	−34.5	−18.2	15.3	66.2	99.7	29.0
Apr	−12.0	−22.2	−6.6	15.5	66.7	84.7	93.6
May	−11.0	−20.8	−5.4	15.7	84.2	78.7	90.4
Jun	−14.4	−31.6	−8.6	15.8	101.7	72.1	100.1
Jul	−13.8	−27.0	−8.0	16.1	107.6	74.6	101.8
Mean	−16.0	−29.0	−10.8	15.5	80.6	89.4	63.4

Source: Organization for Economic Cooperation and Development, *Main Economic Indicators*, various issues.

Notes: Money refers to the M1 measure, and the exchange rate, to dinars per US dollar. The production series come from seasonally adjusted data. The tabular entries themselves are all percentages. Apart from those for unemployment, they represent the annual rate of change as determined from the corresponding month of the previous year; more precisely, the rate for series X equals $100 \cdot (X/X_{-12} - 1)$. The unemployment rate is obtained by dividing the unemployment level by 9,513.8, the labor supply (in thousands) for 1988. Labor supply figures beyond 1988 are not available.

Figure 1.2
Annual Rates of CPI Inflation and Money Growth

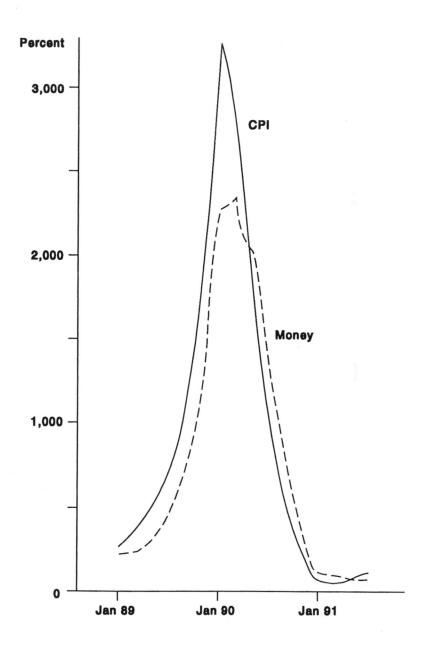

production had managed to expand on balance during 1989, it now dropped by annual rates as large as 16.2 percent. Machine production declined by a staggering 26.2 percent in June, and consumables fell 13.2 percent in May. Output decreased sharply, unemployment increased resolutely, inflation topped 3,000 percent, and the dinar depreciated commensurately. In short, 1990 was a very bad year.

The year 1991 provided some relief from inflation, which retreated to triple or even double digits. Nevertheless, unemployment continued to drift upward, and output continued to slide. In fact, output's retrenchment in March was unquestionably most pronounced: 22.4 percent. Similarly, the cuts in equipment production and consumables production reached record levels in that month, 34.5 percent and 18.2 percent, respectively. The Yugoslavia that had attained great heights in decades past was now presiding over its own economic failure and its own demise. Necessarily and symbolically, data on the country ceased to exist through the Organization for Economic Cooperation and Development (OECD) after July 1991.

1.4 INFLATION AND MONEY GROWTH

Before the discussion turns to questions of theory and practice in Yugoslavia, a final stroke in this sketch of facts deserves mention. Cagan (1956, pp. 25-27, 65-66, 91) observed for hyperinflation that the rate of inflation varies directly with the rate of money growth and that the quantity of real balances declines. As Table 1.2 indicates, both conditions held during Yugoslavia's last months. That inflation and money growth moved together is also shown in Figure 1.2. Furthermore, for the many months where the inflation line lies above the money-expansion line, the chart openly implies a decline in real balances. These features will prove to be useful in explaining Yugoslav price inflation in Chapter 4.

NOTES

1. Besides relying on the authorities cited explicitly, this section appeals to the contributions by Hamilton (1968, p. 9), Ra'anan (1977, pp. 2-3, 11), Rusinow (1977, pp. 1-42, 172-83, 308-42), Lydall (1984, pp. 49-108; 1989, p. 1), and Gapinski, Škegro, and Zuehlke (1989b, pp. 3-46.)
2. Between the reform of 1965 and the Constitution of 1974, another flare-up between the Croats and Serbs occurred. In 1971 Croatia lashed out against what it felt was the long-standing domina-

tion of Yugoslavia by Serbia. It protested that republic's grip on the military, the restrictions imposed on religious groups, and economic exploitation. Tito did not take kindly to the burst of Croatian nationalism and purged the Croatian Communist Party of nationalist sympathizers. Ra'anan (1977, pp. 27-35) discussed the episode.

3. Information for this section comes primarily from the *New York Times* as well as from the Organization for Economic Cooperation and Development (*Main Economic Indicators*, December 1991, p. 170, fn. 3) and Glenny (1992, pp. 30-35).

4. Amplification of the Agrokomerc matter appears in Section 2.3.3.

5. There are two sides to every story. The Serbian logic behind the event maintained that the new money was needed to replace the revenues lost from customs and to relieve an added burden in financing the federation and the less developed areas.

6. This writer vividly recalls his visit to Zagreb during the week before Croatia's declaration of independence. As had become a rule through the years, the stay was a busy one that mixed business with pleasure, but on Thursday, June 20, the day preceding departure for Zürich, two incidents of conflicting impressions occurred. Early that day the writer journeyed with Borislav Škegro and Andrea Mervar, their joint research assistant, into Slovenia for an afternoon at picturesque Lake Bled. Traveling down the two-lane road that connected Zagreb, Croatia's capital city, with Ljubljana, Slovenia's capital, the trio came upon a construction crew erecting what looked like—to an American anyway—a lemonade stand. It soon became evident, however, that the travelers had crossed the border between Croatia and Slovenia and that what was being built was a Checkpoint Charlie. Independence surely was close at hand. Yet that evening the opposite seemed to be true. As the final hours of Thursday approached, the writer decided to walk from his Zagreb apartment at Ekonomski Fakultet to the newly renamed Jelačić Square, a large gathering spot that had undergone first-rate renovation. As usual, the Times Square neon flashed advertising messages while people sat, laughed, and drank. In other words, life went on as though the next week was to be the same as any other.

7. As described by Kornai (1979, pp. 806-9), an avuncular disposition of the state goes hand in hand with soft-budget constraints—whereby firms can cover costs by means other than revenues alone—and with employment tenure. Soft budgets and employment tenure are treated in Sections 2.3.3 and 3.5.

2

Theory and Practice

Reducing an economy to a set of mathematical expressions requires a theory about the way in which the economy is put together. The theory should fit the facts. Whether it does in the case of Yugoslavia is the subject of the present chapter, which begins with a general discussion of the limits to theory. As part of that discussion, Section 2.1 refers to the use of simplifying assumptions and to the need for functional-form assumptions. It also distinguishes optimizing behavior from satisficing conduct. Section 2.2 reviews Illyrian theory, a decidedly nontraditional view of economic structure. It derives principal implications of the theory, compares them with the properties of standard Western logic, and suggests that they bear little resemblance to the facts.

Section 2.3 goes beyond Illyrian theory to review efforts to rectify its strange conclusions. It ventures back into traditional arguments and forward into special characteristics. In addition, it notes the similarities between a Yugoslav business establishment and a Western nonprofit company; it also affirms the reasonableness of satisficing. Section 2.4 explains how traditional dogma and satisficing doctrine converge to provide the basis for model building. It elaborates Yugoslav orthodoxy and follows that presentation with a discussion of heterodoxy. Rational expectations come next. A case against the hypothesis is offered, and an alternative hypothesis known as adaptive rationality is examined. Afterward attention turns to Ricardian equivalence, but David Ricardo's own words written more than a century and a half ago combine with contemporary research to dismiss that idea. Section 2.5 then completes the chapter by bringing together the implications of Yugoslav theory and practice for the modeling effort.

2.1 LIMITS TO THEORY

Economic relationships are complex. Consumers relate to consumers, firms relate to firms, and economies relate to economies. Moreover, there are numerous cross-relationships such as consumers to firms or firms to economies. This complexity is only magnified by the synergistic involvement that the economic order has with the political system and the social setup. Economic events change political nuances and social patterns, and those induced changes in turn impact economic events (Heilbroner, 1970, pp. 89-90). Everything seems to affect everything else.

To advance the understanding of these convoluted relationships, economic theory divides them into small segments and subjects them to simplifying assumptions. The economy is stripped away from the surrounding political and social environment within which it operates and is examined in a clinical vacuum abhorrent to both the radical camp and the Virginia school (Olson and Clague, 1971, pp. 757-58). Consumers are taken to one side and are investigated under the assumption that they maximize utility. Firms are taken to another side and are presumed to maximize profit or to minimize cost. Whole economies are reduced to basic characteristics and are presumed to worry about a small handful of problems like inflation, unemployment, and trade flows.

Some of the assumptions imposed have an intuitive claim to validity. That an individual receives less satisfaction from a twelfth pair of shoes than from the first, that output expands when labor expands, that real-wage movements vary with labor-market conditions, and that international trade responds to currency depreciation are notions that many can embrace and even champion. Other notions have less intuitive appeal, such as the claim that uncertainty alters the mix of saving rather than the level of saving, that—noise aside—individuals always have accurate inflation expectations, that lowering tax rates increases tax collections, or that elected officials put economics before politics.

But perhaps assumptions should not be judged one at a time. Perhaps the true test of assumptions and the theory that houses them is whether they generate implications that hold empirically. In Friedman's (1953, p. 41) words:

> A theory cannot be tested by comparing its "assumptions" directly with "reality." Indeed, there is no meaningful way in which this can be done. Complete "realism" is clearly unattainable, and the question whether a theory is realistic "enough" can be settled only by seeing whether it yields

predictions that are good enough for the purpose in hand or that are better than predictions from alternative theories.

Heilbroner (1970, p. 81) echoed this sentiment when he observed that the purpose of economics is to further an understanding of the economic order. To the extent that the science does further understanding, it is relevant no matter how abstract or farfetched it may appear. By this ends-justify-the-means logic, the litmus test of theory lies in performance. Posed simply, does it work?

To work, theory often needs a particular helping hand. For instance, the static interpretation of the firm maintains that a profit-maximizing enterprise sets capital stock in proportion to the level of output. But which output? Actual or permanent? Permanent sounds about right, but then how does one quantify permanent? By a distributed lag? But then which one? The rate of change in money wage depends upon the inflation rate, inter alia. But which inflation rate? The expected rate is the sensible choice, despite theory's hesitancy on the point. Theory is likewise hesitant on functional form, as questions of linearity, log linearity, or other nonlinearity often remain beyond its grasp. The frequent use of proxies in empirical analysis provides additional testimony on the help that theory needs to work.

On occasion the helping hands blur theoretical distinctions. With an assist from a distributed lag, consumption based on the longsighted permanent-income hypothesis leads to a formulation wherein current consumption depends upon current disposable income and consumption lagged one period. Yet this result is virtually identical to the conclusion reached from shortsightedness, where because of uncertainty consumers jettison their intertemporal utility function in favor of a temporally myopic one. In lending a hand, assumptions may actually distort the character of the theory and create similarities or differences where none exist.

On other occasions the helping hands unwittingly become the center of debate. Attention turns to minute matters, quantitative techniques spring up to study them, and issues of substance fall by the wayside. Sometimes technique invites more technique and in the shuffle crowds the substantive issues onto the wayside. When treated as an end in itself, technique stifles theory rather than stimulates it.

To reach the heart of an economic issue, theory slices away many of the appendages of reality. It blinds itself to many intricacies to enable it to see the fundamental mechanisms more clearly. Succinctly, it places limits on itself. It chooses to ignore, or at least to downplay, the nexus among the economy, the polity, and the society. In what it chooses to consider, it encounters limits that are finessed by resorting to assumptions that have more or less intuitive appeal and that may be more or less successful in penetrating and advancing issues. During good times this simplifying process may be calmly regarded as yielding a reasonable representation of the relevant reality. However, in bad times confusion rules, perceptions waver, and previously solid assumptions crumble. Correspondingly, so does the validity of theory (Heilbroner, 1970, p. 87).

Perhaps theory is asked to do too much given the complexity of economic reality. Because of uncertainty, noninformation, misinformation, and bureaucratic red tape, entrepreneurs may elect to earn a satisfactory profit rather than the maximum profit. To them, "good enough" may be the standard of success. Households may elect to consume at some habitual level rather than at the utility maximum level, and workers may elect to watch their real wage fall rather than to protect it from inflationary policy. In other words, because of the prevalence of uncertainty and the deficiencies of information, economic agents might satisfice rather than optimize.

It was Nobel Laureate Herbert Simon (1957, pp. 198-99, 204-5) who initiated that argument. At its basis lies the principle of bounded rationality, which states that

> the capacity of the human mind for formulating and solving complex problems is very small compared with the size of the problems whose solution is required for objectively rational behavior in the real world—or even for a reasonable approximation to such objective rationality.

Individuals have limited knowledge, limited foresight, limited skill, and limited time, and accordingly they seek solutions that are satisfactory as opposed to optimal. Bounded rationality and satisficing go hand in hand, and, to Simon, explain economic behavior. If they do, then the propositions of optimization theory can hold only as an approximation, or they might not hold at all.

2.2 ILLYRIAN THEORY

It would be a formidable challenge to find a greater disparity between optimization theory and actual practice than that which exists between Illyria and Yugoslavia.[1] Introduced by Ward (1958) to explain economic conditions under worker self-management, Illyrian theory falls short of the mark. In fact, it falls so short that it prompted one scholar to compose a piece entitled "Illyrian Theories in Quest of Application."[2]

In Illyria workers wear two hats. They are indeed workers, but they also are managers. In that latter capacity they strive to maximize income per worker y, which can be written as

$$y = (pQ - rK_o)/L. \tag{2.1}$$

Q denotes the quantity of output, while p denotes its parametric price. K_o is the fixed stock of capital available to the firm. This stock, which belongs not to the firm itself but rather to society as a whole, involves a parametric cost r per machine. L signifies the quantity of labor. Linking inputs L and K_o to output Q is a production function $Q = Q(L, K_o)$ that has the usual properties. Specifically, with the subscript indicating the appropriate partial derivative, $Q_L > 0$ and $Q_{LL} < 0$ for $0 < L < \infty$. Moreover, $Q(0, K_o) = 0$, $Q(\infty, K_o) = \infty$, $Q_L = \infty$ at $L = 0$, and $Q_L = 0$ at $L = \infty$.[3]

Differentiating y with respect to L subject to the production function yields

$$y_L = \frac{p}{L} \left[\left(Q_L - \frac{Q}{L} \right) + \frac{r}{p}\frac{K_o}{L} \right], \tag{2.2}$$

which when set to zero leaves

$$pQ_L = y. \tag{2.3}$$

To maximize income per worker, the labor-managed firm should hire labor to the point where the value of the marginal product pQ_L equals unit labor cost. Thus interpreted, this first-order condition is more than vaguely similar to the first-order condition of a Western entrepreneurial firm. However, as will be seen, the similarity is only skin deep.

In order to make the discussion more pointed without loss of much generality, the production function might be specified as the Cobb-Douglas

$$Q = \gamma L^\alpha K^\beta, \tag{2.4}$$

which satisfies all of the aforementioned properties. Then from equation (2.3) the labor input that maximizes income per worker becomes

$$L^* = \left[\frac{1}{\gamma} \left(\frac{1}{1-\alpha} \right) \left(\frac{r}{p} \right) K_o^{1-\beta} \right]^{1/\alpha} , \tag{2.5}$$

and the corresponding output level becomes

$$Q^* = \left(\frac{1}{1-\alpha} \right) \left(\frac{r}{p} \right) K_o . \tag{2.6}$$

It is at this juncture that Illyrian theory begins to crack; calculus delivers the blows.

First, $\partial L^*/\partial p < 0$ and $\partial Q^*/\partial p < 0$. As the price of output increases, the labor-managed firm *reduces* the quantity of labor to award each surviving partner a greater share of the proceeds. As labor contracts, so does output, and therefore the firm's supply curve has a *negative* slope. Second, $\partial L^*/\partial r > 0$ and $\partial Q^*/\partial r > 0$. Increasing the cost of capital *increases* the size of the work force as worker-managers spread the extra cost among a larger number of participants to lighten the burden borne by any one person. Consonantly, output rises. Third, $\partial L^*/\partial \gamma < 0$ and $\partial Q^*/\partial \gamma = 0$. Technological progress *reduces* the work force again to provide a greater dividend to the remaining partners. Output *remains unchanged*, however. This last implication can be observed more clearly in terms of the total derivative, namely,

$$dQ/d\gamma = Q_\gamma + Q_L dL/d\gamma ,$$

$$dQ/d\gamma = L^\alpha K_o^\beta - L^\alpha K_o^\beta = 0 .$$

Put verbally, technical progress shifts the production function upward, but at the same time it prompts a leftward movement along the function due to its depressing effect on employment. Under the Cobb-Douglas, these two effects exactly cancel.[4]

In its implications Illyrian theory is hardly Western. The Western firm maximizes profit Π, which may be expressed as

$$\Pi = pQ - wL - rK_o , \tag{2.7}$$

w representing the parametric money wage. Optimization soon produces

$$pQ_L = w , \tag{2.8}$$

$$L^* = \left[\gamma\alpha \left(\frac{p}{w} \right) K_o^{\beta} \right]^{1/(1-\alpha)}, \tag{2.9}$$

$$Q^* = \left[\gamma \left(\alpha\frac{p}{w} \right)^{\alpha} K_o^{\beta} \right]^{1/(1-\alpha)} \tag{2.10}$$

Here $\partial L^*/\partial p > 0$ and $\partial Q^*/\partial p > 0$, meaning that a price increase drives employment and output upward and that the firm has a positively sloped supply curve. Since earnings per worker w are fixed, workers cannot gain individually if the employment roster shrinks, and since the entrepreneur makes the decisions, the roster instead expands to improve the entrepreneur's own income. In regard to the effect of capital cost r, $\partial L^*/\partial r = 0$ and $\partial Q^*/\partial r = 0$. Increased r implies increased "fixed cost," whose impact on entrepreneurial income cannot be softened by adjusting the labor input. As a result, the optimal input and output levels remain unchanged. Finally, $\partial L^*/\partial\gamma > 0$ and $\partial Q^*/\partial\gamma > 0$. Technological progress increases the marginal productivity of workers and improves the income potential of the entrepreneur. Taking advantage of that new potential, the entrepreneur expands employment and output. It may be apparent, then, that the sharp differences between the reactions of the Illyrian firm and its entrepreneurial twin are explainable in terms of whose income is being maximized and who controls the maximization process. In an Illyrian firm the worker's income is maximized, and the workers control the process. In an entrepreneurial firm the entrepreneur's income is maximized, and the entrepreneur controls the process.

A visual account of Illyrian behavior appears in Figure 2.1. The upper panel uses the straight line $pQ = yL + rK_o$ to depict income per worker y. Derived from equation (2.1), that line illustrates y as its slope. Curve $pQ(L,K_o)$ depicts revenue as a scalar transformation of the Cobb-Douglas. According to the two solid loci, maximizing y subject to the production function yields point A and the labor input L^*_A. Raising price pivots both lines counterclockwise to the positions marked by large dashes. The optimum switches from point A to point B, the labor input falls to L^*_B, and from equation (2.4) output falls too. The supply curve is negatively sloped. Raising capital cost r boosts the rK_o intercept of line $pQ = yL + rK_o$ and, as the short dashes tell, moves the optimum from A to C. The labor input rises from L^*_A to L^*_C, and by equation (2.4) output rises as well. The technical-progress scenario graphs like the price-increase sequence.

Figure 2.1
Employment Responses by the Illyrian Firm

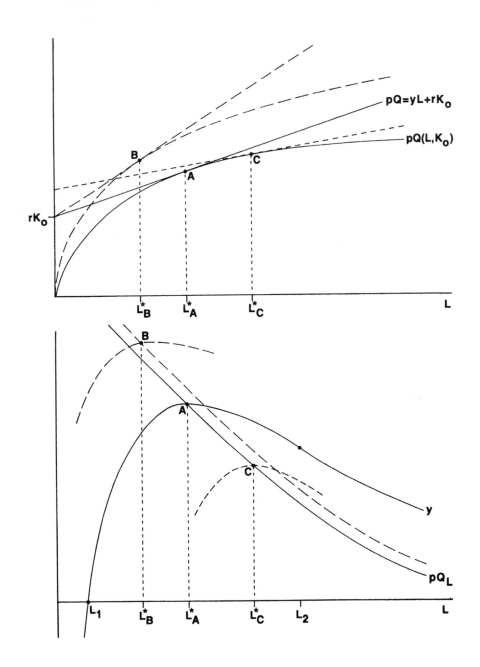

The lower panel of Figure 2.1 sketches y directly.   Under Cobb-Douglas conditions it is easy to show that y = 0 at

$$L_1 = \left[\frac{1}{\gamma} \left(\frac{r}{p} \right) K_o^{1-\beta} \right]^{1/\alpha}$$

and that an inflection point occurs at

$$L_2 = \left[\frac{1}{\gamma} \left(\frac{1}{1-\alpha/2} \right) \left(\frac{1}{1-\alpha} \right) \left(\frac{r}{p} \right) K_o^{1-\beta} \right]^{1/\alpha}$$

By equation (2.5) L_1 and L_2 bracket L^*, which maximizes y. From expression (2.3), that maximum requires a reference to pQ_L, and hence the pQ_L curve is illustrated as well. A few additional calculations reveal that $y_L \gtrless 0$ as $pQ_L \gtrless y$. That is, y rises when it lies below pQ_L, attains a maximum when it equals pQ_L, and falls when it lies above pQ_L. The economic content of this pattern should not be lost. For a new hire to improve the income positions of existing workers, that individual must augment revenue by more than the prevailing income. Otherwise, the hire would force incomes to erode.

A price increase pivots the y curve counterclockwise and simultaneously shifts the marginal revenue line upward. As the large dashes again show, the optimum swings from point A to point B, labor declines to L^*_B, and output declines. Raising capital cost r rotates the y schedule clockwise to the position marked by the short dashes. Since the marginal revenue curve now remains stationary, the optimum moves from A to C, and L^*_C obtains. Raising technology's γ displaces the y and marginal revenue curves in price-increase fashion.

Other implications of Illyrian theory are just around the corner. Since the supply curve has a negative slope, a rightward shift in the demand curve raises price, but it causes quantity to fall.   More demand means less supply, and the price surge associated with the excess demand fails to attract the requisite additional resources. Figure 2.2 graphs the situation. With the demand curve shifting from the solid locus to the dashed one, price rises from p_A to p_B while quantity falls from Q_A to Q_B. Resources are driven away from, not toward, products for which demand increases.

The policy implications from Figure 2.2 are equally strange. To raise output and employment and therefore to reduce unemployment, commodity demand must be reduced. Policy makers would be obliged to *raise* taxes, *cut* government expenditures, or *reduce* money growth (Meade, 1972, p. 415; Horvat, 1986, p. 10). Raising taxes, cutting

Figure 2.2
Illyrian Price and Quantity Adjustments to a Shift in Demand

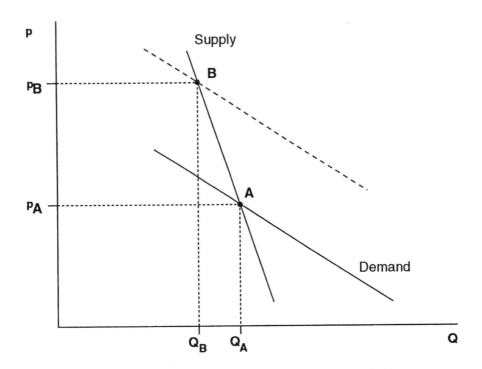

expenditures, or reducing money growth in an unemployment fight makes complete sense in the Illyrian context. However, those same strategies make complete nonsense in the traditional Keynesian context, and consequently, from a prescriptive standpoint, Illyrian theory can be seen as Keynesian theory in reverse.

2.3 BEYOND ILLYRIAN THEORY

Interpreted charitably, the conclusions of Illyrian theory are intriguing; described more frankly in the words of Vanek (1972, p. 259) and Horvat (1986, p. 9), they are absurd. Domar (1966, p. 742) and Dubravčić (1988, p. 7) summed up the theory as unrealistic, and Horvat (1986, p. 11) underscored that thought by sardonically remarking that if something is wrong, it is not the theory but the reality.

2.3.1 Curiosa Resolved

Illyrian theory simply does not fit the facts of worker self-management. For instance, the notion of worker dismissals on which the negatively sloped supply curve rests fails to recognize that under self-management workers are partners in the enterprise. They have membership rights, and as Domar (1966, p. 742), Meade (1972, p. 421), and Bonin and Putterman (1987, p. 23) observed, they cannot be terminated easily. Their employment is virtually tenured. Robinson (1967, p. 222) stressed such group solidarity by asking the insightful question of how workers would choose who is to become unemployed. Vanek (1972, pp. 259-60) took the issue a step further by reasoning that an increased price would hardly prompt workers to fire mates for financial gain, as they would have already gained from the price increase itself. Vanek (1972, pp. 259, 260, 263, 265, 266) concluded that the commodity supply curve is vertical, not negatively sloped. Steinherr and Thisse (1979a; 1979b) reached the same conclusion by a more formal route. They argued that the objective function postulated by Ward is too narrow because it ignores the risk that some workers may lose their jobs. Allowing for this prospect and proceeding with the optimization, they concluded that the level of employment remains unchanged when market conditions improve. Again, the commodity supply curve is vertical.

An even stronger proposition was advanced by Domar (1966, pp. 742-47): The commodity supply curve is positively sloped. What the Wardian analysis misses, said Domar, is the labor supply curve facing the self-managed firm. Workers may have various opportunities for employment, and they surely have an opportunity for leisure. Hence the firm's labor supply curve may assume the usual positive slope. The firm's y schedule may be understood as the labor demand curve, and its interaction with the supply curve determines the firm's operating position.

Figure 2.3 illustrates. There Ls depicts the labor supply curve, while the y and pQ_L curves reproduce in scale-adjusted fashion the corresponding lines presented in the lower panel of Figure 2.1. A price boost shifts the y curve upward from the solid locus to the long-dash contour. As indicated earlier, Wardian economics claims that the operating position shifts from point A to point B, and in the process the labor input declines from L^*_A to L^*_B. By contrast, Domar envisioned that the operating position shifts from point D to point E as the additional demand for labor elicits an increase in supply. Thus employment expands from L_D to L_E. Concomitantly, output expands, giving the commodity supply curve a positive slope. Expressed in terms of the previous mathematics, $\partial Q^*/\partial p > 0$.

Figure 2.3
Employment Responses in the Absence of and Presence of a Labor-Supply Schedule

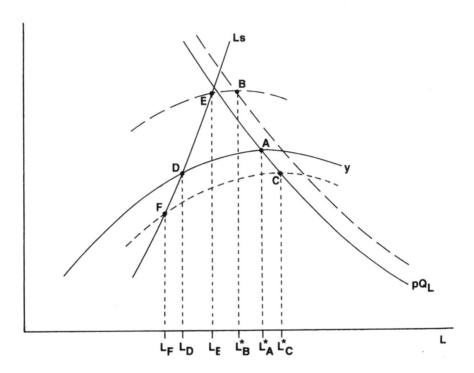

What about the effect of increased capital cost? Such a cost increase drives the y curve downward from the solid contour to the short-dash one. Although Ward imagined that the operating position drops from A to C and employment rises from L^*_A to L^*_C, Domar saw the responses going the other way. More precisely, the firm shifts from D to F, and employment falls from L_D to L_F. Similarly, output falls. Mathematically, $\partial Q^*/\partial r < 0$.

Illyrian curiosa vanish in the shadow of a Domar labor-supply schedule, and with them disappear the odd policy prescriptions. Now to stimulate output and employment and to moderate unemployment, policy makers should reduce taxes, boost government expenditures, or quicken money growth. With Domar's supply curve, theory takes a giant leap back into orthodoxy.

As Figure 2.3 shows by points F, D, and E, Domar anticipated a positive relationship between y and L. Horvat (1986, pp. 16-17) did too but for a different reason, namely, technological progress. In his view technology improves fast enough to shift the production function upward and to the right, thereby enabling L to increase along with y. In the process the Illyrian perversions expire.

Returning to propositions advanced by Steinherr and Thisse (1979a; 1979b), Miyazaki and Neary (1983) argued that workers are concerned about job security. Now, however, this concern leads to a positively sloped commodity supply curve, not merely a vertical one.

Miyazaki and Neary decomposed $\partial L^*/\partial p$, the Wardian total effect of price on employment, into a pure-price effect and a fixed-cost effect, the latter being expressed as $- Q \partial L^*/\partial(rK_o)$ with p being held constant. As Figure 2.1 depicts, Illyrian theory makes $\partial L^*/\partial(rK_o)$ positive. Consequently, the fixed-cost effect becomes negative, and by swamping the positive pure-price effect, it makes $\partial L^*/\partial p$ negative. The trouble, then, arises because $\partial L^*/\partial(rK_o) > 0$.

But if workers are worried about layoffs, then it is not appropriate to assert that they simply seek to maximize income per worker, y in equation (2.1). More appropriate, said Miyazaki and Neary, is the maximization of mean utility, which may be written as

$$V = (L/N)u(y) + (1 - L/N)u(k). \qquad (2.11)$$

Symbol u represents a well-behaved utility function, N denotes the membership size (maximum employment) of the firm, and k signifies the reservation wage income. Since $0 \le L \le N$, V must be a convex combination of the utility levels u(y) and u(k) and must stand between them.

For per-worker income levels above the reservation level, $y > k$, workers prefer employment to layoff. Accordingly, a reduction in fixed cost rK_o releases "funds" that can be used to increase employment, and since u(y) > u(k) in equation (2.11), V must rise with the increased L. Lowering the burden of fixed cost stimulates employment and, contrary to Illyrian theory, makes $\partial L^*/\partial(rK_o) < 0$. It follows that the total effect $\partial L^*/\partial p$ must be positive. However, for $y < k$, workers prefer layoff to employment, and the employment that does occur occurs only to enable the self-managed firm to satisfy its capital-cost obligations. In this situation u(y) < u(k), and a lowering of capital cost rK_o induces L to fall in order to increase V. Thus $\partial L^*/\partial(rK_o) > 0$, and the Illyrian oddity persists. Nevertheless, it persists only in the extreme situation where the firm cannot pay workers a wage that covers their reservation wage.

The entire tale is told in Figure 2.4. There Q_N represents commodity supply when all N partners in the self-managed firm are working, and p_k symbolizes the price that corresponds to the reservation wage income k; that is, $y \gtrless k$ as $p \gtrless p_k$. By Figure 2.4 Illyrian perversion is

Figure 2.4
Commodity Supply Given Worker Concern about Layoff

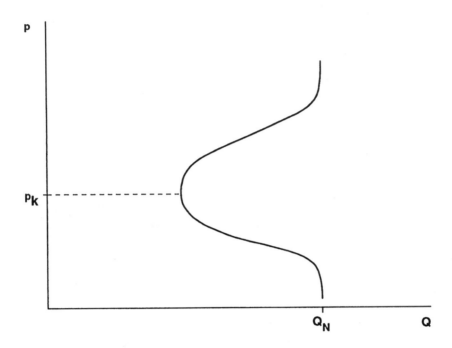

possible only in the special case where $p < p_k$. Actually, even this special case disappears if in Meade (1972, p. 424) fashion the firm compensates dismissed workers. Then allowing the firm to secure temporary hires when its employment maximum is reached tilts the vertical portion of the curve and yields a commodity supply curve that is positively sloped everywhere. Theory takes another giant leap back into orthodoxy.

In portraying the commodity supply curve as negatively sloped, Illyrian theory misses the reality of Yugoslav economic life. It also misses two other aspects of that reality, namely, the effort-incentive structure and the soft-budget constraint.

2.3.2 Effort Disincentives

One of the extolled virtues of self-management is that it brings with it strong effort incentives. Laborers work for themselves rather than for management, and hence the conflicts and tensions that characterize Western labor-management relations do not arise. Instead, cooperation and congeniality rule, stimulating effort and productivity. This sanguine view of Vanek (1970, pp. 244, 247) and Horvat (1986, p. 14) seems reasonable because, as Gapinski, Škegro, and Zuehlke (1989b, p. 40) observed, under self-management workers have a say in all decisions concerning production, investment, and income distribution. In other words, they enjoy an intense form of what Rapping (1988, p. 60) called responsible autonomy, a system of participation that gives employees status and responsibility for the purpose of improving their performance.

Yet this strengthening of cooperation and incentives may be only illusory. Gapinski, Škegro, and Zuehlke (1989b, pp. 33-34, 40-41, 44) remarked that Yugoslav businesses often face a staggering amount of red tape in the form of permissions and other documentation needed to keep their doors open. Moreover, as Mencinger (1987, pp. 410-11) helped chronicle, that legal structure is highly changeable. Even local authorities do their part to undermine initiative. In one case a woman manager of a manufacturing firm patented a product that received international acclaim. Declining offers to sell her patent abroad, she elected to retain the patent right and to make her firm the sole source of the product. However, when she turned to local authorities for support, they asked her to step aside and to leave the managing of her patent to others, who would attend to everything. Such treatment, which Lydall (1989, p. 116) noted is not an isolated case, hardly can be regarded as fanning the flame of incentives.

Healthy incentives are difficult to maintain under the tangle of red tape, the uncertainty of capricious regulations, and the myopia of government officials. They are equally difficult to maintain in the absence of job discipline, for without it, according to Lydall (1984, pp. 237, 242, 291), laggards fare as well as zealots, and free ridership becomes a norm. Meade (1972, p. 426) warned about the lack of discipline in a self-managed environment, and Lydall (1989, pp. 114-19) recited a litany of failed discipline. In one instance the director of an enterprise lamented that the attitude of workers seemed to be defiant: "If you feel like it, work; if not, you need not; no one can do anything to you." In another example two shifts of factory work covering 15 hours of activity ended with the firm's machinery, each piece of which employed one worker, being used for only 2 hours. In a third episode a firm reported that idleness and carelessness kept output to less than 10 percent of its proper level. In a fourth, employees were found during office hours to be playing billiards at a local inn. Said a radio report, "There is nothing unusual in that." A fifth account put the average number of hours worked during an 8-hour period in the social sector at only 3.5 hours and cited absences from work and time wasted on the job as the causes of the lackluster showing.   Anecdotal experience, of course, does not constitute irrefutable proof. Nevertheless, these episodes indicate rather plainly that the effort-incentive advantage of worker self-management may be more valid in the mind's eye than on the shop floor.[5]

2.3.3 Soft Budgets

A second aspect of Yugoslav economic life that remains beyond the scope of Illyrian theory is, in the words of Kornai (1980, pp. 306-7; 1986, p. 4), the soft-budget constraint of the firm. In Yugoslavia firms exert influence over local banks and use that influence to secure loans. In addition, they issue promissory notes to help pay bills in excess of the amount permitted by their own revenues. Known also as interenterprise credits or as unintended credit, these notes circulate throughout the business community and eventually become monetized by the banking system.[6]

Evidence that the volume of interenterprise credits is substantial and hence that the degree of budget softness is substantial as well takes several forms.   One is a report about a scandal surrounding Agrokomerc, a large food-processing outfit situated in the Bosnian town of Velika Kladuša. Controlling a local bank and enjoying the support of several key politicians, management issued interenterprise credits totaling roughly $300 million in a single year.[7] Another account of budget softness comes from Gedeon (1985-86, pp. 215, 217), who quoted statistics disclosing that in Yugoslavia as much as 75 percent of a firm's material costs was covered by bills of exchange. A third illustration comes from Kornai (1986, pp. 18-19), who showed that around 10 percent of the Yugoslav firms under examination operated at a financial loss.

Still other evidence on budget softness can be drawn from the financial constraint of the government and from the ledgers of the banking system. Table 2.1 displays that information. Since the government provides the ultimate backing for interenterprise credits, denoted L1, its budget equation can be understood to certify that expenditures plus credits equal the sum of tax collections, money-stock changes, and borrowing from abroad.[8] Rearranging this expression then yields L1. With M1 representing the standard money-supply aggregate, $ML1 = M1 + L1$ measures total credit, intended and unintended combined. In a similar vein NBSCOTH signifies the residual category of credits in the balances of the republican banks, whereas NBSCTOT symbolizes the banks' total credits. Although the two indicators L1/ML1 and NBSCOTH/NBSCTOT give different impressions regarding the magnitude of interenterprise credits in the

Table 2.1
Indicators of Budget Softness

Years	L1/ ML1	NBSCOTH/ NBSCTOT
1952-64	.265	.016
1965-73	.399	.050
1974-79	.434	.330
1980-88	.482	.656

Note: Entries represent the ratios of means.

early years, they reach the same conclusion in the later years: Interenterprise credits were abundant, and as unintended credit they accounted for half of the total.

Budget softness inclines firms to a larger size than otherwise. Support for this proposition comes from a Western cousin of the Yugoslav enterprise: the nonprofit performing arts company. Typically such a company receives a sizable subsidy that enables it to operate beyond the confines of its own earned income. The subsidy, or patronage, softens its budget constraint and affects its behavior.

In a landmark review of 166 nonprofit performing arts companies in the United States, the Ford Foundation (1974, Appendix B) confirmed the bountifulness of patronage and showed how much patronage relaxed the budget constraint. Gapinski (1984, p. 459) provided similar information on the Royal Shakespeare Company (RSC), a major performing arts organization in the United Kingdom. Table 2.2 selects from both sets of statistics. On average a nonprofit US theater received 30.7 percent of its total income in the form of patronage, and these "soft" funds impelled it to spend 151.8 percent of what it earned on its own. Similarly, US opera collected 34.6 percent of its income in patronage, a fact that explains why opera expenditures amounted to 153.6 percent of earned income. For symphony the percentages were even greater—47.8 percent and 219.5 percent, respectively—while for ballet they read 38.5 percent and 163.9 percent, respectively. As the numbers on the RSC attest, matters were not much different on

Table 2.2
Patronage and Budget Profiles for Nonprofit Performing
Arts Companies

Art Form or Company	Patronage Ratio	Expenditure Ratio
The United States		
Theater	.307	1.518
Opera	.346	1.536
Symphony	.478	2.195
Ballet	.385	1.639
The United Kingdom		
RSC	.300	1.460

Sources: Ford Foundation (1974, Appendix B) and Gapinski (1984, p. 459).

Notes: The patronage ratio equals patronage divided by total income (earned income plus patronage), whereas the expenditure ratio equals total expenditures divided by earned income. All entries are ratios of means. Those for the US refer to multiple organizations in each art form and cover the fiscal years 1965/66 to 1970/71. Those for the RSC cover the financial years 1965/66 to 1979/80.

the eastern side of the Atlantic.

Pursuing the arts' response to subsidy, Gapinski (1980, pp. 582-84) studied the Ford Foundation data and found that the marginal product of labor fell below the real wage in each of the four art forms. Likewise, the marginal product of capital fell below capital's real price in each. Under subsidy, nonprofit arts companies hire more labor and acquire more capital than would an unsubsidized profit maximizer.

Table 2.3 offers additional insights along the same lines. Drawing from inquiries by Gapinski (1984, pp. 463-64; 1988, pp. 761-63), it

Table 2.3
Behavior of Theater Companies with Patronage Present and Absent

| Measure | The Royal Shakespeare Company | | | |
| | Aldwych Theater | | Stratford Theater | |
	Actual Conditions	Profit Maximum	Actual Conditions	Profit Maximum
Labor Input	491,040	29,592	580,280	234,640
Capital Input	299,680	20,053	373,870	162,402
Output	234,045	16,528	414,281	178,536
Profit	-504,571	5,181	-213,843	316,848

| Measure | Representative US Theater Companies | | | |
| | Medium Size | | Large Size | |
	Actual Conditions	Profit Maximum	Actual Conditions	Profit Maximum
Labor Input	90,194	1,489	248,881	6,359
Capital Input	223,364	5,556	697,929	23,730
Output	323,590	15,620	1,031,560	66,716
Profit	-291,760	3,502	-752,030	14,956

Sources: Gapinski (1984, pp. 463-64; 1988, pp. 761-63).

Notes: For the RSC the labor input is quantified in man-hours; capital and profit, in real pounds; and output, in paid attendance. For the US companies labor is calibrated in man-hours, while all other variables are expressed in real dollars. An outfit of medium size lists nominal expenses between $1.0 million and $1.5 million yearly. One of large size lists them in excess of $2.0 million yearly.

first addresses the conditions at the then principal venues of the RSC: the Aldwych and Stratford theaters. Actual conditions refer to company activities under the subsidy, while the profit-maximization sequence projects how the company would function if it were an unsubsidized profit maximizer. As the table shows, the differences are striking. Compared to the profit-maximum standard, the company employed much more labor, the multiples being 16.6 at the Aldwych and 2.5 at the Stratford, and it used much more capital, those factors being 14.9 at the Aldwych and 2.3 at the Stratford. Accordingly, output was considerably greater under the subsidy. Perhaps most significant are the profit comparisons. Calculated in the usual way as earned income minus total costs, profit registered - £504,571 at the Aldwych and - £213,843 at the Stratford. Profit at each venue is actually an enormous loss; yet the curtain still rises. Had the company been a profit maximizer, there would be no losses. In fact, the severely curtailed level of activity would have turned a tidy profit.

The representative subsidized US theater companies documented in Table 2.3 behave like the RSC. Regardless of the organization's size, the subsidy leads to more labor, more capital, and more output. It also leads to losses, which a profit maximizer would have avoided.

Soft budgets give firms a license to operate without looking over their accounting shoulders. They permit firms to escape bankruptcy, and simultaneously they protect the tenure status of employment. It naturally follows that firms may not be terribly responsive to factor-price movements (Kornai, 1980, p. 308; 1986, pp. 9-10). Increased input costs can be met by issuing interenterprise credits rather than by releasing workers and cutting production. Additionally, output price may be raised as output quantity remains unchanged, reinforcing the assertion of Vanek and associates that the commodity supply curve under self-management is anything but perverse. By the same token, soft budgets remove the need to optimize. With financial rescue merely an arm's length away, firms may have little desire to conduct business according to the strict rule of some first-order condition. For them, as Kornai (1986, p. 8) intimated, satisficing may make much more sense. Bureaucratic red tape, capricious regulations, myopic officials, and worker lethargy only strengthen the case for satisficing.

In a resourceful endeavor Lydall (1984, pp. 31-39) described a self-management model characterized by limited markets and limited technical know-how. There each firm has a marginal revenue curve with a Sweezy-style vertical zone through which the marginal cost curve passes. Within this framework the firm sets price and responds to demand changes straightforwardly by increasing supply when demand increases and by decreasing supply when demand decreases. Price changes would occur to discourage entry, and they would be tied to changes in labor costs, nonlabor input costs, and technology. The spirit of Lydall's analysis fits the satisficing pattern, and the traditional kinds of behavioral responses that it elicits match what one might imagine under a "good-enough" philosophy.

2.4 THOUGHTS FROM ORTHODOXY AND HETERODOXY

Illyrian theory does not work; its strict arithmetic generates implications that simply do not fit the facts. Its failures inspire remedial efforts to bring theory closer to practice, but in the process those efforts bring it closer to tradition. Replacing the negatively sloped commodity supply curve with a vertical or positively sloped schedule is a case in point. At the opposite end of the mathematical spectrum lies satisficing, but it too yields traditional results. Given this common destination, perhaps the job of modeling the Yugoslav economy should begin from conventional theory proper and should then modify that conventional wisdom to accommodate the special features of Yugoslavia such as worker solidarity and soft credits. Surely this tack can be no less appropriate than starting from a discredited theory and applying bandages post hoc. It even may be the preferred method since it appeals to a very familiar body of knowledge. In this situation familiarity might not breed contempt.

2.4.1 A Second General Theory

One of the strongest endorsements for grounding the modeling endeavor in traditional theory came from Vanek (1972) despite his plain and repeated insistence that the Yugoslav economy was so different from its Western cousins that Western principles could not be applied. Reading his work is almost equivalent to reviewing the analysis by Patinkin (1965, pp. 229, 232-33, 236-39, 258-61, 268-69), a high priest of orthodoxy.

Vanek (1972, pp. 256-64) set out his formal model in six equations,[9] the first being the equilibrium condition for the commodity market:

$$\overline{Q} = Q(\overline{Q}, p, i, x). \tag{2.12}$$

The left-hand side $\overline{Q}$ denotes commodity supply, while the right-hand side denotes a function representing commodity demand. As before, p signifies price; i and x stand for the interest rate and the exchange rate, respectively. It may be worth noting that one of Vanek's justifications for including price as a determinant of demand is the real balance effect, a canon of Patinkin.

Next in line is equilibrium in the money market, namely,

$$\overline{M}_o = M(\overline{Q}, p, i), \tag{2.13}$$

where $\overline{M}_o$ symbolizes the exogenous supply of money and where the right-hand side describes money demand. Unlike the money supply, bond supply B is endogenous, as is bond demand B, making the equilibrium condition there

$$\overline{B}(\overline{Q},p,i,x) = B(\overline{Q},p,i,x). \tag{2.14}$$

The foreign sector is summarized by a foreign exchange market, which can be specified as

$$pX(p,x) = xZ(\overline{Q},p,i,x), \tag{2.15}$$

whose X and Z denote the quantities exported and imported, respectively. Foreign import prices are presumed to be constant at unity.

Traces of Illyria enter the inquiry through the labor-market condition (2.3) restated as

$$p\partial\overline{Q}/\partial L = (p\overline{Q} - rK_o)/L. \tag{2.16}$$

Closing the paradigm is the production function[10]

$$\overline{Q} = \overline{Q}(L,K_o). \tag{2.17}$$

From Walras's law the bond-market equilibrium (2.14) can be suppressed, and with the exchange rate x taken as constant, the foreign exchange market may be reinterpreted as measuring the trade balance. Furthermore, substituting the production function (2.17) throughout the model and, in accord with the idea of a vertical commodity supply curve, treating L as fixed collapse the system to two equations in two unknowns: equations (2.12) and (2.13) in p and i.

Thus consolidated, the Vanek model has a commodity equation that resembles the Patinkin commodity expression CC and a money equation that resembles the Patinkin money expression LL. These likenesses are more than superficial. For instance, monetary expansion in Vanek's system causes price to rise and the interest rate to fall; it has the same effect in Patinkin's. Moreover, budgetary expansion causes price and interest to rise in both. Admittedly, the two models have their distinguishing characteristics; nevertheless, their strong similarities cannot be denied. Orthodoxy has much to say for the modeling of Yugoslavia.

2.4.2 Incomes Policy

But heterodoxy too has something to offer, and again Vanek (1972, p. 266) led the way by raising the prospect of price controls in Yugoslavia. At the same time, he emphatically dismissed wage controls as being contrary to the essence of self-management.

Wage and price controls must be one of the most controversial issues in contemporary economics. They treat the symptom, not the disease; they disrupt allocative efficiency; they foster destabilizing movements; they create logistical nightmares; and they invite special-interest pressure. In short, wage and price controls, also known as incomes policy, create more problems than they solve. They only make matters worse. Indeed, Friedman (1966), Dildine and Sunley (1978), Rees (1978), Ture (1978), Baumol (1979), and Mencinger (1987) articulated compelling criticisms, and the failures of incomes policy in Brazil and especially in Yugoslavia seem to clinch the point.[11]

The proponents of incomes policy make strong replies to the charges, and their ranks, which swelled with the formulation of a tax-based incomes policy by Wallich and Weintraub (1971), are legion too. Seidman (1976), Okun (1977), Lerner (1978), Colander (1979a), Rockwood (1979), Lerner and Colander (1980), and Canterbery (1983) ably represented them. Moreover, the econometric and simulation analyses for the United States by Perry (1967), Eckstein and Girola (1978), Chirinko and Seidman (1981), Gapinski (1986), and Gapinski and Choudhary (1986-87) indicated that incomes policy could improve macro performance on balance. Christofides and Wilton (1983) reached a similar conclusion for Canada, and Bruno (1989) repeated it powerfully for Israel. To be sure, the inflation rate would tumble.

The rationale behind the Post Keynesian advocacy of incomes policy begins with a conflict over income shares and ends with the belief that expectations drive the inflation process (Lerner, 1972, pp. 81-82; 1979, pp. 219-20). Validation of this expectations basis of inflation evolves from the inquiries by Lipsey (1960, pp. 12-16) and Evans (1969, pp. 263-66).

Labor demand Ld and labor supply Ls have the usual curves drawn with respect to the real wage w/p, simplified to v, and labor-market equilibrium obtains at a positive rate of unemployment U_A. For real wages above the equilibrium level, the unemployment rate exceeds U_A, and for wages below equilibrium, unemployment falls below U_A. The market is stable. Thus the real wage moves toward equilibrium, and it adjusts at a speed that varies directly with the extent of disequilibrium. In more precise terms

$$\Delta v / v_{-1} = f[(Ld - Ls)/Ls]. \tag{2.18}$$

Function f passes through the origin, $0 = f(0)$. In addition, it has a positive slope, $f' > 0$, and it maps out either a concave-upward curve or a straight line, $f'' \geq 0$.

The unobservable excess demand rate $(Ld - Ls)/Ls$ can be tied to the observable unemployment rate U as

$$(Ld - Ls)/Ls = g(U). \tag{2.19}$$

Function g equals zero at the positive rate of unemployment U_A. Too, it is negatively sloped and concave upward. Succinctly, $0 = g(U_A)$, $g' < 0$, and $g'' > 0$.

From equations (2.18) and (2.19), the speed of real-wage adjustment becomes

$$\Delta v/v_{-1} = h(U). \tag{2.20}$$

Since $h(U) = f[g(U)]$, the properties of f and g determine those of h. That is, $0 = h(U_A)$, $h' < 0$, and $h'' > 0$. Function h looks like the famous curve of Phillips (1958), only it explains real-wage inflation rather than money-wage inflation.

With

$$\Delta v/v_{-1} = \Delta w/w_{-1} - \Delta p/p_{-1} \tag{2.21}$$

as an approximation, equation (2.20) gives way to

$$\Delta w/w_{-1} = h(U) + \Delta p/p_{-1}. \tag{2.22}$$

Wage negotiations naturally look to events that might occur over the life of the agreement, and consequently the price inflation term in relation (2.22) ought to be interpreted as the expected inflation rate $E(\Delta p/p_{-1})$, leaving

$$\Delta w/w_{-1} = h(U) + E(\Delta p/p_{-1}). \tag{2.23}$$

If firms follow a price-markup rule, then for some constant ζ

$$p = \zeta w/q, \tag{2.24}$$

where q signifies labor productivity. Converting formula (2.24) into a rate of change makes

$$\Delta p/p_{-1} = \Delta w/w_{-1} - \Delta q/q_{-1}, \tag{2.25}$$

approximately. In light of equation (2.23), this expression expands to

$$\Delta p/p_{-1} = h(U) + E(\Delta p/p_{-1}) - \Delta q/q_{-1}. \tag{2.26}$$

The actual rate of inflation depends upon the unemployment rate in the trade-off fashion of the Phillips curve, but it also depends upon the expectation of inflation and the rate of technical progress. Raising the expected rate of inflation by 1 percentage point raises the actual rate by a full point. Conversely—and here rests the hope of the Post Keynesians—a 1-point reduction in expectations lowers the actual rate by 1 point. Graphically, the Phillips curve shifts downward, freeing the standard fiscal and monetary tools to improve the unemployment situation in a fight against stagflation.

Countries being gripped by hyperinflation presumably have inflation expectations that bear heavily on wage and price dynamics. In that context the United Nations (1986, pp. 70-78), Bresser Pereira and Nakano (1987, p. 7), Cardoso and Dornbusch (1987, pp. 288, 289, 291), Dornbusch (1987, pp. viii-ix), and Dornbusch and Simonsen (1987, pp. 2, 14) endorsed the application of incomes policy, and work on Yugoslavia by Škegro, Gapinski, and Anušić (1989, pp. 104-5) produced a similar endorsement. Such support, together with the fact that Yugoslavia turned to a controls program at the start of 1990, suggests that at least this part of heterodoxy deserves consideration in modeling the Yugoslav economy.

2.4.3 Rational Expectations

In 1961 Muth (pp. 316-17, 333) introduced the concept of rational expectations. He argued that expectations, being the informed predictions of future events, are the same as the predictions from the relevant economic theory. Stated more cleanly, expectations are accurate up to a random disturbance term ξ, namely,

$$E(\Delta p/p_{-1}) = \Delta p/p_{-1} + \xi. \tag{2.27}$$

According to this hypothesis, expectations have no systematic bias.[12] Economic agents cannot be tricked; they cannot be fooled. There are no surprises. A decade after Muth's contribution, a fraternity of economists represented by, say, Sargent and Wallace (1976, pp. 172-78) took the fun out of economics by insisting that countercyclical policy was totally useless. To reduce the unemployment rate, authorities must drive down the real wage, perhaps through the inflationary pressure of a demand stimulus. However, individuals accurately anticipate the inflation response and act to protect the real wage. It does not fall, the unemployment rate does not fall, and the net result of the countercyclical tactic is merely a higher rate of inflation.

The mathematical version of the rational expectations narrative can be presented concisely. Substituting hypothesis (2.27) into the inflation generator (2.26) yields

$$U = h^{-1}(\Delta q/q_{-1} - \xi). \tag{2.28}$$

The unemployment rate depends upon technical progress and random events. More tellingly, it has no connection with inflation or with orthodox policy measures. In effect, the Phillips curve is vertical, and the obvious inference is that countercyclical policy should be scrapped. "Don't do something, just stand there!" becomes the official slogan, as it did earlier under the monetarist banner of the constant-growth-rate rule (Heller, 1969, p. 34).

But the rational expectationists have more mischief to play. If economic agents promptly and accurately revise their expectations, then coefficients in the arithmetic change when conditions change, and economic models obsolesce under the application of policy. By this Lucas critique (Lucas, 1981, pp. 109-11, 126), models really are trying to hit a moving target, and given the fixed nature of their homing devices, the prospects for success are dim. Policy modeling and policy making are doomed from the start—at first glance.

A second glance, however, brings into focus images that inspire a more sanguine judgment. One image relates to the cost of expectation revision. Adjusting expectations implies learning, which is the acquisition of knowledge in much the same way that investment is the acquisition of capital. Rapidly moving ahead with capital expansion pushes production cost and purchase price upward, and accordingly entrepreneurs are advised to go slowly by selecting only a fraction of the desired stock in any period. The counterpart of this flexible acceleration principle posits that partial adjustment governs the acquisition of knowledge. Expectations, then, may not be accurate up to a random disturbance term. Instead they might follow the biased formulation

$$E(\Delta p/p_{-1}) = \Delta p/p_{-1} + \eta e^{-\theta t} + \xi, \tag{2.29}$$

where the ignorance parameter η is nonzero and where the speed-of-learning parameter θ is positive. Expectations have a systematic bias $\eta e^{-\theta t}$ that diminishes through time t and ultimately disappears as individuals accumulate wisdom in the wake of countercyclical policy. This statement of March's (1978, pp. 592-93) adaptive rationality hypothesis combines with equation (2.26) to yield

$$U = h^{-1}(\Delta q/q_{-1} - \eta e^{-\theta t} - \xi).$$

(2.30)

Countercyclical policy can reduce unemployment below the "natural rate" as long as individuals are adjusting their expectations.

The cost issue can be carried further. Economic agents may be envisioned to revise their expectations by weighing the cost against the benefit of doing so. The benefit of information gathering is, of course, the protection of the real wage and the standard of living. Agents seek information until cost equals benefit, but that information hunt may end closer to Simon's Land of Bounded Rationality than to Sargent and Wallace's Kingdom of Unbounded Enlightenment. Again, expectations may not be accurate. Jonung and Laidler (1988, p. 1086) subscribed to this view.[13]

Taylor (1975, pp. 1014, 1017) maintained that proper revision of expectations requires clarity in the signals being transmitted by the government. It is important to know whether the target is stationary or moving; if it is moving, then direction and speed are important considerations as well. Is the United States balancing its federal budget? Certainly! President Carter talked about balancing the budget but left the Oval Office deeper in red ink than when he entered. President Reagan insisted on a balanced budget only to heat the deficit past the boiling point of $212 billion. Politicians argued that the red tide could be turned with a balanced-budget amendment to the US Constitution; nonetheless, the joint resolution articulating that language never passed through Congress. Undaunted, proponents ushered into law the Gramm-Rudman-Hollings Act only to discover that its heralded across-the-board budget-trimming mechanism was unconstitutional. Although rewritten, the act seemed to lose its cutting edge, hefty deficits persisted, and Senator Hollings (1990, p. 11A) publicly questioned the merits of his own invention. Meanwhile the proposal for a balanced-budget amendment accomplished Lazarean feats by making its way into Congress two other times but, like its earlier incarnation, went no further. Put succinctly, the signals transmitted by the budget-balancing rhetoric are less than clear. They are also less than clear for other US policy maneuvers. If "signal extraction" is difficult for a country like the United States, whose strong central government historically has provided policy leadership, then it must have been doubly so for Yugoslavia, whose weak central government historically watched as the country drifted along without a unified economic agenda. Once again, expectations may not be accurate.

Empirical evidence can be cited to expand the case against the rationality hypothesis. For instance, Figlewski and Wachtel (1981, pp. 2-4) tested the inflation expectations of business, academic, and government economists and summarily rejected rationality. In studying expectations data pertinent to personnel executives experienced in labor-market behavior, Leonard (1982, pp. 157-58, 160) likewise rejected the hypothesis. Similarly, surveying a variety of studies, Lovell (1986, p. 119) noted that, contrary to rationality, experienced economic agents are slow learners—their θ is small—and he inferred that the rank and file of inexperienced individuals could hardly fit the rationality mold. This same inference could be drawn from the Figlewski-Wachtel and Leonard investigations as well. In still another inquiry Pollock and Suyderhoud (1992, pp. 320-21, 324) concluded that the expectation about something as fundamental as the length of one's own life is formed in a manner that is inconsistent with rationality.

Figlewski and Wachtel, Leonard, Lovell, and Pollock and Suyderhoud referred to the US experience. By contrast, Shostak (1981, pp. 4-9) examined the South African experience but rejected the hypothesis nevertheless. Kawasaki and Zimmermann (1986, pp. 1343-45) flunked it in the German situation, as did Jonung and Laidler (1988, pp. 1083-86) for Sweden. Gapinski (1992a, pp. 9-11) looked at ten countries, including the so-called Group of Seven: Canada, France, Germany, Italy, Japan, the United Kingdom, and the United States. Maintaining that expectations gravitate toward rationality, he asked how long it takes for them to *become* rational. The answer varies from country to country, but on balance that adjustment time proves to be 5.5 years. From the practical standpoint, then, expectations are not rational. These endeavors—and numerous others—would be heartily applauded by Simon (1979, pp. 504-5, 510).

Even if expectations were accurate, the rational expectationist conclusion that countercyclical policy is ineffective need not hold. Knowing the future is insufficient to protect the real wage. That knowledge must be put into practice: Workers must revise their contracts in step with their revised expectations. If they cannot, then, as Phelps and Taylor (1977, pp. 164-65, 180) and Fischer (1980, pp. 219-20) intimated, the real wage can fall and countercyclical policy can be effective despite rationality. A self-managed environment, where workers have a voice in the wage decision, lends itself to the implementation of revised expectations, and hence the record of the real wage in Yugoslavia should make a bold statement about the relevancy of countercyclical policy. Inasmuch as that record shows the real wage to have fallen economywide almost uninterruptedly since 1977, its statement is a resounding affirmation of relevancy.

2.4.4 Ricardian Equivalence

The policy-ineffectiveness proposition of the rational expectations hypothesis (REH) is typically brought up in the context of monetary initiatives. A similar proposition can be found on the fiscal side of policy. It stems from what is called the Ricardian equivalence hypothesis, which coincidentally has the same acronym as its monetary counterpart.

According to Ricardian equivalence, individuals perceive a fiscal deficit to mean (that is, to be equivalent to) higher future taxes. Consequently, they increase their saving now to prepare themselves for that higher tax bill. The interest that they earn on the extra saving enables them to cover the service charge of the deficit, and the saving principal enables them to satisfy the tax principal when it finally falls due. Should they die beforehand, their children would satisfy that obligation through the estate left behind.

The implication of this private saving response to the public saving maneuver can be grasped from the standard macro identity

$$S_p + S_g = I + (X - R), \tag{2.31}$$

where S_p and S_g denote private saving and public saving, respectively. I represents domestic investment, while X and R signify exports and imports, respectively. All terms are reals. Starting from, say, a balanced budget, the government implements a deficit spending program by cutting taxes. Thus S_g becomes negative. However, individuals react by increasing S_p to the full extent of the S_g decrease—in effect, they save the deficit. As a result, nothing happens to investment,[14] and nothing happens to the trade balance. Moreover, since the newly created disposable income is saved, nothing happens to consumption either. Fiscal action, like monetary action under rational expectations, is neutralized.

Although the equivalence hypothesis is a contemporary issue, it dates all the way back to an article entitled "Funding System" that David Ricardo prepared for the 1820 *Encyclopaedia Britannica*. Therein he equated debt, or deficit, to taxation by writing,

> In point of economy, there is no real difference in either of
> the modes; for twenty millions in one payment, one million
> per annum for ever, or 1,200,000 l. for 45 years, are precisely
> of the same value; ... (Sraffa, 1951, p. 186)

Yet Ricardo finished the passage with the reverse logic:

> ... but the people who pay the taxes never so estimate them,
> and therefore do not manage their private affairs accordingly.

A few lines later he reiterated that view by adding,

> It would be difficult to convince a man possessed of 20,000
> l., or any other sum, that a perpetual payment of 50 l. per
> annum was equally burdensome with a single tax of 1000 l.
> He would have some vague notion that the 50 l. per annum
> would be paid by posterity, and would not be paid by him; ...
> (Sraffa, 1951, p. 187)

Ricardo contended that individuals, in fact, do not perceive the
different financing schemes to be identical. What he was arguing, as
O'Driscoll (1977, pp. 208-9) affirmed, is actually nonequivalence
rather than equivalence. Private saving does not increase to
completely offset the decrease in public saving, and so investment
changes, the trade balance changes, and consumption changes in
orthodox fashion.

Ricardo's own comments notwithstanding, the champions of
equivalence such as Bailey (1962, pp. 75-76) and Barro (1974, pp.
1101-4; 1989, p. 52) offered strong arguments of support. Still, the
critics are unmoved. For instance, Eisner and Pieper (1984, p. 17)
summarily dismissed equivalence. Bernheim (1987, pp. 3-20; 1989,
pp. 63-67) and Sahota (1993, pp. 208-10) compiled exhaustive lists of
theoretical objections to it, and Gapinski (1993, pp. 13-25) rejected it
on empirical grounds.

Perhaps the twin REHs should be interpreted as something of a
contemporary religion. Like a religion, they have their fervent
believers and their ardent disbelievers. Faith is required either way,
services are frequent, and conversions are rare. This volume
subscribes to policy modeling and advocates active policy, whether
monetary or fiscal. Thus, unlike a catechism, it may appeal mainly to
the disbelievers.

2.5 IMPLICATIONS FOR MODELING YUGOSLAVIA

Economic theory has its limits, but Illyrian theory has more than its share. It asserts that commodity supply varies inversely with price. It posits that output varies directly with capital cost and remains steady or falls with technical progress. It holds that more demand means less supply and that resources are diverted away from scarcity. It prescribes increased tax collections, reduced government spending, and slower money growth for reducing unemployment. It ignores the solidarity of workers in the self-management context, it overlooks the soft-budget conditions under which firms operate, and it neglects the work disincentives inherent in the daily business routine. The conceptual weaknesses of Illyrian theory underscore the prudence of traditional reasoning, whereas the complexities of economic life and the softness of enterprise budgets give credibility to a satisficing approach. The latter, however, heads in the same direction as the former, and consequently, traditional precepts modified to reflect the special features of the country should provide a proper framework for the modeling effort.

Consumption, then, is postulated in terms of disposable income and lagged consumption consonant with the longsightedness hypothesis of Friedman (1957, pp. 7-19, 142-47), with the shortsightedness hypothesis of Ball and Drake (1964, pp. 64-68, 75-79), or more basically with the habit-persistence hypothesis of Brown (1952, p. 359). Since the data allow a separation of consumption expenditure by type of product, relative prices enter the specifications as well. So does credit to account for the credit-soaked nature of the economy. Investment, the other private spending stream, begins from the time-honored flexible accelerator expressed in stock-adjustment form or in flow-adjustment fashion. To capture the capital effect of budget softness verified by the nonprofit performing arts, the function is expanded following Gapinski (1990a, pp. 49-55) to include both intended and unintended credit. User cost makes an appearance, though Yugoslavia's persistently negative real interest rate warns of a weak showing by this variable. Given the detail of the data set, the investment schedule is specified by sector.

Wage inflation by sector is set out in the spirit of equation (2.23). Labor-market pressures count, although, due to worker solidarity, the appropriate pressure gauge may be something besides the unemployment rate. In keeping with adaptive rationality, the coefficient of price inflation should be less than unity. Furthermore, as workers have a say in wage decisions, they probably seize a share of their own productivity increase, and thus productivity growth may find its way into the argument set. Tyson (1977, pp. 124, 129-34) and

Gapinski (1991, pp. 39-42) lent support to this interpretation. Bill paying under soft budgets is credit influenced, and as a result wage payments—like investment expenditures—may be credit driven either because credits are used to pay wages directly or because they free other funds for wage payments. It readily follows that credit growth belongs in the wage inflation equation.

Sectoral price inflation takes its cue from the customary cost-push paradigm, which singles out the growth in unit labor cost as a major determinant. From the analysis by Bresser Pereira and Nakano (1987, p. 69), growth in the dinar cost of imports becomes a determinant too. Moreover, the Yugoslav hyperinflation record cited in Chapter 1, coupled with the thoughts by Cagan (1956, pp. 29, 64-66, 88) and Vanek (1972, p. 267) about vestiges of the quantity theory of money, suggests that credit growth should round out the inflation functions.

Other implications deserve at least brief mention. Worker solidarity and soft budgets mean that employment movements are insensitive to current market conditions and instead are characterized by inertia. In other words, they may be governed by some type of ratchet mechanism. From a policy standpoint the role of credit in setting the pace for wages and prices means that remedial monetary initiatives might heed Vanek's (1972, p. 265) advice by aiming at inflation. Moreover, since wage inflation has a basis in adaptively rational expectations and since price inflation depends upon wage inflation, heterodox policy might serve as an important complement to Vanek's orthodox restraint in the inflation fight. Such policy issues warrant careful consideration; however, they must await a full description of the Yugoslav economic structure as it existed before the clouds of disintegration began to gather. That description is the purpose of the next two chapters.

NOTES

1. Lydall (1984, p. 109) expressed a similar belief.

2. On the historical side of this provocative effort, Dubravčić (1988, p. 1) noted that Illyria had been a Roman province situated in part of what came to be called Yugoslavia.

3. Other reviews of Illyrian mechanics were offered by Domar (1966, pp. 736-42), Meade (1972, pp. 403-16), Estrin (1983, pp. 11-42), and Bonin and Putterman (1987, pp. 13-18).

4. Ireland and Law (1982, pp. 124-25) showed that output remains constant under technical progress when the labor-managed firm operates subject to homothetic production conditions marked by factor-augmenting technology. Brewer (1988, pp. 404-5) reached the

same conclusion for the case of Harrod neutrality. The Cobb-Douglas, of course, is consistent with both production models. Actually, a stronger result is possible: Output may *fall* because of technical progress. Estrin (1983, p. 19) raised that possibility, and Brewer (1988, pp. 406, 414-15) confirmed it.

5. The discipline model of labor effort contends that wage incentives alone are insufficient to produce high worker effort and that supervision is needed to that end. Tests by Gordon (1990, pp. 30-32) validated this hypothesis for the United States and implied that in a self-managed environment, where supervision borders on laxity, worker effort is wanting. A companion study for the US by Green and Weisskopf (1990, pp. 242, 244, 246-47) showed that work effort varies directly with the extent of unemployment and that this discipline effect is stronger where labor unionism has shallow root. Again there is a natural implication for Yugoslavia. Self-management, through worker solidarity, undermines the threat of unemployment while solidifying a powerful brand of unionism. It therefore emasculates the discipline effect and discourages worker effort.

6. In other words, the Yugoslav money supply is endogenous. Gedeon (1985-86, pp. 212, 215-18) explicated the situation deductively, whereas Chowdhury, Grubaugh, and Stollar (1990, pp. 640-45) verified it econometrically.

7. Agrokomerc was not the only case of financial abuse in Yugoslavia. Why it received front-page coverage may be explained more by efforts to besmirch the reputation of a political figure associated with the incident than by the pure fact of budget misconduct. Some details of the Agrokomerc affair can be found in "All the Party Chief's Men" (1987, p. 40).

8. Borrowing domestically was not an established practice of the government.

9. An earlier version of the model can be found in Vanek (1970, pp. 172-73, 184-85, 189, 191-92). It, however, omitted the foreign sector.

10. The 1970 version of Vanek's model suggests that the labor market condition and the production function of the 1972 version contain printing errors. Equations (2.16) and (2.17) therefore observe the 1970 format.

11. The Yugoslav experience was recounted by Mencinger (1987, pp. 411-13).

12. Disturbance term ξ has a zero mean. The deterministic special case, where ξ is always zero, may be called perfect foresight in keeping with the language of vintage-capital growth models.

13. Howitt (1981, pp. 259-62) too referred to the cost and benefit of learning, while Colander (1979b, pp. 205-7) and Fischer (1980, pp. 211-12, 225) concurred with the general idea.

14. The insensitivity of investment to the deficit runs deeper than the mathematics of identity (2.31) indicates. Since private saving rises to offset the reduction in public saving, the loanable funds being absorbed by the government are replaced and keep the interest rate stationary. With no movement in interest, there is no movement in investment. In the vernacular, there is no crowding out.

3

Quantity Relationships

Describing the Yugoslav macro economy in equation form is the object of the EIZFSU Mark 4.0. This model, an evolved construction that Appendix B compares against the original formulation, covers a wide range of quantity and price relationships. Quantities are considered here. Section 3.1 looks at consumption and at the propensities and elasticities inherent in the consumption functions. Section 3.2 explores investment. Stock-adjustment and flow-adjustment principles are postulated, and their capacity elements are combined with and ranked against finance factors in the expressions tested. Capital stock is featured in Section 3.3, which comments on the age of capital. Output serves as the theme of Section 3.4, which links actual output to the capacity level. Following the output issues are labor matters such as employment, labor supply, and unemployment; they occupy Section 3.5. Similarly, taxation and government spending come to the fore in Section 3.6. Section 3.7 then switches the emphasis from domestic concerns to international activity by examining trade flows and in the process concludes the inquiry into quantities.

Given its nature, the discussion often identifies variables and equations by their Mark 4.0 names and numbers. Those designations are fully described in Appendix A.

3.1 CONSUMPTION

In keeping with the wealth-theoretic model of either Friedman (1957, pp. 142-47) or Ball and Drake (1964, pp. 67-68) or with the habit-persistence paradigm of Brown (1952, p. 359), real consumption

C is posited to depend upon real disposable income YD and lagged real consumption. To allow for the credit orientation of the Yugoslav economy, it is also taken to depend upon a real credit variable XR. Price effects enter through relative price PR, while vector Z^v representing other determinants shapes the function into

$$C = \alpha_0 + \alpha_Y YD + \alpha_X XR + \alpha_P PR + \alpha_C C_{-1} + \alpha_Z^v Z^v. \qquad (3.1)$$

Coefficient α_Y satisfies the usual restriction on the marginal propensity, namely, $0 < \alpha_Y < 1$. In addition, $0 < \alpha_X < 1$, $\alpha_P < 0$, and $0 < \alpha_C < 1$. The elements of vector α^v_Z are signed consonant with the elements of Z^v.

Disposable income YD, redesignated more elaborately as YDA72 in equation (CN14) of Appendix A, encompasses four kinds of income: earnings in the "productive" sector, earnings in the "nonproductive" sector, social security payments to persons, and remittances from Yugoslavs working abroad. Productive earnings WPROD/PIPDC constitute the biggest component by far, averaging about two-thirds of the four-component total. Nonproductive earnings GWS/PIPDC come third with about 14 percent of the total. Their temporal behavior tends to complement the movement of productive earnings; that is, nonproductive earnings tend to rise when productive earnings fall and to fall when they rise. Social security income SSINC/PIPDC places second at 16 percent, and its share exhibits an upward trend following the reforms of the mid-1960s. Foreign remittances FREMIT/PIPDC finish fourth with a share of about 5 percent. Although small in relation to their counterparts, remittances are not inconsequential, as they represent a source of foreign currency. It may be observed that, by including productive and nonproductive earnings, disposable income automatically includes the real wage. Hence a decline in real wage may be associated with a decline in disposable income, as it is for 1987 and 1988. On the other hand, the behavior of social security and remittances may help to override the action of the real wage, enabling disposable income to rise as real wage drops. Year 1978 substantiates that possibility.

Regressing equation (3.1) separately on the 11 product types yields equations (CN1) to (CN11) in Appendix A. All coefficient estimates conform to a priori anticipations. Lagged STAXAER in beverage equation (CN1) has the negative sign called for by the general notion that taxes stifle demand. Since entertainment often involves reading, the positive coefficients for BOOKSPUB and NEWSCIRC in entertainment equation (CN3) make sense, and since tourists eat, walk, and otherwise travel, the positive coefficients for TOURTOT in food equation (CN4), footwear equation (CN5), and transportation equation (CN11) make sense as well. HOMEAREA displays a positive coefficient in household operation equation (CN8) simply because larger properties are more expensive to maintain than are smaller ones.

The marginal propensity differs appreciably across product types. As Table 3.1 summarizes, the short-run propensity α_Y is smallest for other consumption COTHER72: 0.0052. By contrast, it is largest for food CFOOD72, which—as the means indicate—is the largest consumption item. In that case the propensity equals 0.0551 and exceeds the smallest α_Y by a factor of ten. Summed across all product types, the short-run propensity equals 0.2712, a fairly standard result in consumption research.[1]

The long-run propensity can be extracted from α_Y under the steady-state conditions that, at time T, $C_T = \zeta\, e^{\xi T}$ for positive constants ζ and ξ and therefore that $C_T = e^{\xi} C_{T-1}$, the magnitude of ξ being the growth rate given in Table 3.1. Then calculating $\alpha_Y/(1 - \alpha_C e^{-\xi})$ leaves the long-run propensity, which when summed across the 11 product types registers 0.6300. Evidently, and not atypically, policy effects that work through the multiplier vary dramatically from one time frame to another.

Table 3.2 reports the income and price elasticities, the long-run numbers emerging from the short-run figures after division by $1 - \alpha_C e^{-\xi}$. To assist in the evaluation, elasticities for roughly comparable items in the United States and elsewhere are given in Table 3.3; like those in Table 3.2, they pertain to income and price in real terms.

Food, the lion's share of Yugoslav consumption, appears to be well behaved. Contemporaneously its income elasticity equals 0.1553, and for the long haul it reads 0.4205, a value that lies within hailing distance of the 0.55 elasticity recorded by Stipetić (1982, p. 336) for the 1970s. Together the short-run and long-run numbers exhibit the same pattern shown for food consumed at home in the US. Similarly, food's price elasticity equals -0.2573 and -0.6970 in the two time dimensions. Transportation, the second largest and the fastest-growing component in total consumption, exhibits higher income elasticities than does food and in that regard duplicates the long-run experience of the US. However, unlike the US example, it manifests the lowest price elasticities across product types. Moreover, when compared with the situations in the neighbor countries, it again has price elasticities that rate among the lowest. Apparently, transportation patterns in Yugoslavia are quite unresponsive to price movements.[2]

Table 3.1
Consumption Means, Growth Rates, and Marginal Propensities by Type of Product

Product Type	Mean	Growth Rate	Marginal Propensity Short Run	Marginal Propensity Long Run
Beverages	9,643	.0488	.0252	.0826
Clothing	12,359	.0453	.0343	.0983
Entertainment	4,590	.0905	.0088	.0192
Food	50,376	.0342	.0551	.1492
Footwear	3,412	.0395	.0065	.0092
Furniture	11,708	.0668	.0544	.0836
Health	5,682	.0705	.0338	.0460
House Operation	8,422	.0644	.0062	.0177
Other	5,655	.0438	.0052	.0410
Tobacco	5,019	.0392	.0207	.0284
Transportation	12,483	.1066	.0210	.0548

Notes: Each mean is denominated in millions of 1972 dinars; each growth rate is calculated from the standard exponential rule. Both statistics apply to the years covered by the corresponding regression analysis in Appendix A.

Table 3.2
Income and Price Elasticities by Type of Consumer Product

Product Type	Income Elasticity		Price Elasticity	
	Short Run	Long Run	Short Run	Long Run
Beverages	.3717	1.2161	-.4510	-1.4756
Clothing	.4018	1.1522	-.3808	-1.0919
Entertainment	.2720	.5929	-.1353	-.2950
Food	.1553	.4205	-.2573	-.6970
Footwear	.2772	.3911	-.2676	-.3776
Furniture	.6735	1.0350	-.2538	-.3901
Health	.8622	1.1736	-.5581	-.7597
Household Operation	.1068	.3052	-.5802	-1.6578
Other	.1476	1.1660	-.1994	-1.5747
Tobacco	.5974	.8194	-.4510	-.6186
Transportation	.2441	.6368	-.1113	-.2903

Note: The elasticities for any product type hold at the means applicable to the years covered by the corresponding regression analysis in Appendix A.

Table 3.3
Consumption Elasticities by Type of Product in the United States and in Countries Neighboring Yugoslavia

Product Type	Income Elasticity Short Run	Long Run	Price Elasticity Short Run	Long Run
Beverages, Alcoholic	.2898	.6207		
Clothing	1.1423	.5131		
Entertainment:				
Theater and Opera	.7407	1.2604	-.1827	-.3109
Motion Pictures	.8126	3.4075	-.8748	-3.6685
Appliances	4.1978	2.9950		
Food, at Home	.4972	.7115		
Footwear	.9433		-.9135	
Furniture	2.5975	.5275		
Health, Sundries	.2453	3.7406	-.1993	-3.0391
Household Operation:				
Electricity	.1319	1.9364	-.1289	-1.8926
Electricity (a)			-.1520	-2.3100
Water	.8746	.5861	-.2028	-.1359
Other	.5577	1.2657	-.1272	-.2885
Tobacco Products	.2075	.8615	-.4556	-1.8919
Transportation:				
Bus, Intercity	.1720	1.8944	-.1967	-2.1657
Gasoline	.5493	1.3572		
Gasoline (b)	.3780	1.0300	-.1860	-.5050
in Austria (c)	.7600		-.7900	
in France (c)	1.1400		-.2000	
in Germany (c)	.4000		-.1700	
in Italy (c)	.1200		-.3700	
Railway, Commuter			-.7185	-.9127

Sources: Houthakker and Taylor (1970, pp. xi-xii, 55, 57, 166-67), except for (a) Kraft, Kraft, and Reiser (1976, pp. 19-20, 23, 25); for (b) Alt, Bopp, and Lady (1976, pp. 83-86); and for (c) Baltagi and Griffin (1983, pp. 119-21, 124, 135-36).

Notes: Entries relate to the United States unless otherwise indicated. Those for the neighbor countries are static estimates that do not distinguish between short run and long run.

3.2 INVESTMENT

Managers desire to have available K^* machines by the end of the period, but because of cost considerations they elect to acquire capital slowly. In particular, they follow the partial-adjustment rule of the flexible accelerator (Goodwin, 1948, p. 120; Chenery, 1952, pp. 13-14):

$$K - K_{-1} = \lambda(K^* - K_{-1}), \tag{3.2}$$

where K denotes the actual capital stock at the end of the period and where reaction coefficient λ satisfies the restriction $0 < \lambda < 1$. With K^* being proportional to current output Y, rule (3.2) reduces to

$$I = \mu Y - \lambda K_{-1}, \tag{3.3}$$

whose I signifies net investment $K - K_{-1}$.

Expression (3.3) focuses on stock adjustment and, in recognition of that feature, has been called by Matthews (1959, p. 41) the capital-stock-adjustment principle. However, since the capital stock can be regarded as the amalgamation of current and past investment flows, stock-adjustment principle (3.3) may be reexpressed in flow-adjustment terms. For infinitely lived capital,[3] principle (3.3) implies

$$I = \mu Y - \lambda(I_{-1} + I_{-2} + I_{-3} + \dots). \tag{3.4}$$

Lagging relation (3.4) by one period and subtracting the result from (3.4) itself produce

$$I = \mu \Delta Y + (1 - \lambda)I_{-1}, \tag{3.5}$$

a flow-adjustment model.

Capacity is not the only driving force behind investment. Finance counts too in the general case, as Duesenberry (1958, pp. 87-100) testified, and in the case of Yugoslavia, where firms influence banks and enjoy soft budgets, finance is a force that must be reckoned with. Gapinski (1990a, pp. 49-52) presented the argument. Logically, then, capacity paradigms (3.3) and (3.5) should be extended to capture real credit availability XR and real credit cost UC, which besides the real rate of interest includes the tax rate borne by firms. Incorporating the two finance measures along with other determinants Z^v into the capacity expressions yields

$$I = \alpha_0 + \alpha_Y Y + \alpha_K K_{-1} + \alpha_X XR + \alpha_U UC + \alpha_Z^v Z^v, \qquad (3.6)$$

$$I = \beta_0 + \beta_Y \Delta Y + \beta_I I_{-1} + \beta_X XR + \beta_U UC + \beta_Z^v Z^v, \qquad (3.7)$$

whose sign patterns are straightforward. For statement (3.6), $\alpha_Y > 0$, $\alpha_K < 0$, $\alpha_X > 0$, and $\alpha_U < 0$. Vector $\alpha^v{}_Z$ has elements signed in concert with the elements of Z^v. Signs for the β coefficients match those for their α twins with the exception of β_I, which is positive. Described more completely, $0 < \beta_I < 1$.

Applying the stock-adjustment and flow-adjustment models (3.6) and (3.7) to gross investment in each of the ten sectors produces equations (IN1) to (IN10) of Appendix A. Overall those fits have a high degree of explanatory power, especially given the usual volatility of investment. Only catering, the fastest grower according to Table 3.4, evidences weak explanatory ability.

All coefficients in each equation are properly signed. The positive signs for the coefficients of $\Delta LANDS_{-1}$ and $\Delta LANDP$ in the agriculture equations support the view that larger plot sizes encourage increased mechanization. $OECDA_{-1}$ rightly has a positive coefficient in the catering equation because improved economic fortunes beyond the Yugoslav borders should mean increased foreign tourism and catering activity within them. Wider newspaper circulation means a greater demand for newsprint and perhaps for reading materials generally. Such broader interest has repercussions for investment in forestry and explains the positive coefficient for $NEWSCIRC_{-1}$. Oil is the lifeblood of transportation. Greater quantities quicken its pulse rate and stimulate the heartbeat of its attendant investment. Hence the coefficient of OILUSSR/PZ has a positive sign in transportation equation (IN10).

As regards the capacity and finance coefficients, industry investment IIND72, easily the largest investment series, has an income coefficient of 0.3138 that takes fourth-place honors and a capital coefficient, translated into the flow-adjustment form $1-\lambda$, of 0.9131 that finishes second. However, its finance coefficients of 0.1502 for credit availability and -3483.3 for user cost lead those for the other sectors and finish in first place by substantial margins. The second largest investment component, transportation's ITRA72, displays the greatest income coefficient, 0.8549, and finance coefficients that rank second and third: 0.0238 and -284.40, respectively. At the opposite end of the spectrum stand the two agricultures, particularly private agriculture. Despite its size, private agriculture investment has an income coefficient that is the smallest of the ten.[4] Moreover, its

Table 3.4
Investment Means, Growth Rates, and Causal Shares by Sector

Sector	Mean	Growth Rate	Share for Capacity	Finance	Relative Share
Industry	23,985	.048	.575	.425	1.355
Social Agriculture	3,581	.028	.851	.149	5.690
Private Agriculture	2,428	.051	.678	.322	2.102
Catering	1,782	.095	.572	.428	1.337
Construction	1,797	.067	.687	.313	2.195
Forestry	599	.039	.678	.322	2.106
Handicraft	1,164	.080	.817	.183	4.476
Home Trade	2,383	.049	.796	.204	3.891
Residual	5,757	.046	.495	.505	.980
Transportation	8,753	.049	.663	.337	1.967

Notes: All entries pertain to the years of the corresponding regression inquiry in Appendix A. Growth rates are exponential, capacity share is S_C, and finance share is S_F. Relative share equals S_C /S_F. Capacity and finance shares are reported as means expressed in proportionate, not percentage, terms.

lagged investment coefficient is next to last, and the two credit coefficients are likewise near the bottom. As expected from the basic production methods practiced on Yugoslavia's small-scale family farms, economic matters matter little in the investment decision.[5] Similarly, as expected from the often negative real interest rate and as advised at the end of Chapter 2, the user cost coefficient, although always correctly signed, is never more than weakly significant across the sectors.

The pattern of regression coefficients provides fragmented clues about the relative importance of capacity and finance in investment. Table 3.4 presents a more unified comparison through the investment shares due to capacity S_C and finance S_F. These causal shares are calculated in a "residual" manner resembling the procedure frequently used to quantify technical progress from production function estimates. That is, investment is adjusted for all determinants other than capacity and finance and for the negative effect exerted by UC. From equation (3.7) the adjusted series I_A becomes

$$I_A = I - \beta_0 - \beta_Z^v Z^v - 2\beta_U UC,$$

leaving

$$I_A = \beta_Y \Delta Y + \beta_I I_{-1} + \beta_X XR - \beta_U UC. \tag{3.8}$$

Since $\beta_U < 0$, each of the four terms in statement (3.8) contributes positively to investment, which is now oriented in gross—not net— terms. From statement (3.8) it naturally follows that the shares are

$$S_C = (\beta_Y \Delta Y + \beta_I I_{-1})/I_A,$$

$$S_F = (\beta_X XR - \beta_U UC)/I_A.$$

By Table 3.4 capacity dominates finance.[6] For top-sized industry, capacity explains 57.5 percent of adjusted investment and finance explains 42.5 percent, the relative share being 1.355. Fast-growing catering has roughly the same split between capacity and finance and hence roughly the same relative share, 1.337. Transportation leans further toward capacity, posting 66.3 percent against 33.7 percent, whereas private agriculture, forestry, handicraft, and social agriculture lean even more heavily in the capacity direction. Their biases confirm the intuitive notion that finance is a secondary consideration in farming and in "mom-and-pop" operations. Finance outranks capacity only once—in the portmanteau sector—and then by the slimmest of margins, 50.5 percent to 49.5 percent. Interpreted in the context of the debate recounted by Gapinski (1990a, pp. 45-46), these results say that investment fact supersedes investment fancy, and accordingly the strict accelerationists might find some comfort in them.[7]

Besides investment in plant and equipment, total investment ITOT72 in equation (IN12) of Appendix A contains housing investment IHOU72, which subscribes to stock-adjustment hypothesis (3.6). Equation (IN11) presents the details. Again, the coefficients are properly signed. Credit availability is broadened beyond domestic sources to cover real credit from abroad, namely, the lagged version of ΔFCREDIT/IMPTP. Like ML1/PZ, this variable exerts a positive effect on housing. Similarly, the export of factor services abroad EXFSR relates to housing positively through the remittances that it generates. Yet the greater is the living space already in place—alias HOMEAREA—the weaker is the need for new housing, and the lower is investment. In regard to the fact-or-fancy debate, housing aligns itself fairly closely with construction by registering a capacity share of 65.2 percent and a finance share of 34.8 percent. As before, the calculations pertain to the regression years, when housing investment averaged 18,758 million dinars. That figure places second only to industry investment.

3.3 CAPITAL STOCK

Gross investment I, the total acquisition of new plant and equipment, serves to replace expiring units and to expand the existing stock. With δ denoting the rate of physical depreciation, it naturally follows that

$$I = (K - K_{-1}) + \delta K_{-1}, \tag{3.9}$$

where, as earlier, K represents the capital stock extant at the end of the period. Arithmetic then yields

$$K = I + (1 - \delta) K_{-1}, \tag{3.10}$$

$1 - \delta$ measuring the proportion of old capital still in operation. For purposes of estimation, formula (3.10) may be rewritten as

$$K - I = (1 - \delta) K_{-1}. \tag{3.11}$$

Table 3.5 reports the results of fitting equation (3.11) in the

Table 3.5
Sectoral Capital-Stock Equation (3.11): Estimations and Implications

Sector	Coefficient of K_{-1}	Student-t Value	RBARSQ	RHO	DW	δ	1/δ
Industry	.9706	599.650	.9997	0	1.99	.0294	34.0
Social Agriculture	.9577	114.260	.9921	.510	2.06	.0423	23.6
Private Agriculture	.9822	124.470	.9500	.497	1.93	.0178	56.2
Catering	.9870	264.560	.9988	0	2.12	.0130	76.9
Construction	.9750	275.620	.9988	.132	2.05	.0250	40.0
Forestry	.9427	213.650	.9968	.249	1.91	.0573	17.5
Handicraft	.9471	74.162	.9854	.710	2.41	.0529	18.9
Home Trade	.9734	373.980	.9994	-.137	1.96	.0266	37.6
Residual	.9823	42.938	.9450	.269	1.76	.0177	56.5
Transportation	.9737	232.080	.9973	.395	1.91	.0263	38.0

Notes: RBARSQ denotes the adjusted coefficient of determination; RHO, the first-order autocorrelation coefficient; and DW, the Durbin–Watson statistic. All estimations cover the years 1953–88.

individual sectors. The rate of depreciation implicit in those coefficients ranges from the highs of 0.0573, 0.0529, and 0.0423 for forestry, handicraft, and social agriculture, respectively, to the midlevels of 0.0294, 0.0266, 0.0263, and 0.0250 for industry, home trade, transportation, and construction, respectively. Private agriculture, residual, and catering post the respective lows of 0.0178, 0.0177, and 0.0130. Converting these rates into physical life figures under a straight-line schedule merely involves division. Thus capital lasts 17.5 years in forestry, 18.9 years in handicraft, and 34.0 years in industry, while in some sectors it is almost infinitely lived.

Turned around, long life suggests old age, and compared against the record of major developed countries, Yugoslavia's capital does appear to be dated. Maddison (1987, p. 664), for instance, looked at the average age of capital in France, Germany, Japan, the Netherlands, the UK, and the US. Three years were examined—1950, 1973, and 1984—producing 18 separate estimates of age. Nonetheless, age never exceeded 16.5 years, a benchmark that, by Table 3.5, Yugoslav capital always exceeds. Reliance on less modern capital is not uncommon for a nation undergoing development. Perhaps more to the point, such reliance is neither inconsistent with the weak incentives toward capital that derive from ownership by an amorphous society nor incongruous with a virtual ban on the resale of that society's property.

3.4 OUTPUT: CAPACITY AND ACTUAL

Capacity output can be defined in several ways, but in each case it represents a standard for judging economic performance. For instance, it may be posited as the output level that yields minimum unit cost. Alternatively, it may be interpreted as the output level that could be achieved given full employment of some or all inputs. This second conception, whereby capacity output also can be construed as potential output or simply as maximum output, has been used in macro models such as the Wharton paradigm of the United States (Evans, 1969, p. 435), and it has provided a benchmark for policy analysis by government agencies such as the US Council of Economic Advisers. It may be quantified by first selecting some output value as the base and then projecting values through time at a rate that reflects the trend movements of inputs. Another method, the one adopted here,[8] first identifies output peaks and then either interpolates between them or extrapolates from them.

Panel A of Figure 3.1 illustrates that method in the industry context. Actual output YIND72 is regarded as peaking seven times: in 1953, 1957, 1960, 1964, 1971, 1974, and 1979. Interpolating between those

Figure 3.1
Capacity Utilization in Industry

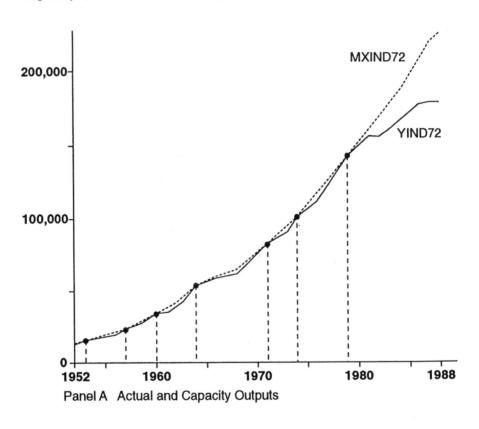

Panel A   Actual and Capacity Outputs

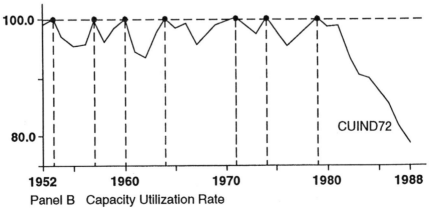

Panel B   Capacity Utilization Rate

seven points and extrapolating outward from the first and last produce the capacity series MXIND72. From this maximum it is possible to define an output gap as MXIND72 - YIND72, which measures the additional output that could have been generated had favorable conditions prevailed. It is also possible to define the rate of capacity utilization as 100·YIND72/MXIND72. Nicknamed CUIND72, it indicates in percentage terms how close industry output comes to its maximum. Panel B of Figure 3.1 depicts industry's capacity utilization rate and, in so doing, highlights its dreadful performance during the 1980s.

The record of capacity utilization is presented more comprehensively in Table 3.6. For all ten sectors combined, utilization averaged 94.8 percent over the 37 years 1952-88, although its minimum value registered 77.7 percent.[9] The sectors themselves exhibited variations on that theme. Handicraft, with an average of 96.2 percent, enjoyed the greatest utilization, whereas construction, with an 89.4 percent mean, suffered the lowest. In fact, its minimum rate sank to the horribly low level of 64.1 percent. For the postreform years 1965-73 and the post-Constitution years 1974-79, utilization remained so impressively high across sectors that even the minimum rates easily exceeded 80 percent. By contrast, in the 1980s and especially in the final five years reported, six of the ten sectors posted all-time low rates. Only social agriculture and transportation managed to withstand the collapse of utilization.

Quantifying capacity output is one thing; explaining it is another. Equations (MX1) to (MX9) in Appendix A offer explanations for nine of the ten sectors, the capacity level for private agriculture being treated as exogenous. Manifestly, the fundamental determinant of capacity output is the capital stock *available*. Other determinants may augment the expressions, and the complementary capacity variables in industry and residual exemplify such refinements. Nevertheless, capital anchors capacity.[10]

As the equations show, capacity's capital elasticity ranges from a high of 2.684 for forestry to a low of 0.049 for transportation. Perhaps not surprisingly, this ordering roughly matches—in reverse—the pattern of available capital across the sectors. Forestry's top-ranked elasticity corresponds to a bottom-ranked capital share, 100·KFOR72/KSUM72, of 0.9 percent. In like manner, the third-ranked construction elasticity of 0.530 lines up with the third-from-the-bottom capital share of 3.2 percent, and the bottom three elasticities for industry, residual, and transportation team with the top three shares. Ceteris paribus, less capital means more capital opportunities and greater elasticities.

With capacity output in hand, actual output can be specified as a

Table 3.6
Capacity Utilization Rates by Sector and Period

Sector	1952-88		1952-64		1965-73		1974-79		1980-88		1984-88	
	mean	min	mean	min	mean	min	mean	min	mean	min	mean	min
All	94.8	77.7	95.4	90.2	98.6	95.3	98.3	96.0	88.0	77.7	83.0	77.7
Industry	95.8	78.9	97.4	93.2	98.4	95.6	98.2	95.3	89.3	78.9	84.5	78.9
Social Agriculture	93.9	72.4	90.0	72.4	95.3	86.9	96.6	89.3	96.4	92.4	96.5	92.4
Private Agriculture	92.8	75.9	90.4	75.9	94.3	85.0	96.7	91.3	92.2	81.4	88.7	81.4
Catering	93.9	80.2	91.3	82.1	97.4	91.8	96.2	93.1	92.7	80.2	88.2	80.2
Construction	89.4	64.1	89.1	75.8	97.8	93.1	96.8	94.8	76.5	64.1	67.7	64.1
Forestry	92.8	78.0	89.3	78.0	95.5	82.4	97.0	92.8	92.4	85.3	89.4	85.3
Handicraft	96.2	77.4	95.9	85.1	98.7	97.5	99.3	98.5	91.8	77.4	87.0	77.4
Home Trade	93.2	70.5	93.8	86.3	98.2	95.3	96.5	91.1	85.1	70.4	78.4	70.5
Residual	92.8	69.2	94.8	80.4	96.8	89.5	99.0	97.4	81.9	69.2	73.9	69.2
Transportation	94.7	86.0	94.9	86.0	94.9	86.4	96.3	92.2	93.1	90.5	91.3	90.5

Note: Entries are percentages.

proportional function of the sort YIND72 = α·MXIND72. Proportionality term α is envisioned to reflect secular developments, demand pressures, and price movements, inter alia. As equations (YA1) to (YA10) of Appendix A disclose, secular occurrences exert a negative effect on output over the sectors. However, in Keynesian fashion, demand always stimulates it. Whether demand is represented by the aggregate measure DEMD72, by food and beverage consumption CFOOD72 + CBEVER72, by investment spending ITOT72 and exports EXNFSR, or by economic activity abroad OECDA, its coefficient proves to be uniformly positive. Positive too is the coefficient of relative price, a typical determinant of supply.

Social product, Y72 in equation (YA11), equals the sum of its sectoral parts. It excludes government services; including them creates YSTAR72 by equation (YA12).

3.5 LABOR

Explaining employment in the West commonly appeals to a production function, invokes an optimization rule, and then solves for the labor variable. For instance, when the technology imparts constancy to the elasticity of factor substitution σ, the production function may be written as

$$Y = \zeta(\xi_L L^{-\rho} + \xi_K K^{-\rho})^{-1/\rho}, \tag{3.12}$$

where Y denotes output and where L and K denote, respectively, labor and capital inputs. Parameters ζ, ξ_L, and ξ_K are positive, while $\xi_L + \xi_K = 1$. Parameter ρ, which relates to σ as $1/\sigma - 1$, cannot drop below -1. Optimization subject to equation (3.12) then leaves

$$\partial Y/\partial L = W/P, \tag{3.13}$$

whose W and P stand for the money wage and the price level, respectively. Taken together, expressions (3.12) and (3.13) imply that

$$L = (\zeta^{\rho}/\xi)^{-(1+\rho)}(W/P)^{-(1+\rho)}Y, \tag{3.14}$$

namely, that employment depends negatively upon the real wage and positively upon output.

According to statement (3.14), employment adjustments are symmetric: Employment falls as fast as it rises given equal but opposite perturbations. For Yugoslavia, however, budget softness and the employment tenure that goes with it argue against symmetry. Slack times need not translate into dismissals, as partners may elect to have economic activity drop progressively below the production surface. Table 3.7 reports on this pattern. More precisely, it shows the recent movements of output and employment in those sectors where employment is endogenous.[11] For industry, output declined in 1982 and 1988, but employment did not follow suit. In fact, it increased. Similarly, output for social agriculture declined in 1985, 1987, and 1988, but employment increased. Employment in construction fell as output sank, but it fell only during half of the construction recession. Much the same conclusion can be drawn from the remaining sectors.

One way to capture this asymmetry is by introducing a ratchet into the employment equations. The spirit of the ratchet is shown in Figure 3.2. There economic activity is gauged by commodity demand D rather than by output, hardly a major substitution since employment represents a derived demand. As long as demand is expanding, employment advances along the ray EF. But once demand begins to decline from its peak level D_0, the ratchet becomes operative, and employment falls along the segment GH, not GE. Consequently, the recession-level demand D_1 is associated with L_I workers instead of L_J, and $L_I - L_J$ jobs are preserved.[12]

Modifying a linear version of equation (3.14) to include the ratchet yields, after other revisions,

$$L = \alpha_0 + \alpha_R R + \alpha_{WP}(W/P) + \alpha_D D + \alpha_{DD}(D_0 - D) \\ + \alpha_L L_{-1}. \tag{3.15}$$

This schedule allows for the 1965 reform through dummy variable R and for employment inertia through lagged employment L_{-1}. Variable D_0 signifies peak demand, whether current or past, and thus $D_0 - D$ must be nonnegative. During secular expansion $D_0 - D$ vanishes, making $\partial L/\partial D = \alpha_D$, whereas during contraction it holds, rendering $\partial L/\partial D = \alpha_D - \alpha_{DD}$. From Figure 3.2, $\alpha_D > 0$, $\alpha_D - \alpha_{DD} > 0$, and $\alpha_D > \alpha_D - \alpha_{DD}$. Consequently, $\alpha_D > \alpha_{DD} > 0$. It is instructive to observe that condition $\alpha_D - \alpha_{DD} > 0$ echoes the traditional sentiment that flagging demand, by itself,[13] cannot stimulate output, and accordingly it reiterates a main conclusion of the case against Wardian economics.

The fitted versions of expression (3.15) appear as equations (LB1) to (LB11) in Appendix A, where, for improved understanding, the residual sector is split into four components: commercial and financial, education, health, and general government. To its credit,

Table 3.7
Output and Employment by Sector over the Decade 1979-88

Year	Industry Out.	Industry Emp.	Soc. Agr. Out.	Soc. Agr. Emp.	Catering Out.	Catering Emp.	Construction Out.	Construction Emp.
1979	142.9	2,102	14.5	205	10.4	209	41.9	622
1980	148.8	2,162	14.8	208	10.6	218	42.0	644
1981	155.3*	2,242	15.2	218	10.7	229	40.0*	645*
1982	155.1*	2,313	16.6	228	11.0	237	37.0*	635*
1983	157.3	2,374	16.7	237	11.2	244	32.2*	623*
1984	165.4	2,445	18.3	245	11.5	254	30.8*	615*
1985	169.8	2,529	17.3*	251	11.7	262	30.3*	608*
1986	176.4	2,625	18.8	259	11.0*	269	29.9*	613
1987	177.8	2,706	18.5*	264	10.4*	274	29.6*	615
1988	176.6*	2,716	18.5*	265	10.6	284	27.8*	585*

Year	Handicraft Out.	Handicraft Emp.	Home Trade Out.	Home Trade Emp.	Residual Out.	Residual Emp.	Transportation Out.	Transportation Emp.
1979	11.3	210	66.4	558	13.4	1,258	30.9	388
1980	11.8	222	67.0	582	13.4	1,299	32.1	400
1981	12.0	230	65.4*	596	13.8	1,333	32.5*	409
1982	12.6	238	65.9	607	14.2	1,364	31.6*	416
1983	12.8	242	64.5*	621	13.9*	1,391	32.0	423
1984	13.2	248	62.9*	631	13.2*	1,419	33.3	431
1985	13.7	254	62.6*	641	13.7	1,460	34.4	441
1986	12.9*	266	64.2	658	14.0	1,503	36.0	453
1987	12.3*	272	60.4*	669	14.5*	1,544	37.2	452*
1988	12.3	278	57.9*	676	14.3*	1,554	37.9	458

Notes: Output is expressed in billions of 1972 dinars; employment, in thousands of persons. An asterisk identifies a decline in a series. In those cases where rounding conceals movement, the direction of change can be inferred from the presence or absence of an asterisk.

Figure 3.2
An Employment Ratchet

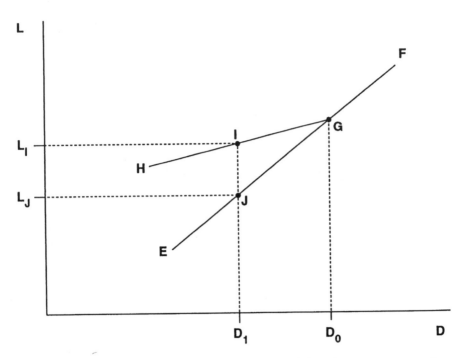

the real-wage coefficient α_{WP} always enters with the correct negative sign. Also to their credit, the demand coefficient α_D and the inertial coefficient α_L always exhibit the correct positive signs. These patterns for α_{WP}, α_D, and α_L are more than vaguely reminiscent of the configurations for Western economies and give credence to the thought expressed in Section 2.5 that traditional theoretics have much to say about economic relationships in Yugoslavia.

Without exception, ratchet coefficient α_{DD} satisfies the inequalities $\alpha_D > \alpha_{DD} > 0$. Economic distress hits the employment rolls, but tenure cushions the blow. In construction, for example, ratchet α_{DD} $(D_0 - D)$ saved an average of 73.7 thousand jobs per year from 1984 to 1988. In health it saved 12.4 thousand annually over that period, while in industry it salvaged another 12.1 thousand. All in all, tenure spared 111.5 thousand jobs annually.

As equation (LB12) of Appendix A indicates, total employment EMPTOT is obtained by summing employment across the nine homogeneous sectors and the four components of the residual. This figure, however, differs from the officially recorded statistic, which omits agricultural employment except for those farmers who are part of the social security system. The relationship between the official count ETOT and total employment EMPTOT is shown in equation (LB13).

Labor supply LSTOT is posited in formula (LB14) as the product of the target population and the participation rate, both of which are exogenous. Unemployment rate URATE flows naturally from LSTOT, as equation (LB15) tells. A second unemployment measure URATEYU is calculated to reflect more closely the official definition; identity (LB16) has that information.

3.6 FISCAL FACTORS

Government influences the flow of quantities through instruments that include taxes and expenditures. In Yugoslavia the tax system can be thought of as involving five different levies: a personal income tax, a sales tax, a firm tax, an import tax, and an "other" tax, which in turn entails a household tax and a portmanteau nonhousehold tax. Government consumption, on the other hand, includes commodity purchases, wages and salaries, and financial depreciation of capital. Real tax collections (TOTTAX/P) generally increased through time, although they sagged almost continually during the economic adversity of the 1980s. Real government consumption GOVC72, described by equation (OR4) in Appendix A, followed a similar pattern. However, by remaining below revenue levels, it resulted in a surplus that filtered through the remaining items of the government's budget constraint, equation (OR8).

Table 3.8 provides a closer look at the fiscal ledger. As regards taxes, it is evident that there have been substantial modifications in the code since the early 1950s. Prior to the reform events of 1965, other tax—principally other nonhousehold tax—represented the main revenue raiser. Second in importance was sales tax, while firm tax ranked third. Personal tax came fourth, producing only a third of the revenue generated by other tax. Yet in the wake of the 1974 Constitution, personal tax became the chief revenue source, as other tax tumbled to roughly the level of the sales tax. In addition to disclosing this ordering reversal, Table 3.8 notes that firm tax became inoperative between the reform and Constitution years and that other tax was the levy which made up the difference.

On the expense side of the ledger, purchases and earnings exhibit their own ordering reversals and re-reversals, although purchases dominated over the years 1952-88 taken as a whole. Numerically, they accounted for slightly more than half of government consumption, whereas earnings registered about ten percentage points below

Table 3.8
Total Tax and Government Consumption by Share and Period

Share of

Period	Total Tax from				Other Tax			Government Consumption from		
	Personal Tax	Sales Tax	Firm Tax	Import Tax	Total	Household	Nonhousehold	Commodity Purchases	Wages and Salaries	Capital Depreciation
1952-64	.134	.255	.194	.035	.382	.038	.343	.597	.330	.073
1965-73	.124	.180	.001	.086	.609	.031	.578	.469	.490	.042
1974-79	.371	.201	.113	.109	.206	.038	.168	.478	.485	.037
1980-88	.332	.208	.160	.076	.224	.049	.175	.509	.447	.044
1984-88	.333	.197	.171	.079	.220	.048	.171	.516	.437	.047

Note: All entries are means expressed in proportionate terms.

purchases. Depreciation amounted to one-tenth of purchases.

Since the major components of government consumption are regarded as exogenous, econometric interest turns to taxes. However, specifying a tax equation straightforwardly in level form renews the possibility, observed in earlier testing, that the fit would produce one-sided residuals at either end of the sample. To circumvent this prospect, the dependent variable is converted into an average effective tax rate by dividing the nominal tax level by some nominal base variable. For example, the average rate for the personal income tax equals personal tax divided by the wage bill. Similarly, the average rate for the firm tax divides firm tax by the social product exclusive of government services, and that for other tax adjusts by the social product inclusive of such services. Figure 3.3 depicts the three rates. Panel A highlights the steep hike in the personal rate for the post-Constitution era, and Panel C shows the corresponding drop in other's rate. Panel B makes unmistakable the suspension years for the firm tax.

Apart from illustrating previously cited properties, Figure 3.3 emphasizes the jerky motions exhibited by the average rates as they jump from one plateau to another. Dummy variables are incorporated into the estimation equations to capture such leaps, and their years of coverage can be inferred from the vertical dashes in the figure. Underlying systematic tendencies are represented by continuous measures such as time and price inflation, which together with the dummies explain the average rates. Determining tax levels from the rates is then easily accomplished by multiplying by the base variables.

3.7 VOLUMES OF EXPORTS AND IMPORTS

A retrospective on Yugoslav exports and imports uncovers two different patterns in relation to overall economic activity. Total exports averaged about 14 percent of social product during the period 1952-64, but following the 1965 reform, that share became virtually constant at 20 percent. By contrast, total imports, which averaged roughly 18 percent before the reform, climbed to 24 percent immediately afterward and went on to 27 percent during the years 1974-79. Their share subsequently declined, dropping below 20 percent for the years 1984-88. As these cursory numbers suggest, imports usually outstripped exports, making net exports negative. Nevertheless, by the late 1980s the situation reversed, and net exports turned in positive values.

Yugoslav exports EXGNFSR fall into three groups. The first group consists of merchandise exports to Western countries, whose currencies

**Figure 3.3
Selected Average Tax Rates**

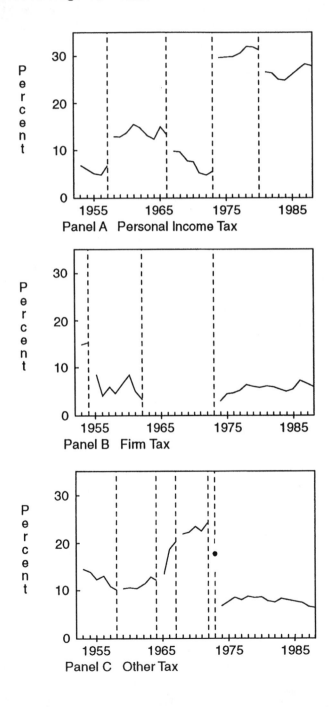

Panel A   Personal Income Tax

Panel B   Firm Tax

Panel C   Other Tax

are convertible in foreign exchange markets. The second group encompasses merchandise exports to Eastern nations, whose currencies are not convertible, while the third involves exports of nonfactor services, services like those associated with construction, consulting, insurance, international transportation, and tourism. Table 3.9 compares the three types by expressing their volumes as fractions of the total. In the early period 1952-64 exports to the West EXPTNSR accounted for the bulk of sales abroad. Their fraction of 0.641 exceeded that for nonfactor services EXNFSR by a multiple of three and that for exports to the East EXPTSR by a multiple of four. This weak showing by Eastern exports can be traced in part to the Soviet conflict that provoked a temporary suspension of trade with the socialist states. As time advanced, Western exports shrank in relative magnitude, whereas Eastern exports and nonfactor services both gained strength to the point where, loosely speaking, each series represented a third of total exports during the 1980s.

Explaining merchandise exports to the West follows a fairly typical format. For instance, the real exchange rate matters. Its backbone is the nominal rate DINDOAV, denominated in dinars per US dollar. As Table 1.1 showed, DINDOAV remained constant from 1952 to 1964, reflecting the Bretton Woods system of fixed exchange rates. Devaluation from 3.00 to 6.96 occurred in 1965 and to 12.50 in 1966, consonant with the accommodation of fundamental disequilibria allowed by that system. Further depreciation took place in 1971 and 1972 and then routinely as Bretton Woods faded into the past. By 1980 DINDOAV stood at 24.64, and by 1988 it easily topped 2,500.00. Such massive depreciation, observed as well in the "official" accounting exchange rate ERSTAT, helped to keep Yugoslav exports from drying up altogether during a time of intense domestic inflation. In other words, depreciation tended to protect exports by protecting the real exchange rate PRELIND, expressed as (DINDOAV /PIND)·IMPTP. In fact, it failed to keep pace with inflation from 1985 to 1987, and as a result the real rate declined to the detriment of merchandise exports. Equation (IA1) of Appendix A confirms that relationship.

Since Yugoslav exports to the West are imports there, it follows that the economic health of those countries should be an export determinant. Improved Western fortunes, measured by the index OECDA, mean improved fortunes for Yugoslav business abroad. Comparative advantage too might come into play. Relative to the West, Yugoslavia held an advantage in the production of labor-intensive and land-intensive commodities. Consequently, the decided increase in the capital intensity of industry production—namely, in KIND72/EIND—implies a move away from comparative advantage and

Table 3.9
Export and Import Shares by Period

Period	Export Share of			Import Share of			
	EXPTNSR	EXPTSR	EXNFSR	IMPTIR	IMPTKR	IMPTCR	IMNFSR
1952–64	.641	.167	.192	.541	.201	.172	.085
1965–73	.458	.247	.295	.581	.191	.119	.110
1974–79	.407	.269	.324	.598	.200	.064	.138
1980–88	.390	.314	.296	.591	.124	.047	.238
1984–88	.426	.302	.273	.603	.119	.052	.226

Note: Export shares are calculated relative to the total exports of goods and nonfactor services, EXGNFSR. Import shares are computed relative to the corresponding input total, IMGNFSR.

a sacrifice of exports.[14] Two other determinants might be foreign credit and exports to the East. Credit acts as a proxy for the ease with which trade can be financed (Leamer and Stern, 1970, p. 16) and should exert a positive effect on EXPTNSR. Conversely, Eastern exports, whose manufacture competes for productive resources, should carry a negative weight. Equation (IA1) confirms these four hypotheses.

Trade with the nonconvertible East is conducted through bilateral arrangements that amount to a form of barter whereby a temporary imbalance in the bilateral account triggers a series of transactions designed to restore balance. One such balancing item is oil from the USSR. Oil compensates Yugoslavia for exporting there, and as its price PML3 rises, the demand for those exports can rise as well. Equation (IA2) of Appendix A makes that linkage clear. It should be noted, however, that bilateral trade need not operate smoothly. At various times during the 1980s, Yugoslavia experienced large surpluses vis-à-vis the East, and ultimately those surpluses brought about the creation of dinars by the National Bank to reimburse exporters. Equation (IA2) reflects this situation through the ML1/PZ term.

While it is surely unfair to characterize the East as a "dumping ground" for inferior products, it is fair to say that Eastern markets are willing to accept lower-grade material that would not be acceptable to the West or sellable at home. Inventory accumulations $KIZREAL_{-1}$ and expanded production $\Delta YIND72$ that might lead to new accumulations thus induce EXPTSR. Moreover, inasmuch as merchandise exports to the East reflect construction activity by Yugoslav firms, nonfactor services become a requisite complement. Besides, the foreign exchange earnings generated from all exports of nonfactor services weaken the inclination of exporters to trade with the more exacting West and release merchandise for trade with the East. Equation (IA2) captures these thoughts.

Exports of nonfactor services resemble goods exports to the West in the sense that they depend upon credit and the real exchange rate PREXZ. However, more specific to their own composition, they also vary with the demand by foreigners for Yugoslav sun, food, and song and with the price of international transport services. Equation (IA3) presents the details.

The import side of Yugoslav international activity IMGNFSR has four components: intermediate goods, capital goods, consumer goods, and nonfactor services. As Table 3.9 indicates, intermediate goods imports IMPTIR constitute by far the largest portion of the total—more than half—and that portion has tended to expand through time. On the other hand, capital goods imports IMPTKR and their consumer goods counterpart IMPTCR experienced relative declines that put their shares at 12.4 percent and 4.7 percent, respectively, for the 1980s. That severe capital contraction coincided with a sharp drop in the *level* of capital imports and raises a question about the productive capacity of the economy. Similarly, the share contraction for consumer items during the 1980s corresponded to a hefty decline in that import level and prompts a question about the standard of living. Nonfactor services, unlike capital and consumer goods, enjoyed a continual increase in their imports both in level IMNFSR and, as Table 3.9 notes, in share.

Despite differences in their temporal movements, the three classes of goods imports have several explanatory points in common. The real exchange rate matters, but now it matters negatively rather than positively as in the case of exports. An increase in the real rate PRELIND or PRELC, either from nominal depreciation or from domestic disinflation, makes foreign goods more expensive and thus less attractive. Hard currencies to pay the import bills count positively, and their volume swings directly with exports to the West EXPTNSR, with remittances from Yugoslavs working abroad EXFSR, and with foreign borrowing FB and ΔFCREDIT. Of course, an import tax ITAXAER hurts all three types of goods.

A few other factors might lie behind the import streams. For example, industry has an insatiable appetite for intermediate goods, and consequently the more that it contributes to total output, the greater should be the need for (and the volume of) intermediate imports. Yet some of those basic materials might be produced by domestic farms or might come from domestic inventories, thereby reducing that need. Similar reasoning might be applied to consumer goods imports. Moreover, the move away from comparative advantage evidenced by the growth of KIND72/EIND may create a consumer goods vacuum to be filled by purchases abroad. Finally, capital goods imports might respond favorably in concert with domestic capital-stock initiatives and in keeping with the level of aggregate demand. Indeed, the latter determinant is a fixture of the standard theory referred to earlier.

Equations (IA4) to (IA6) appeal to all of these considerations to explain goods imports. The import of nonfactor services can be equated in identity fashion to the amount spent on shipping, travel, and other services "overseas." Equation (IA12) takes that tack.

NOTES

1. For instance, the United States models by Fair (1974, p. 287) and by Liu and Hwa (1974, p. 347) have total short-run propensities in

that vicinity.

2. Owing to the modest reason for introducing Table 3.3, no attempt was made to render items exactly comparable across countries. Where compositions differ, the interpretation of results warrants caution, and such caution certainly applies to transportation inasmuch as only the Yugoslav elasticities include automobile purchases.

3. As the next section discloses, this assumption is not without merit for the case of Yugoslavia.

4. The finding that the income coefficient for private agriculture investment (0.0070) falls below its social sector equivalent (0.1335) agrees with the conclusion by Boyd (1987, pp. 210-11) that machinery has a lower output elasticity in private agriculture than in social agriculture. By the usual calculus the income coefficient varies directly with the output elasticity, and thus a smaller value for the latter implies a smaller value for the former.

5. Stipetić (1982, pp. 333, 346) offered a few words on the credit position and production scale of private agriculture.

6. The share arithmetic behind Table 3.4 converts the stock-adjustment equation for industry and for catering into flow-adjustment language by substituting $\mu \Delta Y$ for μY and $(1 - \lambda)I_{-1}$ for $-\lambda K_{-1}$ while keeping the remainder of the equation unchanged.

7. The weight of capacity should not be construed to imply that, contrary to the remarks in Sections 2.3.3 and 2.5, soft credit is unimportant for investment. Hardly. Recalculating the shares by quantifying XR as M1/PZ rather than as (M1 + L1)/PZ provides some idea about the effect of soft credit L1/PZ on investment. For instance, absent L1/PZ the capacity share in industry equals 68.0 percent rather than 57.5 percent, and the finance share registers 32.0 percent instead of 42.5. Therefore, the relative share reads 2.122 as opposed to 1.355. Similarly, without L1/PZ transportation shows a split of 75.6 percent versus 24.4 percent and a relative share of 3.092, whereas social agriculture posts numbers of 90.2 percent, 9.8 percent, and 9.179, respectively. On average over the ten sectors, soft credit raises the finance share and lowers the capacity share by 8.2 percentage points.

8. Behrman (1977, pp. 143-44), who likewise adopted the trends-through-the-peaks method, reviewed its strengths and weaknesses. Further discussion was offered by Phillips (1963, pp. 282, 290-91).

9. The utilization rate for the ten sectors combined is calculated as 100·MXY72/Y72, whose component variables are described in equations (MX10) and (YA11) of Appendix A.

10. The US models by Data Resources, Inc. (1976, p. 75) and Chase Econometrics (1983, eqs. 2-11) similarly use capital to anchor capacity.

11. Employment is presumed to be exogenous for private agriculture and forestry. In the former situation it declined continually from 1956 to 1985, when the counts became unavailable. In the latter case it remained roughly constant at a low level, 66,000 workers.

12. The kinship between this employment ratchet and the consumption ratchets of Duesenberry (1949, p. 114) and Modigliani (1949, p. 393) should be obvious.

13. Table 3.7 exhibits the response of employment to all determinants combined and therefore masks the pure ratchet effect.

14. Industry's capital/labor ratio averaged 90,100 (real) dinars per worker for the years 1952-64. It jumped to 143,800 for the period 1965-73 and then to 193,000 and 225,000 for the respective epochs 1974-79 and 1980-88.

4

Prices and Values

Quantities in Yugoslavia reveal fascinating details about the country's economic structure. Prices too have a story to tell, and it begins in Section 4.1 with wage inflation. There the determinants of wage inflation are defended on theoretical grounds, and the relative strengths of those causal forces are established on empirical grounds. Section 4.2 extends that treatment to price inflation. Since wage inflation and price inflation react to each other, they form a network of inflation. Section 4.3 examines the network, while Section 4.4 identifies the counterfactual policy implications that naturally derive from it.[1] Bridging from the equations in the network to those that actually appear in the Mark 4.0 requires a few economic planks, which are supplied by Section 4.5. Afterward, Section 4.6 moves to consumer price inflation. Section 4.7 presents additional reflections on price indices, and Section 4.8 concludes the discussion by turning attention from domestic price relationships to international value relationships in the balance of payments.

4.1 SECTORAL WAGE INFLATION

Equation (2.23) provides the starting point for the explanation of wage inflation—and therefore of wage level—by sector. It maintains that

$$\Delta W/W_{-1} = h(U) + E(\Delta P/P_{-1}), \tag{4.1}$$

where W denotes the money wage; U, the unemployment rate; P, the price level; and $E(\Delta P/P_{-1})$, the expected rate of price inflation.

Section 2.5, however, suggests that such a Western formulation might be refined to more appropriately reflect the special features of Yugoslavia. For instance, the principle of worker self-management gives workers a voice in the conduct of business affairs, including wage decisions, and consequently they are in a position to extract a productivity premium. In other words, they are able to appropriate for themselves some of their own productivity increase. As a result, productivity growth $\Delta Q/Q_{-1}$, Q being output per worker, warrants insertion into formula (4.1).

Worker solidarity and the employment tenure that comes with it caution that the unemployment rate may be a bad gauge of labor-market pressure in Yugoslavia, where slack times need not lead to new dismissals and where boom periods need not lead to new hires. A more sensitive indicator may be cast in terms of capital. Variations in labor pressure should reflect themselves as variations in capital usage, which can be specified by $\ln(K_{-1} \cdot V)$, K signifying the end-of-period capital and V symbolizing the import of intermediate goods. That intermediate imports belong in a utilization measure can be justified by the shortages of intermediates which Yugoslavia often encounters and by the work disruptions which they cause. Succinctly, then, $\ln(K_{-1} \cdot V)$ replaces h(U) in expression (4.1).

How are inflation expectations $E(\Delta P/P_{-1})$ to be modeled? Owing to the annual nature of the data, elaborate functional forms would likely provide little insight beyond the information conveyed by a basic structure, and hence $E(\Delta P/P_{-1})$ is postulated as a linear function of the current actual inflation rate $\Delta P/P_{-1}$. A formal defense of this retreat to simplicity comes from Gapinski (1991, pp. 40-41), who used annual data to study Yugoslav wage inflation at the aggregate level. Postulating expectations by alternative polynomial distributed lags of current and past actual inflations produces inflation coefficients that decline sharply in magnitude and in statistical significance from the current year's. Restricting the lag structure to the present and immediate past year then leaves only the former coefficient significant, thereby supporting the idea of a linear structure in current inflation. Discussion by Wyzan and Utter (1982, pp. 398-401) lends further support to this formulation.[2]

In a soft-budget environment wage payments are connected to soft credits. Consummate actors playing Shakespearean leads in London or New York command stellar fees that may be specifically identified in the grant packages from the Arts Council of Great Britain or the National Endowment for the Arts. Or those subsidies might cover other costs, enabling the fees to be paid from box-office receipts. Either way, subsidies affect wages positively. Applying a similar argument to the Yugoslav situation, after encouragement from Gedeon

(1985-86, pp. 215, 217), broadens equation (4.1) to include a nominal credit variable X.

Taken together, self-management, worker solidarity, inflation contemporaneity, and soft budgets convert equation (4.1) into

$$\Delta W/W_{-1} = \alpha_0 + \alpha_R R + \alpha_Q \Delta Q/Q_{-1} + \alpha_K \ln(K_{-1} \cdot V) \\ + \alpha_P \Delta P/P_{-1} + \alpha_X \Delta X/X_{-1}. \tag{4.2}$$

R signifies a shift variable for the reforms of 1965. Except for α_0, whose sign is ambiguous, all α coefficients should be positive. According to the equations in Table 4.1, they are.[3]

Although the 1965 reforms swept across all productive sectors, their effects were not uniform. As the REFORM coefficients manifest, handicraft reacted most strongly (0.4454); catering, most weakly (0.1317). The market-pressure variable $\ln(\cdot)$ performs surprisingly well. The aforementioned work by Gapinski (1991, pp. 41-42) at the aggregate level found pressure to be statistically insignificant over the years 1953-87; yet the results here for virtually the same period indicate that it was alive and well at the sectoral level. Perhaps the process of aggregating variables across different sectors masks the true relationship and might account for a rather standard belief that in Yugoslavia market forces do not extend to the labor input.

Consonant with comments offered in Sections 2.4.3 and 2.5 and with findings by Wyzan and Utter (1982, p. 399), the coefficient of inflation $\Delta PZ/PZ_{-1}$ always falls below unity, ranging from a high of 0.5162 for social agriculture to a low of 0.2097 for construction. Inflation expectations sway wage decisions, but, ceteris paribus, wage advances fall short of price advances, causing the real wage to fall. Protection of the real wage therefore must rely on other factors such as productivity increases. This possibility will be explored more fully later. Also explored more fully later is the way in which credit quickens the wage-price spiral. As the equations affirm, credit growth $\Delta ML1/ML1_{-1}$ stimulates wage inflation in each sector, and the stimulus cannot be regarded as small. For example, an increase of 10 percentage points in credit growth raises wage inflation by 5.5 points in construction, 4.4 points in industry, and even 2.7 points in social agriculture. But by the cost-push philosophy of equation (2.25), accelerated wage inflation prompts accelerated price inflation, which, from equation (4.2) or from the more precise relations in Table 4.1, prompts a further acceleration of wage inflation. To complicate the sequence, price inflation may have its own direct dependency on credit growth. In other words, price inflation may be affected by

Table 4.1
Sectoral Wage Inflation Equations

Equation for $\Delta W12.../W12..._{-1}$ in

Coefficients and [Student-t Values]

Explanatory Variable	Industry	Soc. Agr.	Catering	Construct.	Forestry	Handicraft	Home Trade	Residual	Transport.
CONSTANT	-.3029 [-1.822]	-.2074 [-1.805]	-.1290 [-.922]	-.1310 [-.986]	-.3582 [-2.119]	-.2934 [-1.346]	-.2305 [-1.561]	-.4614 [-2.552]	.1179 [7.133]
REFORM	.2319 [4.986]	.2117 [4.750]	.1317 [2.307]	.1724 [3.395]	.2169 [3.968]	.4454 [5.792]	.2456 [4.784]	.2851 [5.526]	.1976 [3.753]
$\Delta Q.../Q..._{-1}$	.1497 [.340]	.1092 [1.486]		.0566 [.271]	.0069 [.030]	.1537 [.569]	.3399 [1.103]	.1064 [.485]	
$\ln(K...72_{-1}\cdot \text{IMPTIR})$	.0190 [2.489]	.0151 [2.483]	.0122 [1.629]	.0143 [2.011]	.0258 [2.708]	.0212 [1.758]	.0180 [2.374]	.0272 [3.062]	
$\Delta PZ/PZ_{-1}$	.3380 [3.413]	.5162 [6.220]	.4574 [4.746]	.2097 [2.097]	.4173 [4.613]	.4381 [4.097]	.2845 [2.541]	.3975 [5.565]	.4882 [7.378]
$\text{DUM8488}\cdot \Delta ML1/ML1_{-1}$	.4445 [5.660]	.2707 [3.949]	.3524 [4.426]	.5450 [6.601]	.3537 [4.723]	.3531 [4.080]	.5269 [5.842]	.3735 [6.535]	.3122 [5.477]
Addendum									
RBARSQ	.9690	.9716	.9549	.9652	.9618	.9409	.9643	.9606	.9554
RHO	-.460	-.357	-.251	-.476	-.305	-.162	-.500	0	0
DW	1.99	2.04	2.16	1.96	2.25	2.00	2.32	1.95	2.01
Years	53-88	53-88	53-88	53-88	53-88	53-88	53-88	53-88	53-88

Notes: CONSTANT refers to the unit vector in the equation intercept. An ellipsis mark (...) substitutes for the sectoral acronyms used in Appendix A, which defines the remaining symbols.

credit movement twice: once directly and once indirectly through wage inflation.

Table 4.2 decomposes wage inflation into its causal shares, which are calculated along the lines of the investment shares S_C and S_F in Section 3.2. Conceptually, wage inflation is corrected to $Z = \Delta W/W_{-1} - \alpha_0 - \alpha_R R$ giving way to the labor productivity share $S_Q = \alpha_Q (\Delta Q/Q_{-1})/Z$, the market-pressure share $S_K = \alpha_K (\ln(K_{-1} \cdot V))/Z$, the inflation expectation share $S_P = \alpha_P (\Delta P/P_{-1})/Z$, and the credit-growth share $S_X = \alpha_X(\Delta X/X_{-1})/Z$. Because the regression analysis posits credit as pertinent only during the last five years of the sample— namely, from 1984 to 1988—the share computations are restricted to that period.

One striking lesson to be learned from the share information is that the deterioration of economic fortunes in Yugoslavia transformed the productivity premium into a productivity discount. The productivity share was negative in industry, construction, handicraft, home trade, and "everything else," meaning that productivity caused money wages to advance at a slower rate than they otherwise would have. Even where S_Q manages to be positive, it is positive by a negligible amount. Such a dismal showing, of course, may be due more to business-cycle fluctuation than to worker lethargy. Nevertheless, it reinforces the point of Section 2.3.2 that the rosy vision sensed by Vanek and Horvat from the work-incentive structure of self-management may be the figment of rose-colored glasses. Seen clearly, the productivity record under self-management must be rated as awful, and workers paid the price in a way that hit close to home.

Corroborating the earlier remarks about market pressure, share S_K normally is large; in fact, it is the largest wage contributor in industry, forestry, handicraft, and residual. Its lowest value, transportation aside, occurs for catering, but even there it equals 26.6 percent. With conditions in the labor market accounting for more than one-quarter of money-wage advances, it seems inappropriate to dismiss them as inoperative.

Like the market-pressure variable, inflation expectations and credit growth carry their own weight in the wage-determination process. The low mark for the expectation share S_P equals a respectable 19.5 percent in construction,whereas the low posting for credit is 23.9 percent in social agriculture. This latter figure happens to be the smallest of all (nonproductivity) shares in social agriculture. Forestry and handicraft join social agriculture in that regard, and the three together nicely repeat their ranking of credit in the investment context reviewed by Table 3.4. Judged in terms of either investment or wage inflation, credit plays an important, though secondary, role in those three sectors.

Table 4.2
Wage Inflation Means and Causal Shares by Sector for the Years 1984–88

Sector	Mean	Labor Productivity	Market Pressure	Inflation Expectations	Credit Growth
			Share for		
Industry	1.007	-.00016	.387	.265	.349
Soc. Agr.	.970	.00024	.315	.445	.239
Catering	1.024	.00000	.266	.412	.322
Construction	.996	-.00096	.312	.195	.495
Forestry	1.012	.00004	.418	.313	.269
Handicraft	1.023	-.00370	.377	.345	.282
Home Trade	1.030	-.01119	.350	.234	.427
Residual	1.024	-.00162	.458	.278	.266
Transportation	1.013	.00000	.000	.605	.395

Notes: Wage inflation means pertain to $\Delta W / W_{-1}$ and hence are proportionate, not percentage, rates. Shares are likewise means expressed in proportionate terms.

4.2 SECTORAL PRICE INFLATION

Explaining Yugoslav price inflation begins with the popular cost-push model sketched by equations (2.24) and (2.25). As Horvat (1971, p. 150) remarked, "If average personal incomes do not increase faster than the productivity of labor, other things being equal, prices in the Yugoslav economy will be perfectly stable." Following Horvat's lead, Mencinger (1975, pp. 30-38), Tyson (1977, pp. 139-43), and Sapir (1981, pp. 157, 165) formulated cost-push equations and successfully tested them on data through the early 1970s. Bresser Pereira and Nakano (1987, p. 69), who devoted their energies to the inflation problems of Brazil and Argentina, extended the basic formulation (2.25) to include the domestic cost of imported materials. Soon thereafter, Bruno (1989, pp. 288-89), investigating circumstances in Israel, echoed the sentiment that import cost critically affects inflation. Accordingly, the cost-push paradigm can be written as

$$\Delta P/P_{-1} = \zeta_0 + \zeta_{WQ}(\Delta W/W_{-1} - \Delta Q/Q_{-1}) + \zeta_D \Delta D/D_{-1}, \tag{4.3}$$

where D denotes in dinars the unit cost of imports. Of course, $\zeta_{WQ} > 0$. Moreover, $\zeta_D > 0$, as dinar depreciation, by raising the domestic cost of imports, increases the rate of inflation.[4]

Cagan's (1956, pp. 25-27, 65-66, 91) classic work involving the quantity theory of money showed for bouts of hyperinflation that price inflation moved directly with money growth and that real balances fell when nominal balances rose. That these conditions held for contemporary Yugoslavia is easily documented. In 1980 the inflation rate $\Delta PZ/PZ_{-1}$ stood at 0.334 when credit growth $\Delta ML1/ML_{-1}$ hovered at 0.205. Simultaneously, real credit $ML1/PZ$ equaled 220.8 billion dinars. In 1984 the inflation rate equaled 0.426, credit growth registered 0.537, and real credit measured 166.6 billion dinars. By 1988 inflation and credit expansion reached 2.004 and 2.284, respectively, while real credit fell to 160.3 billion dinars. Cagan's analysis, these statistics, the even more recent evidence presented in Table 1.2 and Figure 1.2, and finally the thoughts by Vanek (1972, p. 267) about traces of the quantity theory in Yugoslavia advise that hypothesis (4.3) be broadened to capture credit growth; more precisely,

$$\Delta P/P_{-1} = \beta_0 + \beta_R R + \beta_{WQ}(\Delta W/W_{-1} - \Delta Q/Q_{-1}) + \beta_D \Delta D/D_{-1} + \beta_X \Delta X/X_{-1}. \tag{4.4}$$

As in the case of wage inflation, R enters to isolate the effects of the 1965 reforms, and X represents the volume of nominal credit.

Table 4.3 reports the econometrics of synthesis model (4.4).[5] Those regressions disclose an almost uniformly negative reform coefficient β_R despite the upward spikes that in 1965 characterized price inflation across most of the sectors. This paradoxical result means that prices rose during the reform years more slowly than they otherwise might have and gives credence to the notion that the mid-1960s price controls cited by Drutter and Lacković (1982, p. 108) had their desired effect. It also gives further credence to the evidence cited in Section 2.4.2 concerning a Post Keynesian call for incomes policy in Yugoslavia.

Validating the cost-push model, advances in unit labor cost $\Delta W/W_{-1}$ - $\Delta Q/Q_{-1}$ fueled price inflation. Cost pass-through was almost complete in catering, where 94.7 percent of increased labor-cost growth became an inflation increase. Industry passed forward 76.9 percent, while private agriculture passed 35.2 percent. Its percentage and the 40.7 percent for social agriculture are, respectively, the smallest and the second smallest pass-through rates in the nine relevant sectors. The explanation for this pattern is elementary. A firm's ability to carry cost increases forward depends in part upon the shape of the demand curve for its product. The more elastic is the curve, the more limited is that ability. Agricultural outfits commonly face rather flat demand curves, and consequently their pass-through prospects should be more limited than those for firms in other sectors.[6]

On the reverse side of the cost-push coin, the β_D coefficients for import cost are noticeably lower than their β_{WQ} counterparts. Evidently import cost carries smaller weight in the price mechanism, and therefore it exhibits a lower pass-through rate.[7]

At first blush, the results for the credit coefficient β_X are confusing because they put social agriculture first with 0.3494, mom-and-pop handicraft second with 0.2119, and private agriculture third with 0.1795. Yet industry, where credit ranks among the top determinants for investment and for wage inflation regardless of whether the standard involves regression coefficients or causal shares, is sixth in the club of nine. This confusion dissipates, however, when it is remembered that paradigm (4.4) entails a synthesis hypothesis of inflation. It combines cost push with credit expansion, which can be thought of as a demand-pull factor. Thus interpreted, the β_X configuration says, not unreasonably, that demand pull is more important in the agricultures and handicraft than in industry. The causal shares in Table 4.4, besides documenting the consistent dominance of labor cost over both import cost and demand pull in

Table 4.3
Sectoral Price Inflation Equations

Explanatory Variable	Industry	Soc. Agr.	Pri. Agr.	Catering	Construct.	Forestry	Handicraft	Home Trade	Transport
				Equation for $\Delta PIPD.../PIPD..._{-1}$ in					
				Coefficients and [Student-t Values]					
CONSTANT	-.0482 [-2.660]	-.0364 [-2.833]	.0366 [1.301]	.0256 [.705]	.0017 [.098]	.0181 [.817]	-.0114 [-.371]	.0290 [1.027]	-.0100 [-.457]
REFORM	-.4970 [-6.466]	-.2259 [-3.929]	-.1992 [-1.921]	.1081 [1.333]	-.0587 [-.765]	-.2109 [-2.760]	-.2871 [-2.626]	-.0955 [-.776]	-.2846 [-3.296]
$\Delta W12.../W12..._{-1}$ $-\Delta Q.../Q..._{-1}$	.7693 [5.882]	.4073 [7.095]	.3521 [3.991]	.9471 [5.612]	.7266 [7.466]	.8358 [8.055]	.8173 [7.561]	.6574 [3.812]	.5754 [5.560]
$\Delta D/D_{-1}$	.3258 [5.413]	.2974 [7.259]	.2758 [4.236]		.1023 [1.909]	.1311 [2.388]		.2520 [2.820]	.2158 [3.682]
$\Delta ML1/ML1_{-1}$	.0614 [.618]	.3494 [7.049]	.1795 [2.854]		.1098 [1.393]	.0367 [.575]	.2119 [2.334]	.0290 [.208]	.1500 [2.276]
DUM8488 $\Delta ML1/ML1_{-1}$				.0080 [.060]					
DUM87				.4573 [2.506]					
				Addendum					
RBARSQ	.9682	.9784	.8790	.9319	.9480	.9583	.8824	.8919	.9317
RHO	-.699	-.677	.188	-.478	-.615	0	0	-.494	0
DW	2.11	1.91	1.89	2.07	1.99	2.02	2.07	1.93	1.94
Years	53-88	53-88	53-88	53-88	53-88	61-88	53-88	53-88	53-88

Notes: D is measured as DINDOAV·IMPTP. Symbols are defined in Table 4.1 and in Appendix A.

Table 4.4
Price Inflation Means and Causal Shares by Sector for the Years 1984–88

Sector	Mean	Share for		
		Labor Cost	Import Cost	Credit Growth
Industry	1.135	.660	.284	.056
Social Agriculture	1.076	.366	.289	.345
Private Agriculture	.879	.402	.353	.245
Catering	1.117	.991	.000	.009
Construction	.961	.764	.116	.121
Forestry	1.034	.827	.134	.039
Handicraft	i.130	.794	.000	.206
Home Trade	1.040	.707	.261	.031
Transportation	1.004	.598	.235	.167

Notes: Based on the expression $\Delta P/P_{-1}$, the entries for inflation means are proportionate rates. Shares are means expressed in proportionate terms too.

explaining price inflation, describe the contribution of demand pull in vivid terms: Demand pull accounts for 34.5 percent of price inflation in social agriculture, 24.5 percent in private agriculture, and 20.6 percent in handicraft, but only 5.6 percent in industry. The frame of reference for these numbers, as in the case of wage inflation, is the period 1984-88 owing to the definition of the credit variable in catering.

Sectoral prices respond individually to the movements of labor cost, import cost, and credit. They then combine to relate those movements to overall price PZ by an average whose weights equal the sector output shares and hence vary through time. Equation (PR11) in Appendix A describes the linkage.[8] Since industry accounts for the largest portion of total output, its share is the largest, averaging 36.6 percent for the years 1961 to 1988. Second in PZ impact is home trade, whose share stands at 16.8 percent. Private agriculture ranks third with 13.4 percent, social agriculture places sixth with 4.3 percent, and forestry comes last with 1.1 percent. Even major happenings in forestry would have minor consequences for price PZ; the same insensitivity obviously does not hold for industry.

4.3 THE INFLATION NETWORK

Equation (4.2) indicates that sectoral wage inflation, through the PZ index, depends upon sectoral price inflation. According to equation (4.4), sectoral price inflation depends upon sectoral wage inflation. Wage inflation and price inflation depend upon each other, and they do so through a network of interactions that is rich in implications.

To extract those implications, the inflation network may be written compactly as

$$w_j = \alpha_0^j + \alpha_R^j R + \alpha_Q^j q_j + \alpha_K^j k_j + \alpha_{PZ}^j pz + \alpha_X^j x, \qquad (4.5)$$

$$p_j = \beta_0^j + \beta_R^j R + \beta_{WQ}^j (w_j - q_j) + \beta_D^j d + \beta_X^j x, \qquad (4.6)$$

$$pz = \Sigma_j \, \theta_j p_j. \qquad (4.7)$$

Lowercase letters w, q, pz, x, p, and d signify the corresponding proportionate rates of change; for instance, w abbreviates $\Delta W/W_{-1}$. Lowercase k denotes the logarithmic capital usage term $\ln (K_{-1} \cdot V)$, and index j identifies the sector. Coefficient θ_j is the weight of sector j inflation p_j in overall inflation pz; more precisely, $\theta_j = \phi_j (P_j/PZ)_{-1}$, where—by equation (PR11) in Appendix A—ϕ_j represents the fraction of sector-j output in total output and where P_j and PZ represent the respective price levels. For expository convenience but without loss of generality, the q_j and k_j are treated as exogenous, and the network is understood to involve two sectors, $j = 1, 2$. Moreover, θ_1 and θ_2 are posited to be temporally constant.

Inspection of the arithmetic soon reveals that a wage inflation increase anywhere in the network affects wage and price inflation everywhere in the network. To demonstrate, if w_1 increases, perhaps from a structural shock to α^1_0, then p_1 increases via equation (4.6). But the higher p_1 implies a higher pz from equation (4.7) and a higher w_2 from equation (4.5). The elevated w_2 then elevates p_2 from formula (4.6). By the same token, an initial increase in p_1 through, say, β^1_0 triggers a similar sequence and yields the companion conclusion that a price inflation increase anywhere affects wage and price inflation everywhere.

Credit growth x impacts each sectoral wage inflation and price inflation measure directly and indirectly, and since the relevant α and β coefficients are all positive, the inflation rates always move in the same direction as x. Thus an increase in x quickens the wage-price spiral, while a decrease in x slows it. Figure 4.1 sketches the credit-expansion scenario, the top half of the diagram illustrating the events in Sector 1. There the x increase directly raises w_1, which then raises p_1, causing w_1 to rise again via pz. But the x increase also raises p_1 directly, thereby intensifying the w_1 increase. Simultaneously, identical reactions are occurring in Sector 2, and all the while developments in one spiral are transmitted to the other through the connector pz. Structural shocks involving α^1_0 or β^1_0 would activate the network at point A or point B, respectively, and import cost increases escalating d—either through dinar depreciation or through world-price hikes—would start the circuits at points B and C.

Since $\alpha^1_Q > 0$, a productivity boost in Sector 1 boosts w_1. But with $\alpha^1_Q < 1$, w_1 rises by less than q_1, prompting $w_1 - q_1$ to fall. Consequently, with $\beta^1_{WQ} > 0$, p_1 declines, lowering w_1 through pz. In other words, the full effect on w_1 of a q_1 increase can go either way. Not ambiguous, however, is the effect of q_1 on w_2. The lowered p_1 brought about by the higher q_1 means a lowered pz and a lowered w_2; hence q_1 and w_2 move in opposite directions. Market-pressure variable k_1 influences w_1 and thus p_1. Of course, by provoking p_1 it provokes w_2 through pz and therefore p_2 as well. Still, because direct effects should be stronger than indirect effects, it is likely that k_1 has a stronger grip on w_1 and p_1 than on w_2 and p_2.

These properties can be seen more clearly by translating the network into its reduced form, which relates the five endogenous variables w_1,

Figure 4.1
Reaction of the Inflation Network to Faster Credit Growth

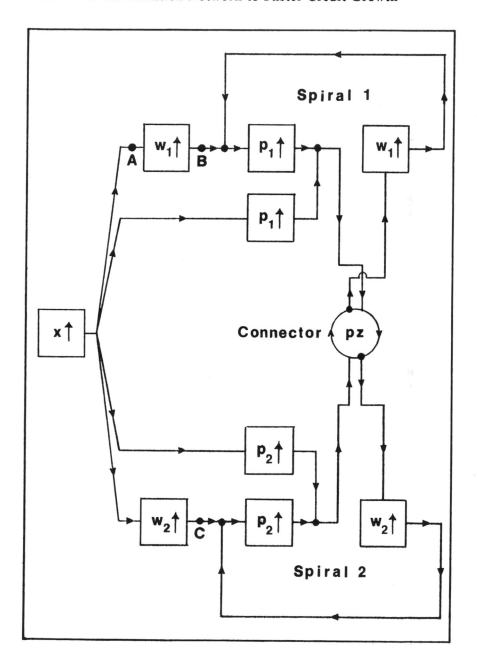

p_1, w_2, p_2, and pz each to the eight exogenous variables 1, R, q_1, q_2, k_1, k_2, d, and x. Industry is selected as Sector 1 and social agriculture as Sector 2. Although somewhat arbitrary, those selections have intuitive appeal. They embody the customary focal points of the development process, they capture the largest single sector (industry) in Yugoslavia, and they involve marked quantitative contrasts between sectors. That is, as Tables 4.1 and 4.3 confirm, the credit-growth coefficient β^1_X in industry-price inflation is less than the credit coefficient α^1_X in industry-wage inflation, while the opposite holds for social agriculture, namely, $\beta^2_X > \alpha^2_X$. In addition, industry has a wage inflation coefficient β^1_{WQ} in price inflation that exceeds the price inflation coefficient α^1_{PZ} in wage inflation, whereas social agriculture exhibits the reverse ordering: $\beta^2_{WQ} < \alpha^2_{PZ}$. Moreover, demand pull is strong in social agriculture but weak in industry: $\beta^2_X > \beta^1_X$. Proportions θ_1 and θ_2 are calculated, respectively, for industry and social agriculture as the means for the period 1984 to 1988, the years to which α^j_X applies.

Table 4.5 presents the reduced-form coefficients for the two-sector network. The first five columns, labeled w_1 to pz, cover the network's five endogenous variables individually. Column 6, labeled w_1 - pz, gives the coefficients for real-wage growth in industry, and column 7, w_2 - pz, does likewise for social agriculture. Since workers in any sector buy goods and services from all sectors, pz—not p_j—is used to track their real-wage movements.

As explained earlier, the reform of 1965 kept prices from rising as fast as they otherwise might have, and this restraint surfaces in the negative reduced-form coefficients of R on p_1, p_2, and pz. Because the reforms supplemented money wages, they enhanced real wages in both sectors. The positive coefficients on w_1 - pz and w_2 - pz make the point.

That own-sector productivity gains have ambiguous effects on money-wage inflation can be seen from the coefficients of q_1 on w_1 and q_2 on w_2. The former coefficient is negative, but the latter is positive. As anticipated, cross-sector productivity improvements dampen wage inflation; more bluntly, the coefficients of q_1 on w_2 and q_2 on w_1 are both negative. Verifying another anticipation, market pressure prompts a stronger reaction in the own sector than in the cross sector. Numerically, the coefficients of k_1 on w_1 and p_1 exceed their counterparts on w_2 and p_2, while the coefficients of k_2 on w_2 and p_2 exceed those on w_1 and p_1.

Faster growth in import cost or credit volume speeds up wage and price inflation, although, as Table 4.5 shows, credit expansion is the more powerful force. Figure 4.1 illustrates why: Credit expansion enters the inflation sequence at the very beginning, whereas import

Table 4.5
Reduced-Form Coefficients on Inflation

Argument	Equation for								
	w_1 (1)	p_1 (2)	w_2 (3)	p_2 (4)	pz (5)	w_1-pz (6)	w_2-pz (7)	$w^*_1-pz^*$ (8)	pz^{**} (9)
1	-.4223	-.3731	-.3898	-.1952	-.3534	-.0689	-.0364	-.0875	-.2443
R	.0965	-.4227	.0049	-.2239	-.4007	.4972	.4056	.2402	-.3977
q_1	-.1140	-.8570	-.4028	-.1641	-.7802	.6662	.1353	.2430	-.5091
q_2	-.0182	-.0140	.0813	-.3742	-.0539	.0357	.3775	.2074	-.0352
k_1	.0249	.0192	.0090	.0037	.0175	.0075	.0147	.0129	.0114
k_2	.0003	.0002	.0156	.0064	.0009	-.0006	-.0085	-.0052	.0006
d	.1463	.4384	.2235	.3884	.4329	-.2865	-.2094	-.1097	.3766
x	.6303	.5463	.5544	.5752	.5495	.0808	.0048	-.0489	.3858

Sources: Coefficients for industry, social agriculture, and handicraft in Tables 4.1 and 4.3 along with 1984–88 data on price and output for those sectors and for all sectors combined. The data are required in calculating θ_j.

Notes: For all columns except column 8, subscript 1 represents industry; subscript 2, social agriculture. In column 8, the 1 represents social agriculture; the 2, handicraft. Column 9 presumes that incomes policy decreases α^j_{PZ} and β^j_{WQ} to 75.0 percent of their initial values. For the industry and social agriculture pairings, $\theta_1 = 0.8892$ and $\theta_2 = 0.1108$. For social agriculture and handicraft, $\theta_1 = 0.5516$ and $\theta_2 = 0.4484$. Argument means over the years 1984–88 in the industry-agriculture context are $q_1 = -0.0037$, $q_2 = -0.0006$, $k_1 = 23.9986$, $k_2 = 21.8216$, $d = 1.1095$, and $x = 1.1126$.

phenomena enter at points B and C, thereby missing the initial wage response.

Credit growth is indeed powerful. For instance, a 10-percentage-point increase in x leads to a 5.5-point increase in the overall rate of inflation—more than half of any new credit growth becomes new inflation. Moreover, distributional consequences lie in the wake. A 10-point increase in x increases industry's real wage growth w_1 - pz by 0.8 point but leaves agriculture's wage growth w_2 - pz virtually unchanged. Pairing social agriculture with handicraft, not industry, produces an even more striking contrast, for then agriculture's wage growth w_1^* - pz^* actually declines by 0.5 point when x rises by 10 points. Distributional disparities of this sort would be lost in an aggregative inquiry and underscore the merit of a sectoral analysis.

4.4 COUNTERFACTUAL POLICY IMPLICATIONS

By quantifying the relationships within the inflation network, Table 4.5 identifies policy actions that would have eased the Yugoslav inflation problem. Perhaps the most obvious action regards credit growth: It should have been cut drastically. Table 2.1, which reviews the magnitude of unintended credit, sharpens that recommendation and takes dead aim at the soft-budget constraint. Yet Table 4.5 cautions that a policy strategy designed only to mop up credits, whether they be soft or hard, could have seriously undermined the real wage, as in the case of industry. Therefore, to ease such withdrawal symptoms and simultaneously to strike a second blow in the inflation fight, policy might have encouraged productivity improvement especially in industry, where (by the q_1 coefficient on pz) progress played a decisive role. Dinar appreciation permitted by antiinflation successes would have been beneficial too.

Sections 2.4.2 and 2.5 called attention to incomes policy as a method for reining inflation. That thought can be pursued further by supposing that incomes policy has the intended effect of lowering the expected rate of inflation or, in the language of equation (4.5), of tempering the reaction of w_j to a change in pz. Similarly, in the vocabulary of equation (4.6), incomes policy tempers the reaction of p_j to a change in w_j. Inflation's sensitivity to inflation is reduced, and accordingly α^j_{PZ} and β^j_{WQ} fall by, say, 25.0 percent across the board. The new reduced-form coefficients for overall inflation are listed as column 9, marked pz^{**}, in Table 4.5. Relative to the original coefficients, column 5, they are uniformly smaller in absolute value, and credit expansion, whose 10-percentage-point increase previously pushed up inflation by 5.5 points, now advances it by only 3.9 points.

Calculating pz from the argument means over the period 1984-88 provides additional insight into the capability of incomes policy. Under the original set of coefficients, pz computes to 1.180: Systemwide prices rose at an annual rate of 118.0 percent. By contrast, the new coefficients put pz at 0.891, implying an inflation rate of 89.1 percent, a decrease of almost 30 percentage points.

From the numbers posted in Table 4.5, it seems that combining antiinflation strategies into a comprehensive package would have had impressive results. For example, steps taken to convert the technical *regress* in industry and social agriculture into technical *progress* might have improved q_1 from -0.0037 to 0.02 and q_2 from -0.0006 to 0.01. The dinar growth of import costs might have been trimmed from a d of 1.1095 to one of 1.00, and credit growth x might have been slashed from 1.1126 to 0.50. Together with incomes policy, these maneuvers would have cut pz from 1.180 to 0.601 as annual inflation fell by almost 60 percentage points.[9] It must be remembered, however, that this conclusion is based on thinking which includes the assumptions that the Yugoslav economy only consists of industry and social agriculture, that productivity and market pressure are exogenous forces, that an incomes policy can be implemented, and that the National Bank can control credit. Being simplifications, these assumptions hold only approximately, and the approximation may be rather crude in some cases. Nevertheless, the conclusion from the exercise must be regarded as striking.

4.5 BRIDGING TO THE MARK

Wage inflation equation (4.2) and price inflation equation (4.4) serve as the basis for analyzing the Yugoslav inflation network. They also serve as the basis for developing the wage and price blocks of the Mark 4.0. In fact, as equations (PR1) to (PR8) along with (PR10) indicate, the Mark 4.0 faithfully duplicates price expression (4.4) apart from adjustments for special features such as date-specific events, bogus accountancy, and capacity utilization. Similarly, wage expression (4.2) is the unmistakable origin of equations (WG2), (WG5), and (WG8). Yet other "productive-sector" wage equations seem to have an alternative root, which may be written in stylized fashion as

$$\Delta W/W_{-1} = \alpha_0 + \alpha_R R + \alpha_{CU}\Delta CU + \alpha_{CPI}\Delta CPI/CPI_{-1} + \alpha_{CW}(\Delta CPI/CPI_{-1} - \Delta W/W_{-1})_{-1}. \tag{4.8}$$

Symbols W and R retain their previous interpretations, and CU denotes the capacity utilization index that expresses actual output as a percentage of capacity output. CPI stands for itself. Save for α_0, all coefficients are necessarily positive.

Despite their seeming disparity, expressions (4.2) and (4.8) are closely related. Hypothesis (4.8) dismisses the productivity premium espoused by statement (4.2), but it still holds to the idea of measuring market pressure by something besides the unemployment rate. Its particular choice is the capacity utilization index CU rather than the import-augmented capital series. Moreover, expression (4.8) retains the linkage between wage inflation and price inflation, and its use of CPI inflation instead of PZ inflation must be regarded as a distinction without much of a difference. As equation (PR16) teamed with equation (PR15) show, CPI is a transparent transformation of PZ.

The main dissimilarity between formulations (4.2) and (4.8) is the replacement of credit growth $\Delta X/X_{-1}$ by the real-wage erosion rate $\Delta CPI/CPI_{-1} - \Delta W/W_{-1}$. This replacement represents a change in emphasis away from the firm's ability to meet wage demands out of a soft budget and toward the worker's intensity of wage demands to protect household living standards. Nonetheless, this reorientation does not break the connection with credit growth. Since CPI inflation depends upon PZ inflation, it also depends upon the sectoral price inflations, which in turn depend upon credit growth. Thus equation (4.8) makes implicit the positive link between wage inflation and credit growth, whereas expression (4.2) makes that link explicit. The two hypotheses are essentially variations on the same theme.[10]

4.6 CONSUMER PRICE INFLATION

Logic maintains that the price of a consumer good reflects the prices of the "raw materials" used in creating the good. For example, the consumer price of food PIPDCFOD should be tied to agricultural prices PIPDAGRS and PIPDAGRP, and the consumer price of transportation PIPDCTRA should be related to transportation costs PIPDTRA. Following this idea, the inquiry first associated each consumer inflation rate with the full set of ten sectoral inflation rates in the hope of detecting a sensible chain of relationships. Then for each consumption item, the full set of sectoral rates was narrowed to a subset that had a proper sign configuration and that displayed a reasonable substantive connection to the good in question. In the end, this two-step procedure yielded some successful matches, such as the coupling of food inflation with the inflation rates in social agriculture, private agriculture, and transportation. Yet some matches proved to be unsatisfactory, such as that for clothing, where greater inflations in home trade and transportation were depicted as actually weakening clothing-price increases. Equally disturbing was the consistent inability of industry-price behavior to find its way into the sectoral subset. These failures advised a less energetic approach, by which each category of consumer inflation $\Delta P/P_{-1}$ is explained by overall "producer" inflation $\Delta PZ/PZ_{-1}$. Thus

$$\Delta P/P_{-1} = \alpha_0 + \alpha_{PZ} \, \Delta PZ/PZ_{-1}. \tag{4.9}$$

According to this hypothesis, all sectoral prices, including industry's, influence each consumption price.

Table 4.6 tests hypothesis (4.9). Despite their simplicity, the equations have respectable explanatory power. Furthermore, they capture the movement of relative prices in the consumer's market basket. More specifically, health, furniture, and transportation advance most rapidly in price, whereas footwear, tobacco, and household operation advance least rapidly.

Upon weighting, the separate consumption price indices combine to explain the price index PIPDC pertinent to total consumption. Appendix A equation (PR12), written in price levels rather than in inflation rates, gives the particulars. The weight applied to each component price index involves a fixed coefficient and a consumption ratio that varies through time. As a result, the weights vary through time, and in this regard PIPDC resembles PZ, equation (PR11). Food price exerts by far the greatest effect on PIPDC. Evaluated at the mean over the years covered by equation (PR12), its weight equals 0.409 or 40.9 percent of the weight distribution. Second place goes to furniture, whose share amounts to 9.7 percent. Third place belongs to clothing, which enters at 8.6 percent. Transportation is fourth at 8.3 percent, and footwear is last at 2.7 percent. As with index PZ, index PIPDC has a heavily skewed weight distribution.

4.7 FURTHER REFLECTIONS ON PRICE INDICES

In addition to the price information already presented, a few other details deserve at least brief mention. They involve six indices. Four have an economywide orientation, namely, the implicit price deflator for investment PIPDI, the official (uncorrected) price index for social product P, the retail price index PRETALL, and the CPI. The remaining two measures are sector specific, namely, the price indices for industrial products PIND and for agricultural products PAGR.

One detail worth attention is the mean growth rate. Table 4.7, which, for purposes of completeness and comparison, also covers the

Table 4.6

Consumer Price Inflation Equations by Type of Product

Product Type	Hypothesis (4.9)		RBARSQ	RHO	DW
	Coefficients and [Student-t Values]				
	α_0	α_{PZ}			
Beverages	.0281 [1.721]	.9673 [26.086]	.9512	-.424	1.76
Clothing	-.0158 [-.967]	.9923 [27.255]	.9552	-.333	1.74
Entertainment	.0125 [.712]	.9580 [24.070]	.9440	-.438	1.84
Food	.0196 [2.328]	.9923 [50.217]	.9864	-.689	1.71
Footwear	.0149 [.645]	.9363 [19.608]	.9164	0	2.11
Furniture	.0133 [.513]	1.0161 [18.958]	.9110	0	2.12
Health	-.0343 [-2.200]	1.1080 [31.371]	.9658	-.423	1.99
Household Operation	.0392 [2.310]	.8417 [22.644]	.9366	-.228	1.91
Other	.0246 [.891]	.9929 [18.646]	.9204	0	1.78
Tobacco	.0295 [2.033]	.8662 [26.467]	.9529	-.397	2.03
Transportation	-.0017 [-.092]	1.0075 [23.494]	.9410	-.527	1.94

Notes: Symbol definitions appear in Appendix A. Apart from the equation for other-consumption inflation, all estimations cover the years 1953-88. Data limitations restrict the exception to the years 1958-88.

Table 4.7
Growth–Rate Properties for Selected Price Indices

Period	PZ	PIPDC	PIPDI	P	PRETALL	CPI	PIND	PAGR
					Mean Rate			
1953–64	7.0	8.0	5.8	7.6	4.1	6.4	1.3	9.8
1965–73	13.4	15.4	13.5	13.9	14.5	15.5	9.0	16.9
1974–79	18.1	17.6	21.1	17.6	18.3	18.1	14.7	15.1
1980–88	75.4	76.8	73.6	77.1	75.8	74.7	71.9	73.7
1984–88	106.9	109.4	105.7	110.3	107.4	106.1	104.0	98.9
				Coefficient of Variation				
1953–64	119.0	48.9	86.6	67.4	103.7	67.1	186.5	75.2
1965–73	63.0	49.9	32.8	55.8	54.6	57.7	60.8	84.1
1974–79	51.7	20.5	18.4	19.4	35.0	24.4	57.0	31.7
1980–88	72.1	69.6	67.7	70.8	67.7	68.2	73.3	69.7
1984–88	51.8	47.9	43.9	48.6	46.2	46.4	49.5	57.9

Notes: Mean rate is reported in percentage terms. By construction so is the coefficient of variation, which equals 100·standard deviation/mean. Symbols are described in Appendix A.

(corrected) price index PZ and the implicit price deflator for consumption PIPDC, reveals that the mean rate varies markedly across indicators. For the prereform period 1953-64, the lowest rate amounts to 1.3 percent for PIND, while the highest rate equals 9.8 percent for PAGR. In regard to the post-Constitution years 1974-79, index PIND again has the low rate, 14.7 percent, but now index PIPDI registers the high mark, 21.1 percent. For the 1980s the low remains with PIND, at 71.9 percent, as the high moves to index P, at 77.1 percent. Finally, for the half decade 1984-88, the low of 98.9 occurs with PAGR, and the high of 110.3 associates with P. In that period the reported inflation rate can differ by more than 10 percentage points, depending upon the particular index being referenced.

The second detail also regards indicator variability. It is the coefficient of variation, which expresses the standard deviation as a percentage of the mean; it likewise comes to the conclusion that the indices exhibit significant temporal differences. To illustrate from Table 4.7, for the post-Constitution years 1974-79, PIPDI has the lowest coefficient, 18.4 percent, and PIND has the highest, 57.0 percent. In fact, PIPDI evidences the lowest coefficient generally, while PIND often reveals the highest value. From this record and from the record for mean rates, it is plain that PIPDI sees inflation as more intense, albeit more steady, than does PIND. The portraits are the same, but the brush strokes are different.

Such empirical discrepancies lead to the third detail, which is equation specification. Combined with theoretical notions, they suggest that different arguments should be used in specifying the index equations, and as formulas (PR11) to (PR18) of Appendix A attest, the Mark 4.0 holds to that belief.

4.8 BALANCE OF PAYMENTS

Spinning in an open circle are the payments associated with trade among nations. One measure of spin is the current account balance, which equals the payments to Yugoslavia (credits) minus the payments from Yugoslavia (debits) as they relate to the exchange of goods and nonfactor services, the efforts of individuals working abroad, the financing of interest obligations, and the transfer of gifts.

Table 4.8 reports the shares for each category. Payments to Yugoslavia arising from the export of goods comprise more than half of the total, while about a quarter of the credits originates from tourism and other nonfactor services. Remittances from Yugoslavs working elsewhere come next. Starting from nil before the implementation of reform, they gathered steam and reached a 22.1 percent share

Table 4.8
Shares in the Current Account

Period	Goods	Nonfactor Services	Remittances	Interest	Transfers
			Payments to Yugoslavia		
1952–64	.648	.170	.000	.002	.180
1965–73	.589	.252	.110	.005	.044
1974–79	.504	.230	.221	.011	.034
1980–88	.551	.220	.186	.011	.031
1984–88	.574	.214	.165	.010	.037
			Payments from Yugoslavia		
1952–64	.908	.073	.000	.019	.000
1965–73	.843	.111	.000	.041	.005
1974–79	.818	.082	.060	.037	.003
1980–88	.696	.073	.131	.098	.004
1984–88	.689	.071	.132	.104	.004

Note: Entries are means expressed in proportionate terms.

in the immediate post-Constitution era. Their strength then waned modestly during the 1980s. Rounding out the credit entries are transfers and interest, respectively by magnitude.

Debits exhibit a pattern somewhat similar to credits', although goods now prove to be a much more dominant force: Their share in total debits registers 82.6 percent over the entire period 1952-88, whereas their corresponding share in credits amounts to 58.7 percent. Payment for nonfactor services, albeit second in rank, equals about 10 percent, less than half of its credit counterpart. Remittances to other countries, like the moneys going the other way, began at zero before the reform and then gained momentum. Also gaining momentum—unfortunately—were the interest payments by Yugoslavia. For the latter part of the 1980s, those outgoes constituted a full 10 percent of all debits and greatly overshadowed the 1 percent interest share seen on the credit side. Yugoslavia's status as a debtor nation is all too evident in these statistics.

The current account balance can be thought of in ways other than the difference between credits and debits. For instance, it can be imagined as being split into the receipts from net exports of goods and nonfactor services on the one hand and net factor income from abroad, NFI, on the other. From that construction it is possible to tie the nominal balance, BPCABL, explicitly to the real quantities of goods and nonfactor services being traded, NETEX72. That is,

$$BPCABL = NETEX72 \cdot (EXPTP/17) + NFI + Z, \qquad (4.10)$$

where the magnitude in parentheses represents the price of Yugoslav exports and where the Z denotes a discrepancy item.[11] Any term on the right half of identity (4.10) can be positive or negative; yet the tendency for NETEX72 and BPCABL to post the same sign should be clear. Moreover, since foreign borrowing FB from equation (IA16) of Appendix A varies inversely with BPCABL, it follows that a negative NETEX72 promotes a negative BPCABL and a positive FB. Net importing of quantities likely means a current account deficit and borrowing from abroad. The converse also applies.

Figure 4.2 illustrates these tendencies. NETEX72 and BPCABL, the latter converted into the former's scale for visual effect, usually lie on the same side of zero, whereas FB, rescaled the same way for appearance, usually falls on the opposite side. The years just before Tito's death stand out in bold relief. Yugoslavia went on an import binge, drove the current account through the floor, and borrowed through the ceiling.

Another link between quantities and payments is seen in equation (IA7) for transportation. As capacity utilization intensifies in

Figure 4.2
International Balances and Borrowing

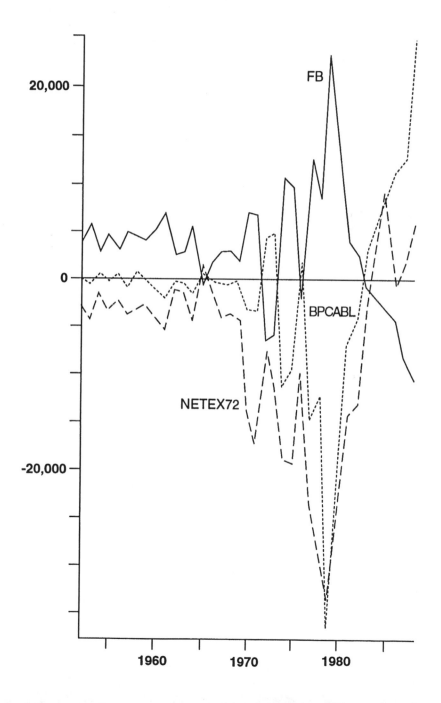

transportation, the need for transportation-related products grows. Some of those items are imported, boosting the payment outflow. By contrast, more domestic investment in transportation helps to satisfy that need, while currency depreciation discourages its satisfaction. In either case, transportation imports fall, as does the payment outgo. Consumer demand and trade volume count as well—both positively.

Interest payments from Yugoslavia are explained by equation (IA8). Not surprisingly, worldwide interest rates, represented by the US Treasury bill rate, affect them directly. The contractual nature of those payments is also discernible.

NOTES

1. Sections 4.1 to 4.4 constitute a reincarnation of a paper written by Gapinski (1992b) and published by Western Illinois University. That material is used with permission.

2. Linearity does not presuppose rational expectations except in the special case where, as Figlewski and Wachtel (1981, p. 3) along with Lovell (1986, p. 112) noted, the intercept equals zero and the slope equals unity. Results presented later show that the special case does not obtain.

3. Wage data are not available for private agriculture, and thus no equation appears for it.

4. The capability of currency depreciation to worsen domestic inflation is dramatized by the Brazilian experience of the early 1980s. Bresser Pereira (1990, p. 512) reviewed the situation.

5. Endorsement of a synthesis explanation for price inflation comes from developing and developed countries alike. Behrman (1977, pp. 190-91) verified it in studying Chile, whereas Stockton and Struckmeyer (1989, p. 283) implied it in examining the United States. More to the point, Mencinger (1987, pp. 402, 406-8) confirmed it in researching Yugoslavia. For the residual sector, where the synthesis model fails, the price level is tied to the industrial price index in a manner that allows for the possibility of a changing relationship between the two sectors. Appendix equation (PR9) illustrates.

6. Price controls and subsidies designed to moderate price increases further explain why agricultural price inflation manifests a relatively limited response to labor-cost growth.

7. A generalized version of price rule (2.24) is $P = \nu e^{\tau T} (W/Q)^{\chi} D^{\psi}$, where T stands for time. Logarithmic transformation and time differentiation leave $\dot{P}/P = \tau + \chi(\dot{W}/W - \dot{Q}/Q) + \psi(\dot{D}/D)$, the dots identifying time derivatives. If import cost has the smaller weight in the price rule, $\psi < \chi$, then it also has the smaller pass-through rate.

8. Treating the weighted sectoral prices as regressors checks equation (PR11) econometrically. The resulting intercept is zero, each price coefficient is unity, and the RBARSQ is unity as well. The regression spans the period 1961 to 1988 because of zeros for PIPDRES in the earlier years.

9. The policy package also has favorable implications for real wages. Along the baseline, the path followed in the absence of new policy, industry real wage falls at an annual rate of 13.3 percent, as the argument means multiplied by the coefficients in the w_1-pz column of Table 4.5 indicate when summed. Cutting x to 0.50, ceteris paribus, merely hastens the real-wage erosion to 18.3 percent, consonant with the earlier warning; yet the policy package manages to slow that erosion to 7.0 percent. A similar result occurs for social agriculture. There, by the means and the w_2-pz coefficients, the real wage declines at a 9.6 percent rate on the baseline. Restraining x to 0.50 accelerates that decay to 9.9 percent, but implementing the package slows it to 6.4 percent.

10. That both constructions fit the data well corroborates empirically their theoretical affinity.

11. Normalizing factor 17 is the 1972 value of the exchange rate between the dinar and the US dollar.

5

Domestic Counterfactual Scenarios

As Chapter 1 recounted, the 1970s were among the best of economic times for Yugoslavia. Even so, the worst of times set in during the 1980s and contributed to the country's bloody disintegration at the dawn of the 1990s. Could that economic failure have been prevented? What steps might have been taken, and what good would they have done? These questions guide the present chapter, which has a domestic orientation. Section 5.1 looks at price and wage policies. In the process it examines the connection between relative price movements and resource reallocations, and it goes on to quantify the macro consequences of a balanced wage-price program. Section 5.2 addresses output growth. Prompted by government action or by business interests, output expands in alternative sequences. One scenario involves a broad-based effort that covers ten sectors, whereas another selectively limits the program to four.

With exogenous price reductions tackled in Section 5.1 and exogenous quantity expansions handled in Section 5.2, Section 5.3 moves to the reallocation of a given amount of investment dinars across sectors. Through testing it quickly rejects a popular prescription for development. Turning that recommendation upside down, it arrives at a twin paradox of investment, and from there it extends the reallocation system to include infrastructure undertakings such as housing investment. Section 5.4 continues the theme of resource reallocation by redistributing expenditure from government activities to investment. Initially the recipients are five investment lines, including infrastructure, but later they expand to encompass all investment endeavors. During the exercise Section 5.4 uncovers a second paradox, this one pertaining to commodity demand.

Credit contraction is the subject of Section 5.5. After reviewing the historical behavior of credit and its components, this section imposes credit restraint and records the ensuing aggregate responses. Next it reconsiders the employment findings in light of the implications that sustained credit restraint would have for soft budgets, job tenure, and disembodied progress. This reinterpretation leads to a more comprehensive treatment of the country's reaction to tight credit.

Given the shattered hopes, the destroyed fortunes, the human suffering, and the lost lives associated with the collapse of Yugoslavia, it is almost natural for thoughts to drift to an extreme. The breakup was inevitable. "Nothing could have been done to stop it." Or it might be imagined that major good would have been accomplished by minor remedies and that economic failure could have been easily avoided. "If only this had been done or if only that had been established, Yugoslavia would have remained tall and strong." Either of these readings may represent an accurate assessment of the facts. Yet both may reflect more sentiment than scholarship. To assure that the discipline of the latter is maintained throughout the inquiry, the counterfactual scenarios are to be conducted within the confines of the Mark 4.0. By imposing the structure which existed at the time that remedial action would have been taken, the model limits the outcomes to the range of the possible. It guards against exaggerated claims while accounting for the complex interrelationships within the Yugoslav system. It also provides the frame of reference for judging success. That reference, called the baseline path, is the model's rendering of economic conditions extant in the absence of any corrective.

5.1 PRICE AND WAGE ADJUSTMENTS

One aspect of economic life in market-oriented countries is that relative prices influence the allocation of resources across sectors and thereby affect aggregate performance. Not only does the mix of output change, the level of output changes as well. The same can be said for employment, investment, capital, and other aggregates. Another feature of economic life is that government action frequently impacts relative prices. Such intervention may be simply an unintended outcome of a strategy designed for quite a different purpose, or it may be a deliberate part of a program that is believed to be either beneficial to disadvantaged groups or essential for improving the economic climate generally.

In Yugoslavia government price interventions have been commonplace. Mencinger (1987, pp. 410-11), for instance, presented a long list of major decrees and laws that were intended to curb inflation, although many more incursions into the price system could be identified. Those incursions greatly distorted relative prices. Figure 5.1 demonstrates the point by charting the movement of PIND/PAGR, the ratio of industry price to agriculture price. From 1955 to 1959 and again from 1961 to 1963 industry price remained frozen while agriculture price advanced, and as a result the price relative dove. Moreover, the imposition of new strictures and the repeal of old ones compounded the jerkiness of relative prices, as the latter portion of Figure 5.1 suggests.

Despite the antiinflation intention of the government price interventions, Yugoslav inflation thrived, and the economy faltered badly. Such moribund behavior naturally raises the question of whether relative price policy could have any favorable effects in Yugoslavia. The case of industry price might be examined first.

Lowering industry price PIPDIND initially lowers the absolute level of overall price PZ, and since industry carries the lion's share of the weight in PZ—33.7 percent for the years 1952-88 and 41.9 percent for the period 1980-88—that reduction is not negligible. However, because PIPDIND must fall by more than PZ does, relative price PIPDIND/PZ falls too. Its cousin PIND/PZ similarly declines, thus reducing industry output YIND72. Inasmuch as prices in the other sectors are not targeted for shock, relative prices there increase. For instance, relative price in social agriculture PIPDAGRS/PZ moves upward, stimulating social agriculture output YAGR72S. At first, then, the relative price change alters the composition of output: The share of industry in total output falls, while the shares of other sectors rise.

But much more happens beyond these responses. The reduced PZ implies greater real balances ML1/PZ and therefore greater sectoral investments in varying degrees consonant with the different credit sensitivities of the sectors. Similarly, higher real consumer credit CREDC/PIPDC fosters higher consumption C72, whereas lower domestic inflation promotes net exports NETEX72. Expanded investment, consumption, and net exports translate into expanded total commodity demand DEMD72, which in turn stimulates the sectoral outputs and helps industry output to recover from the initial setback at the hands of relative price. Increased demand also boosts employment in industry EIND and elsewhere, but again the reactions are not identical across the board. In particular, employment in industry may grow relative to employment for social agriculture EAGRS, which depends inversely upon a likely rising real wage.

To give some quantitative depth to this theoretical sketch, inflation of industry price might be imagined to drop, ceteris paribus, by 3 percentage points compared to baseline in 1980, by 6 points relative to baseline in 1981, and by 9 points versus baseline in each year from

Figure 5.1
Ratio of Industry Price to Agriculture Price

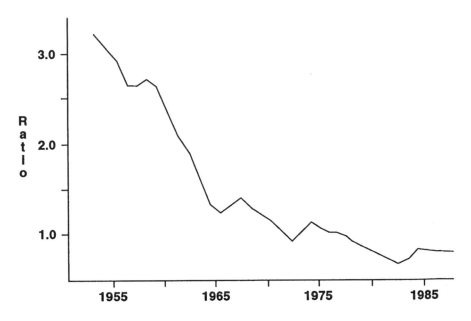

1982 to 1988.   A gradually implemented, formal price control is perhaps the most obvious force behind such movement, but it is not the only possibility.   Other possibilities that come to mind include subsidy management, soft-credit variation, tax concessions, and international trade adjustments.

The effects on relative prices are portrayed in Panel A of Figure 5.2. The solid line shows the percentage difference between relative industry price PIPDIND/PZ under the shock and along the baseline. Similarly, the dashed line traces the percentage difference for relative social agriculture price PIPDAGRS/PZ.   As is evident, relative industry price declines in comparison with the baseline.   In 1980 it lies 1.4 percent below baseline, and by 1988 it lies 23.2 percent below.   On the other hand, relative agriculture price increases; it is 1.1 percent above baseline in 1980 and 30.7 percent above in 1988.

Quantity responses at the sector level continue the story of relative prices.   Industry output advances vis-à-vis baseline, but, presumably because of the negative impact of the relative price disturbance, it advances by less than does social agriculture output.   For example, in triennium 3, years 1986-88, industry production exceeds the baseline level by 8.4 percent on average, while social agriculture production passes its baseline mark by 9.2 percent.   However, circumstances are

Figure 5.2
Relative Prices in Industry and Social Agriculture Compared with Baseline Levels

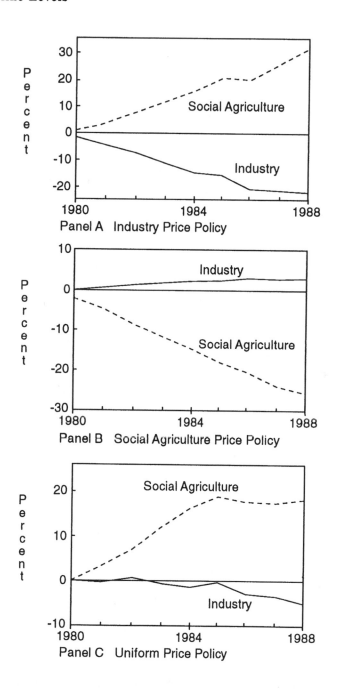

reversed for investment and employment. In triennium 3 industry investment averages 29.1 percent above baseline, and as a result its share of total investment grows from 36.2 percent on the baseline to 37.9 percent. By contrast, social agriculture investment averages 11.7 percent above baseline, and shrinks in investment share from 4.5 percent to 3.8 percent. More strikingly, industry employment in the triennium rises against baseline, whereas social agriculture employment actually falls given that norm. Relative price changes do cause resource reallocations.

The aggregate consequences of the relative price changes are summarized in the first three columns of Table 5.1. Reduced PZ inflation, seen in the CPI inflation numbers, contributes to the increase in investment, which for triennium 3 stands at 25.9 percent above baseline. Likewise, consumption exceeds baseline by 5.0 percent in the triennium. Reflecting depreciation of the real exchange rate PRELIND, exports exceed baseline by 5.6 percent, and imports fall by 10.2 percent. Net exports advance in the process. This enlarged demand, together with the relative price adjustments, explains the 10.2 percent gain in output. Employment too rises—by 2.1 percent. As suggested by the decline in social agriculture employment, real wage rises relative to baseline.

The extent to which a change in sectoral price impacts the macro system depends in no small way upon how powerfully it impacts overall price PZ. Commanding the largest portion of PZ, industry price has a strong presence in the economy. According to Section 4.2, agriculture prices account for much smaller shares of PZ, namely, 13.4 percent for private agriculture and 4.3 percent for social agriculture. Therefore, it follows that a given shock to the twin agriculture prices should generate weaker macro responses than it does in the case of industry price. Furthermore, it follows that the now-*lowered* agriculture price relative PIPDAGRS/PZ should cause social agriculture output to first fall, not rise, and that the smaller demand gain may be insufficient to completely offset the forgone output. In short, social agriculture output actually may decline against baseline.

Duplicating the previous policy pattern, the price inflations in social agriculture and private agriculture both fall, ceteris paribus, by 3 percentage points in 1980, by 6 points in 1981, and by 9 points afterward. No interventions apply to industry inflation. As Panel B of Figure 5.2 illustrates, the relative price of social agriculture now erodes from 1.6 percent below baseline in 1980 to 26.7 percent below in 1988. Conversely, relative industry price grows vis-à-vis baseline, but because agriculture prices influence overall price only weakly, that increase is slight, amounting to 3.1 percent by 1988.

As surmised, output in social agriculture falls by baseline standards.

Table 5.1
Economic Conditions under Price and Wage Policies

Series	Industry-Price Policy			Social Agriculture-Price Policy			Balanced Wage-Price Policy		
	1980-82	1983-85	1986-88	1980-82	1983-85	1986-88	1980-82	1983-85	1986-88
	Percentage Differences of Levels								
Output	1.0	4.2	10.2	0.2	0.5	0.5	1.9	7.0	10.7
Employment	0.1	0.6	2.1	0	0	0	0.3	1.0	1.8
Real Wage	1.5	4.0	5.1	0.4	0.8	0.7	0.8	2.2	-1.2
Disposable Income	1.7	4.9	7.4	0.4	0.8	0.6	1.6	4.3	1.5
Consumption	0.8	2.8	5.0	0.2	0.2	-0.3	0.8	1.1	2.4
Investment	3.3	13.6	25.9	0.8	2.3	2.3	8.9	32.1	42.4
Exports	0.7	3.1	5.6	0.1	0	-0.3	1.2	3.6	3.0
Imports	-1.4	-7.4	-10.2	0.1	0	0.2	-1.1	-7.8	-7.5
	Differences in Percentage Rates								
Output Growth	0.6	1.2	2.6	-0.1	-0.1	0.1	1.2	1.6	1.0
Unemployment	-0.1	-0.5	-1.8	0	0	0	-0.3	-0.9	-1.6
Money-Wage Inflation	-3.2	-5.2	-4.6	-0.8	-0.7	0.5	-10.7	-12.1	-2.3
CPI Inflation	-4.0	-6.6	-6.1	-1.0	-0.9	-0.6	-10.5	-13.0	-0.5

Notes: In the nomenclature of the Mark 4.0, output is Y72; employment, EMPTOT; real wage, money wage/PZ; and disposable income, YDA72. Furthermore, consumption is C72; investment, ITOT72; exports, EXGNFSR; and imports, IMGNFSR. Additionally, unemployment is URATE, and CPI is itself. For any series X expressed as a level, the percentage difference equals $100 \cdot (X - X_{baseline}) / X_{baseline}$, whereas the difference in percentage rates equals $100 \cdot (X - X_{-1})/X_{-1} - 100 \cdot [(X - X_{-1})/X_{-1}]_{baseline}$. All entries are arithmetic averages.

For triennium 3 the shortfall is 6.4 percent and occurs at the same time that industry output stands 0.6 percent above base. This gain by industry output testifies to the resource reallocation that occurs under the price change. Corroboration comes from the investment statistics: in comparison with baseline, investment declines in social agriculture but rises in industry.

That the agriculture-price shocks prompt small macro responses can be gathered from columns 4 to 6 of Table 5.1. Although a price disturbance in industry yields an output response of 10.2 percent in triennium 3, the same disturbance in both agricultures yields an output response of only 0.5 percent. Whereas investment rises by 25.9 percent for the industry perturbation, it advances by only 2.3 percent under the agriculture initiative. Moreover, while CPI inflation is cut by 6.1 percentage points in the former case, it is trimmed by 0.6 point in the latter. Interpreted loosely, a given price shock has only one-tenth the effect when applied to agriculture rather than to industry.

From the logic of the industry-price and agriculture-price sequences, it is reasonable to infer that an initiative which restricts prices uniformly across sectors should have a small effect on all relative prices but a substantial effect on overall price. More to the point, uniform price changes should cause general price to change to the same degree, thus leaving price ratios unaltered ex ante. Panel C of Figure 5.2 attests ex post to such diminished sensitivity of both industry and social agriculture price relatives. There the industry relative departs from baseline by at most 5.2 percent, and the social agriculture relative differs by at most 18.9 percent, about two-thirds of its previous high values. For Panel C price inflation in all ten sectors is tempered according to the 3-6-9 rule.

Mirroring PZ inflation, CPI inflation under uniform price policy declines from baseline by 9.3 percentage points in triennium 1, by 13.6 points in triennium 2, and by 5.6 points in triennium 3. The first two figures are roughly double those associated with the industry-price change in Table 5.1, and the third roughly matches its industry-price counterpart. To keep the focus on triennium 3, output rises relative to baseline by 17.9 percent as opposed to 10.2 percent for industry-price policy. Furthermore, employment expands by 3.5 percent as opposed to 2.1 percent. Real wage climbs by 11.3 percent versus 5.1 percent, consumption grows by 5.3 percent instead of 5.0 percent, and investment soars by 54.8 percent compared to 25.9 percent. Across-the-board price controls can be potent medicine.

Section 4.4 examined the situation where the sensitivity of inflation to inflation was reduced. That is, price inflation and wage inflation became less responsive to each other due to the introduction of an incomes policy. All sectors—the two of them, industry and social agriculture—were shocked equivalently, and in the end macro performance improved as inflation fell. The same issue can be pursued on a larger scale. As before, price inflation in the 10 sectors can be restrained, ceteris paribus, by the 3-6-9 rule. Wage inflation too can be restrained, but its sectors number 12: the 9 "productive" sectors beyond private agriculture and the 3 government or "nonproductive" sectors covering education, health, and general services. Appropriate magnitudes may be assigned to the wage restrictions by insisting that the real wage remain basically fixed under the controls program. That proviso leads to a 2-3-2 rule: Wage inflation in the 12 sectors is reduced, ceteris paribus, by 2 percentage points from baseline in 1980, by 3 points in 1981, and by 2 points from 1982 to 1988. The last three columns of Table 5.1 present the results of this balanced wage-price package.

By experimental design the real wage stays virtually unchanged, deviating from baseline by merely 0.6 percent on average over the entire nine years. Not unexpectedly, consumption remains rather flat across subperiods. Restricting wage advances restricts both the productive and the nonproductive sides of the wage bill, and correspondingly, disposable income and its consumption offshoot become moderated. For instance, consumption increases in triennium 3 by 2.4 percent against baseline under the balanced wage-price program, whereas it expands by a full 5.3 percent under the uniform price control program. Nonetheless, it must be emphasized that consumption does not fall in the wake of the balanced program.

In accord with the drill in Section 4.4, CPI inflation under balanced action falls nicely relative to baseline. Simultaneously, unemployment falls too in accord with a Phillips curve that shifts downward in response to cooled inflation expectations. Equation (2.26) has the mathematical details. Concomitantly with the unemployment reduction, employment expands; so do output, investment, and net exports.

Of the conclusions that can be drawn from the price and wage adjustments, several deserve special note. First, policy designed to change relative prices is effective or ineffective depending upon which prices are targeted for change. Industry price offers substantial promise, while agriculture price offers little. Second, efficacy of a relative price campaign is not unrelated to the determination with which the campaign is conducted. To be successful, the initiative should be unflagging. Applied to ancillary prices or applied in an erratic manner, relative price action is inclined to fail just as it did in Yugoslav practice. Finally, a program of balanced wage-price controls can improve macro performance on a broad front without necessarily sacrificing the household's standard of living.

5.2 INCREASED OUTPUT GROWTH

Rather than disrupt the macro system through price, the shock may impact quantity. Motivation behind a quantity perturbation could again come from the government, or it could originate from other sources. As Section 2.3.2 observed, the government imposes on business a staggering amount of regulations, permissions, and paperwork, and this burden surely impairs output. Bureaucratic red tape simply snarls the production process. Furthermore, as that section also noted, the self-management style of business operation fosters work disincentives. Individuals who have little or no desire to work can act accordingly without fear of discipline. For multiple reasons, then, production likely occurs below the theoretical frontier, and that very prospect urged the modeling of actual output through capacity schedules instead of through production functions.

Whether externally inspired by government efforts to cut red tape or internally induced by worker-sponsored incentive programs, a boost in output pushes up labor productivity (output per worker), whose increase amounts to disembodied technical progress. That Yugoslavia failed to enjoy such progress during the 1980s is clear from the aggregate record cited in Table 1.1 and from the experiences at the sector level. For example, productivity in industry declined at an average annual rate of 0.5 percent during the years 1980-88 and, as Table 4.5 posited, by 0.4 percent over the half decade 1984-88. Social agriculture had productivity fall by 0.1 percent annually over the three trienniums and the half decade. Catering posted rates of -3.1 percent and -4.0 percent, respectively, while construction did likewise: -3.7 percent and -1.6 percent. In fact, seven of the ten sectors evidenced negative productivity-growth rates for both time frames. One of the few bright spots was transportation, its growth being positive at 0.5 percent and 1.8 percent, respectively.

Confronted by this dismal situation, government and business take action to bolster the rate of output growth equally in each of the ten sectors. The magnitude of increase is 0.5 percentage point, a prudent amount given Yugoslavia's past experience and Maddison's (1987, pp. 650, 676) appraisal of Western countries. The output drive lasts from 1980 to the end of 1982. Though temporary, the drive generates permanent effects since it thrusts the economy to a higher expansion path. On that path the enhanced productivity growth means lower price inflation, consonant with equation (2.26). Lower inflation in turn means greater commodity demand from both domestic and foreign buyers, and consequently employment increases. Output increases too, now by the induced route.

At the sector level the gains in productivity are laudable. For instance, annual productivity growth in industry exceeds the baseline rate by 1.3 percentage points on average over the nine years 1980-88. In social agriculture productivity growth exceeds baseline by 1.0 percentage point over the same period. Catering reports an identical gain—1.0 point—whereas construction's rate is 0.5 point higher than base. Transportation, whose history tells of technical progress in contrast to technical regress, essentially duplicates its baseline productivity profile. Carried into the aggregate, the sectoral responses imply that annual productivity growth nationwide exceeds base by 1.2 points for the nine-year period.

Table 5.2 continues the aggregate accountancy in its first three columns. There are no surprises. In triennium 3 the CPI inflation rate drops below baseline by 9.0 percentage points. Consumption rises by 7.0 percent against baseline, investment advances by 16.3 percent, and net exports climb by an ample amount as well since exports increase by 4.4 percent when imports decrease by 9.8 percent. Similarly, output and employment advance: by 11.9 percent and 2.0 percent, respectively. As regards the real wage, Section 4.4 stressed the ability of productivity growth to affect it favorably, and Table 5.2 attests to that capability. Productivity policy raises the real wage much as the price initiatives of Section 5.1 do. The mechanisms are different—price contraction versus quantity expansion—but the consequences are the same. Moreover, inflation and unemployment again fall together as the Phillips curve shifts downward. However, according to equation (2.26), the reason is different: strengthened productivity versus tempered expectations.

Efforts to stimulate output growth, of course, need not apply to all sectors; they may be conducted on a selective basis. If speeding up economic development is the concern, then four sectors might be singled out: industry, catering, construction, and transportation. Although catering might not be an obvious choice, it merits inclusion because it covers the Yugoslav tourist industry, which provides ready access to foreign exchange. Moreover, catering has one of the largest productivity coefficients in the sectoral price equations (namely, -0.7589), suggesting that progress there would have significant beneficial effects on inflation. With the output drive narrowed in focus, it might be pursued more intensively, and thus the rate of output growth is imagined to increase by a full percentage point in each of the four sectors. As before, the program begins in 1980 and expires at the end of 1982.

In its last three columns, Table 5.2 discloses that the narrow-but-intense initiative generates stronger results than does the broad-but-modest venture. For instance, CPI inflation now lies 13.2 percentage points below baseline in triennium 3. Consumption and investment

Table 5.2
Economic Consequences of Increased Output Growth

Series	All Sectors			Industry, Catering, Construction, and Transportation		
	1980-82	1983-85	1986-88	1980-82	1983-85	1986-88
	Percentage Differences of Levels					
Output	2.0	6.6	11.9	2.6	9.0	16.6
Employment	0.1	0.6	2.0	0.1	0.8	2.9
Real Wage	0.9	3.7	5.7	1.2	5.5	8.6
Disposable Income	1.1	4.4	8.0	1.3	6.5	12.1
Consumption	0.6	3.1	7.0	0.7	4.5	10.7
Investment	2.9	10.3	16.3	3.8	14.6	21.7
Exports	0.6	2.5	4.4	1.0	4.2	7.3
Imports	-0.5	-5.2	-9.8	-0.5	-6.8	-14.8
	Differences in Percentage Rates					
Output Growth	1.2	1.5	1.8	1.5	2.1	2.4
Unemployment	-0.1	-0.5	-1.8	-0.1	-0.7	-2.6
Money-Wage Inflation	-0.7	-5.0	-7.1	-1.2	-8.2	-10.2
CPI Inflation	-1.2	-6.3	-9.0	-1.9	-10.2	-13.2

Notes: See Table 5.1.

top baseline levels by 10.7 percent and 21.7 percent, respectively, in that triennium, and output finishes 16.6 percent above that norm.

An interesting corollary to the selective campaign involves the investment share. For the "big-four" sectors, the combined share of investment in total investment averages 1 percentage point above baseline during the nine years. By contrast, the big-four share does not depart at all from baseline for the across-the-board endeavor. In other words, selective policy is not without its resource redistribution, albeit slight.

5.3 INVESTMENT REALLOCATION

Thoughts of intersectoral shifts in investment have special import in the case of Yugoslavia, where social ownership means the absence of market signals for allocating capital. At times investment funds were distributed in keeping with a system of total planning, and hence allocation was more a matter of politics or chance than economics. The duplication of factories across regions, combined with the scarcity of equipment in certain pursuits such as family farming, only verifies the historical perspective.

If capital allocation has a decided political or accidental basis to it, then reallocation may have beneficial consequences. One straightforward plan favors industry at the expense of agriculture, following a standard development prescription that calls for an enlargement of the "modern" sector and a shrinkage of its "traditional" counterpart. Yet exercising that plan in the Yugoslav context actually worsens economic conditions. Although industry investment first rises relative to baseline levels, it eventually falls when judged by that norm. Moreover, social agriculture investment, private agriculture investment, and even total investment almost always remain below baseline. Total output too deteriorates against base, and inflation intensifies. For Yugoslavia the standard development proposition proves to be unwise. Perhaps capital surpluses in industry and shortages in agriculture make capital's marginal product lower in industry, and hence reallocations in that direction undermine performance. Evidence on the capital/output ratios provides some support for this view. For industry, the ratio averages 3.4 over the period 1980-88, but for social and private agriculture combined, it equals 2.8 on average. Further support comes from the capacity-output elasticities with respect to capital. As equations (MX1) and (MX2) of Appendix A reveal, industry has a lower elasticity than does social agriculture.

Given the failure of the agriculture-to-industry plan, logic advises going the other way. The particular package envisioned has industry investment decline, ceteris paribus, by 1,400 million dinars relative to baseline in 1980, by 2,800 million in 1981, and by 4,200 million in each year from 1982 to 1988. The 1,400-million-dinar decrement represents 3 percent of actual industry investment in 1980, and therefore this adjustment pattern in a sense duplicates the 3-6-9 rule used in Section 5.1 for prices. The dinars so released find their way to social agriculture, private agriculture, and catering in proportion to their investment shares.[1]   Thus social agriculture receives 40.0 percent of the money; private agriculture, 38.2 percent; and catering, 21.8 percent.

Table 5.3 reports in its first three columns the macro implications of this investment swap. In comparison with baseline, output and employment rise by 6.4 percent and 1.9 percent, respectively, for triennium 3 while unemployment and inflation fall—by 1.7 and 5.2 percentage points, respectively. Perhaps more fascinating, however, are the investment results. Because of the ex ante loss of dinars, industry investment ex post first falls below baseline figures but then rises above them. Moreover, despite the dinar-for-dinar transfer ex ante, total investment rises ex post. These reactions demonstrate a twin paradox of investment: *For industry, less investment means more investment, and for the economy as a whole, constant investment means more investment.* From Table 5.3 the aggregate gain amounts to 17.9 percent in triennium 3. A tidy sum, this gain illustrates the extent to which socialist dogma favoring industry, especially heavy industry, undermined economic activity.[2]

The shortage of housing in Yugoslavia, the need for new structures generally, and the overburdened nature of a dated transportation network urge a reallocation system that goes beyond the two agricultures and catering to include infrastructure activities. In addition to stimulating the previous three sectors, it would also enhance housing, construction, and transportation, all in proportion to their investment shares. In numbers, 8.7 percent of the dinars made available from industry investment by the 3-6-9 rule now flow to social agriculture; 8.3 percent, to private agriculture; and 4.9 percent, to catering. Newly included housing receives 46.1 percent; construction, 5.4 percent; and transportation, 26.6 percent. Housing investment, which increases commodity demand by creating living space HOMEAREA, thus bolstering expenditure on household operation CHELMA72, is the major beneficiary of the investment switch.

From the last three columns of Table 5.3 it should be apparent that the broader reallocation package has smaller macro repercussions than does the narrower scheme. For instance, triennium 3 output exceeds baseline by 5.3 percent rather than 6.4 percent, employment increases

Table 5.3

Aggregate Implications of Investment Reallocation Plans

Series	The Agricultures and Catering			The Agricultures, Catering, and Infrastructure		
	1980–82	1983–85	1986–88	1980–82	1983–85	1986–88
	Percentage Differences of Levels					
Output	0.4	3.0	6.4	0.4	2.5	5.3
Employment	0.1	0.8	1.9	0.1	0.7	1.6
Real Wage	0.1	1.0	2.1	0.1	0.8	1.7
Disposable Income	0.2	1.7	3.9	0.2	1.5	3.3
Consumption	0.1	0.5	1.8	0.1	0.5	1.6
Investment	1.9	12.5	17.9	1.6	10.1	24.4
Exports	0.4	1.4	2.5	0.4	1.4	2.3
Imports	0.2	-0.4	-2.8	0.1	-0.5	-3.4
	Differences in Percentage Rates					
Output Growth	0.3	1.0	1.2	0.3	0.8	1.0
Unemployment	-0.1	-0.7	-1.7	-0.1	-0.6	-1.5
Money–Wage Inflation	0.1	-0.9	-4.5	0.1	-0.9	-3.8
CPI Inflation	0.1	-1.1	-5.2	0	-1.0	-4.4

Notes: See Table 5.1.

by 1.6 percent instead of 1.9 percent, and inflation falls by 4.4 percentage points as opposed to 5.2 points. But if housing, construction, and transportation are truly important, then the broader plan hardly can be criticized. For triennium 3 it pushes housing investment 29.4 percent above baseline levels when the three-sector effort yields a 12.3 percent increase. Similarly, construction investment improves by 29.0 percent versus 7.4 percent, and transportation investment strengthens by 24.1 percent versus 3.4 percent. Aggregative gains trade off against disaggregative gains, leaving policy makers to choose along a Phillips-type curve where "more of both" is not an option.

5.4 REALLOCATIONS FROM GOVERNMENT ACTIVITIES TO INVESTMENT

Concern about the size of government has been traditional and widespread. In the United States, for instance, government expenditure on goods and services has historically represented the second largest share of gross national product and outstripped private investment by a substantial margin. The numbers for 1970, 1980, and 1990 demonstrate the situation. In 1970 the government's share amounted to 23.7 percent, second only to consumption's gigantic 61.7 percent. By comparison, investment registered 15.8 percent. Year 1980 saw a similar circumstance, with 19.5 percent for government and 16.0 percent for investment, and 1990 produced like results: 19.8 percent versus 16.6 percent. This large presence of government has drawn fire from many economists, who maintain that government activities are less productive than nongovernment activities.[3] Furthermore, they continue, government spending crowds out nongovernment investment and thus detrimentally alters the mix of output. In the case of government, bigness is badness.

Yugoslavia has seen the same kind of problem. As Panel A of Figure 5.3 shows, investment ITOT72 expressed as a share of social product Y72 initially rose from 30.1 percent in 1974 but later fell continually to 18.9 percent in 1988. At the same time, government spending G72 + GWS72 treated as a share of social product first rose from 18.0 percent and then fell until it became somewhat constant at 16.0 percent. By implication, government expenditure must have risen relative to investment on balance. Panel B confirms this intuition, as it traces the movement of the government-to-investment ratio 100·(G72 + GWS72)/ITOT72 from 59.9 percent in 1974 to 84.8 percent in 1988.[4]

If the hypothesis of the comparative inferiority of government

Figure 5.3
Historical Profiles of the Relationship Between Government
Expenditure and Investment

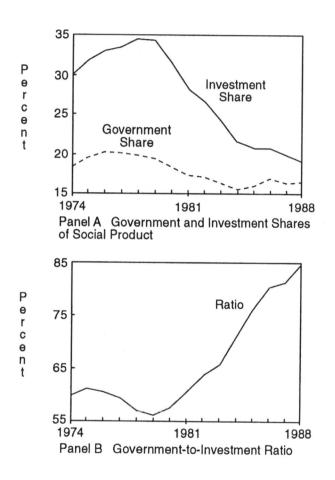

Panel A Government and Investment Shares
of Social Product

Panel B Government-to-Investment Ratio

activity is anywhere near correct for Yugoslavia–and anecdotal experiences all but clinch the point–then decreasing government spending while increasing investment by an equal amount should improve economic performance. In other words, rearranging demand from government to investment should make a positive difference.

The specific reallocation scenario imagined reduces government purchases G72 by 3 percent in 1980, by 6 percent of 1980 purchases in 1981, and by 9 percent of that standard in every year from 1982 to 1988, all reductions being measured against baseline. Wages and salaries paid to government employees GWS72 are equivalently curtailed by the 3-6-9 rule, and hence total expenditure G72 + GWS72 follows the same pattern. Dinars so freed up are redistributed by transfers favoring investment in industry, catering, construction, transportation, and housing based on their proportions in total investment. As a result, industry and housing receive the majority of the funds, 45.2 percent and 30.5 percent, respectively, whereas catering receives the least, 3.2 percent. It may be recognized that the present group of five investment lines encompasses the big-four sectors treated in an output drill of Section 5.2 and the infrastructure factors examined in an investment drill of Section 5.3.

Cutting government wages and salaries reduces employment in "nonproductive" endeavors such as education EMPEDU and general services EMPSPC since those pursuits depend directly upon that spending stream. Employment in construction depends directly upon total investment and must increase as dinars are transferred into that sector. Yet industry employment, which responds negatively to industry investment because of input substitution, must fall. Exerting its own effect is total commodity demand DEMD72, which, if it were to rise eventually, would boost employment in the "productive" sectors generally. In short, the reallocation program sets into motion a complicated series of employment shifts, but, complexity notwithstanding, employment in the entire productive sector should expand at the expense of the nonproductive sector.

These a priori conclusions are confirmed by the model. For triennium 3, education employment slips by 2.0 percent relative to baseline, while general-service employment slides by 0.4 percent. Of the productive sectors, construction is the chief winner, with triennium 3 employment registering 3.5 percent above base. The main loser is industry, which suffers an employment forfeiture of 1.2 percent. Observed from a distance, however, the productive sector gains employment vis-à-vis its counterpart. Specifically, the ratio of nonproductive employment to productive employment for triennium 3 equals 14.8 percent, which is less than the baseline value of 15.0 percent.[5]

The reasoned increase in aggregate commodity demand amounts to 1.3 percent relative to base in triennium 3. Although ex ante the reallocation tactic affects only the components of demand, ex post it affects the level as well. Evidently, a paradox of demand characterizes the adjustment process; that is, *constancy in the level of commodity demand changes the level of commodity demand.*

Other macroeconomic responses are quantified in the first three columns of Table 5.4 Output advances against baseline in all three trienniums, and inflation declines in the last two. Moreover, total investment finishes the nine-year period 13.3 percent above base.

Table 5.4

Macroeconomic Effects of Reallocating Expenditures from the Government to Investment

Series	Five Investment Lines Including Infrastructure			All Investment Lines		
	1980-82	1983-85	1986-88	1980-82	1983-85	1986-88
	Percentage Differences of Levels					
Output	0.3	1.1	2.0	0.5	2.5	6.0
Employment	0	-0.1	-0.2	0.1	0.1	0.5
Real Wage	-1.0	-1.3	-0.6	-1.0	-0.9	0.6
Disposable Income	-1.0	-1.4	-0.7	-0.9	-0.8	1.1
Consumption	-0.5	-1.1	-0.9	-0.5	-0.9	0.3
Investment	5.6	13.1	13.3	6.2	17.2	21.2
Exports	-0.2	-0.7	-0.3	-0.1	-0.3	0.9
Imports	1.0	0.1	-1.3	1.1	-0.2	-3.7
	Differences in Percentage Rates					
Output Growth	0.2	0.2	0.4	0.3	0.8	1.4
Unemployment	0	0.1	0.2	-0.1	-0.1	-0.4
Money-Wage Inflation	0	-0.2	-2.4	0	-0.6	-5.2
CPI Inflation	0.8	-0.1	-2.6	-0.8	-0.7	-5.9

Notes: See Table 5.1.

Consumption, however, falls—by 0.9 percent in triennium 3. The decrease in government wages and salaries is not met by a sufficiently strong increase in the productive-sector wage bill to prevent the total wage bill from falling in real terms. Erosion of that bill drags down disposable income, and as it falls, consumption falls too.

A lesson learned from the tests on the investment mix in Section 5.3 may help to improve performance in the present situation. Rearrangement of investment away from industry toward the agricultures was shown to quicken the pace of activity, and such a redistribution can be implemented here by distributing the government dinars to all 11 investment lines, housing included, rather than to just 5. Distribution again proceeds by the fraction of investment in total investment, and accordingly industry's portion of the government money declines from 45.2 percent to 34.4 percent, while the portions for social agriculture and private agriculture rise from 0 to 4.4 percent and 4.2 percent, respectively. The weights for forestry, handicraft, home trade, and residual also climb from 0.

The improvement in performance is noticeable. For triennium 3 employment in construction now stands 5.5 percent above baseline as opposed to the earlier 3.5 percent. Industry employment falls by less than before, 0.5 percent instead of 1.2 percent. Correspondingly, the productive sector gains more employment compared with the nonproductive sector, namely, the nonproductive-to-productive ratio lies further below the baseline's than previously. Moreover, total output advances more briskly, as the last three columns of Table 5.4 indicate. For triennium 3, output exceeds base by 6.0 percent rather than 2.0 percent, and inflation is 5.9 percentage points less, not 2.6 points. Even the real wage, disposable income, and consumption now expand.

Transferring demand from government to investment does matter, but so does the way in which that transfer is distributed *within* investment. Two reallocation decisions are involved, and both are important.

5.5 CREDIT CONTRACTION

Credit in Yugoslavia has led a turbulent life. Both its intended (or officially sanctioned) component M1 and its unintended (or firm-induced) component L1 have fluctuated wildly through time, although beneath their volatile exteriors lie two basic tendencies. First, the level of credit has been expanding at progressively faster rates, and, second, the mix of credit has been leaning more heavily toward the unintended type. These properties are demonstrated in Tables 5.5 and 2.1.

According to the coefficients of variation and the minimum and maximum values in Table 5.5, the money supply M1 paid little attention to a constant-growth-rate rule. For the postreform period 1965-73, its growth rate varied by 81.3 percent of the mean as it swung from a low of -5.6 percent to a high of 42.3 percent. The post-Constitution years 1974-79 witnessed rates that ranged from 19.0 percent to 55.6 percent, whereas the 1980s saw a swing of more than 200 percentage points, from 20.1 percent to 223.6 percent. Unintended credit was even more unruly. Its coefficient of variation always exceeded that for M1, and its range was always greater. Total credit ML1 necessarily mirrored its component parts.

Turbulence aside, however, Table 5.5 shows that the fundamental movement of credit growth was upward. For the 1965-73 period, total credit advanced at an average rate of 19.4 percent yearly. But for the 1974-79 stretch, it averaged 31.9 percent, and for the 1980s it registered 71.2 percent. The later part of the 1980s (namely, 1984-88) was particularly chaotic, for then credit grew at the heady rate of 111.3 percent.[6] Along with this accelerated growth, as Table 2.1 reminds, the share of L1 in ML1 continually increased from 39.9 percent for 1965-73 to 48.2 percent for 1980-88.

Even students in the principles course know the proposition that inflation is a monetary phenomenon. The inflation equations (PR1) to (PR10), excepting (PR9), of Appendix A confirm that monetarist caveat for Yugoslavia, and they, together with the remarks by Prasnikar and Pregl (1991, p. 193) on the program of four nominal anchors, suggest tackling the country's historically worsening inflation problem through credit restraint. The exercises in Sections 4.3 and 4.4 act on that suggestion in the context of a two-sector system, but the inquiry can be pursued more aggressively with the Mark 4.0. In doing so it is tempting to shape the experiment so as to force credit growth, especially unintended credit growth, to zero; yet such a draconian maneuver would be impossible to accomplish in practice. A more reasonable design draws from Section 4.3 and postulates that M1 and L1 each expand annually at 10 percentage points below actual from 1980 to 1985. Then, when the actual rates catapult, the experimental rates hold steady at about 50 percent, the rate tested in Section 4.4. The resulting growth profile for ML1 is sketched by the solid line in Figure 5.4; the actual path, which underlies the baseline simulation, is illustrated by the dashed line.[7]

Numerical implications of tightening credit are displayed in the first trio of columns in Table 5.6. Clearly, inflation control through credit restraint has its price. For triennium 1 the 10-percentage-point

Table 5.5
Characteristics of Credit Growth in Yugoslavia

Period	Mean Rate	Coefficient of Variation	Minimum Value	Maximum Value
		Intended Credit M1		
1965–73	17.7	81.3	-5.6	42.3
1974–79	29.2	43.0	19.0	55.6
1980–88	68.7	91.7	20.1	223.6
1984–88	104.4	62.6	43.1	223.6
		Unintended Credit L1		
1965–73	29.9	182.3	-41.9	142.1
1974–79	37.0	60.3	15.2	84.7
1980–88	75.5	102.1	16.6	233.8
1984–88	121.9	62.7	49.1	233.8
		Total Credit ML1		
1965–73	19.4	103.2	-12.2	43.2
1974–79	31.9	35.2	18.0	48.0
1980–88	71.2	95.1	18.7	228.4
1984–88	111.3	61.3	53.7	228.4

Notes: All entries are percentages. The coefficient of variation equals 100·standard deviation/mean.

Figure 5.4
**Rates of Total Credit Growth along the Baseline and under Credit
Contraction**

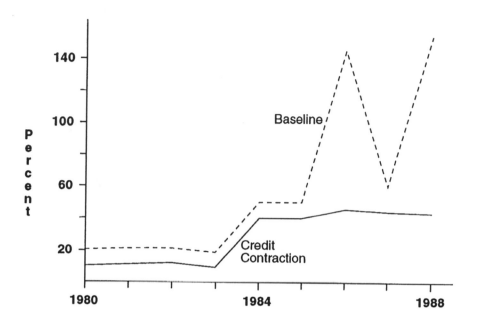

reduction in credit growth shaves the CPI inflation rate by 2.1 points,
but simultaneously it raises unemployment by 0.2 point as the
economy slides along its Phillips curve. This response contrasts with
the reaction to a balanced wage-price controls program, where by
Table 5.1 inflation and unemployment *both* decline as the Phillips
curve shifts downward. For triennium 3 the gradualism of orthodoxy
lowers inflation by 11.2 points while raising unemployment by 1.6
points.[8] Similarly, output drops by 11.1 percent; employment, by 1.8
percent; consumption, by 3.5 percent; and investment, by 44.6 percent.
These larger responses reflect the much greater credit reductions that
occur during triennium 3.

Total employment EMPTOT under credit contraction is depicted by
the solid line in Figure 5.5, which plots the baseline movement by
large dashes. For 1980 the employment loss relative to baseline is 11.7
thousand jobs; for 1981, 22.2 thousand; and for 1982, 29.8 thousand.
These numbers appear to be unrealistically small given the nature of
the perturbation. Continually tightening unintended credit implies a
hardening of the firm's budget constraint and a termination, or at least
a weakening, of employment tenure. Jobs that had been propped up

Table 5.6
Economywide Responses to Credit Contraction

Series	Credit Contraction Alone			Credit Contraction with Workplace Reorganization		
	1980–82	1983–85	1986–88	1980–82	1983–85	1986–88
	Percentage Differences of Levels					
Output	-1.4	-3.8	-11.1	-2.2	-2.7	-8.0
Employment	-0.3	-0.5	-1.8	-2.2	-1.7	-1.8
Real Wage	0.2	-0.5	-0.4	0.8	0.4	1.5
Disposable Income	0	-0.9	-1.7	-1.4	-1.1	0.3
Consumption	-0.5	-1.6	-3.5	-1.1	-2.1	-2.5
Investment	-6.9	-17.3	-44.6	-7.6	-14.9	-40.0
Exports	-0.5	-0.9	-2.9	-1.6	-0.6	-1.8
Imports	-1.1	0.2	-2.3	-1.2	-1.8	-5.3
	Differences in Percentage Rates					
Output Growth	-0.7	-0.9	-3.8	-1.0	0	-3.1
Unemployment	0.2	0.4	1.6	2.0	1.5	1.6
Money-Wage Inflation	-2.0	-0.2	-12.6	-2.2	-0.9	-15.7
CPI Inflation	-2.1	-0.1	-11.2	-2.7	-0.8	-14.9

Notes: See Table 5.1.

Figure 5.5
Employment Profiles along the Baseline and under Credit Contraction

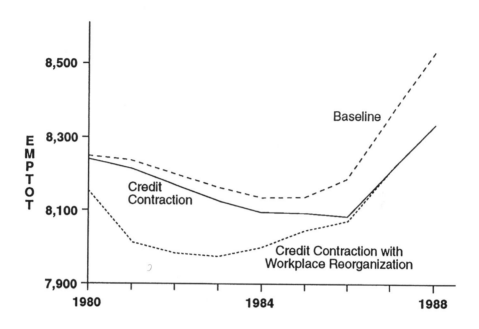

by unbacked promissory notes lose their support as businesses find it necessary to trim fat in an effort to cover costs out of their own revenues. Some firms even go bankrupt, thereby causing a wholesale liquidation of jobs.[9] In short, persistent credit cuts ought to provoke increasingly greater employment forfeitures for a time. Still, those same forfeitures should stimulate the worker incentives that, as Section 2.3.2 observes, likely became dormant under tenure. Rekindled incentives, in turn, should boost output in disembodied fashion and should help to reverse the employment slump.

Modeling the workplace reorganization prompted by hardened budgets is not entirely without guidelines. Section 3.5 estimated that employment tenure protects 111.5 thousand jobs annually, and thus elimination of tenure probably would eliminate a like number of slots initially. Furthermore, if reorganization is not to be overturned by worker revolt, then consonant with the view of Gapinski (1990b, pp. 399, 402), the job cutbacks must be fully restored at some near-future date. Moreover, the "new" disembodied progress that constitutes an integral part of reorganization might take place, as in Section 5.2, only during the first triennium but at an annual rate of 0.25 percent, half the across-the-board benchmark posited earlier. This progress and the two employment targets generate the path traced by short dashes in Figure 5.5. Plainly, workplace reorganization first causes employment to drop below the levels associated with credit contraction alone, but those losses are wiped out over the course of a few years.[10] It may be noted that reorganization applies to all productive sectors except private agriculture, whose rudimentary style of operation renders it unreceptive to such restructuring.

From the macro standpoint workplace reorganization matters a great deal. According to Table 5.6 employment now declines during triennium 1 by 2.2 percent rather than by 0.3 percent or, in terms of head count, by 103.4 thousand workers in 1980, 220.0 thousand in 1981, and 214.7 thousand in 1982. Correspondingly, unemployment increases by 2.0 percentage points instead of 0.2 point. Intensification of unemployment prompts a lowering of the wage bill, a reduction in disposable income by 1.4 percent rather than by 0 percent, and a decline in consumption by 1.1 percent versus 0.5 percent. Investment too drops by more than before: 7.6 percent in comparison with 6.9 percent. Credit contraction coupled with the workplace reorganization that associates with hardened budgets brings about a more precipitous drop in economic activity than does credit contraction alone.

Nevertheless, the news is not all bad. Restructuring improves the two inflation rates and the real wage in triennium 1, and in triennium 3 it improves disposable income and net exports as well. Moreover, in that epoch output, consumption, and investment all fare more favorably than they do under a pure credit sequence. Such news is indeed good.[11]

NOTES

1. Catering is included with the agricultures to lessen the number of dinars being channeled to them, thereby softening the shock of the transfer. Besides, as Section 5.2 described, catering represents Yugoslavia's tourist business, and as such it is important in its own right. Investment shares are taken as the averages of the 1980 and 1988 values.

2. It must be said, however, that deviating from dogma within the Yugoslav framework would have involved political difficulties not unrelated to the uneven distribution of industry and its mix across republics. Some republics would have been hard hit by an antiindustry reallocation.

3. Orzechowski (1977, pp. 250-51) and Bennett and Johnson (1980, pp. 27-30) back up the claim of inferior productivity.

4. Shares for either investment or government spending are not strictly comparable between the United States and Yugoslavia since they are based on different output concepts; that is, gross national product versus social product.

5. It may be noted parenthetically that the weakness of this employment response is quite consistent with the basic inertia underlying Yugoslav employment in general and nonproductive employment in particular. Recent statistics verify this asymmetric robustness by indicating that nonproductive employment declined by 2.3 percent from February 1990 to February 1991 when productive employment dropped by a full 7.7 percent.

6. The years 1989 and 1990 continued the story by recording M1 growth rates of 635.1 percent and 1,426.6 percent, respectively. Table 1.2 elaborates the tale.

7. Behind the choice of a modest path for ML1 restriction lies the belief that tightening credit is tricky business. For instance, mopping up unintended credit might have fostered a more permissive posture in terms of intended credit. An extreme case of such substitution was the Serbian move in December 1990 to unleash new money without legal authority. Efforts to control credit might have been further frustrated by the Social Accounting Service, which often strove to clear accounts payable and receivable by computer rather than by normal channels of debt settlement.

8. Discussion regarding the gradualism of orthodoxy versus the spontaneity of heterodoxy can be found in Okun (1978) and Rockwood (1979).

9. Bankruptcies reached unprecedented heights in 1990 and 1991.

10. In simulation language the steering mechanisms for the movement of total employment are add-factor (intercept) adjustments to the individual employment equations (LB1) to (LB8) of Appendix A and to the exogenous employment series EMPFOR. For sector j the adjustment term equals $b[\Delta L1/L1_{-1} - (\Delta L1/L1_{-1})_{baseline}](E_j)_{baseline}$, where b denotes a time-dependent scalar. $(E_j)_{baseline}$ denotes baseline employment for sector j in 1980 and essentially distributes the total employment loss proportionally across sectors. The bracketed expression, which is always negative due to credit contraction, focuses on unintended credit L1 rather than on total credit ML1, albeit with virtually no difference in numerical results. Elements of vector b are chosen by trial and error. This add-factor adjustment follows the scheme adopted by Gapinski (1990b, p. 397).

11. A similar rebound was imagined by van Bergeijk and Lensink (1990, pp. 11-13) for the grander transitions of Bulgaria, Czechoslovakia, Hungary, Poland, and Romania from centrally planned to market-oriented economies.

6

International Counterfactual
Maneuvers

Remedial actions need not be fashioned only in the domestic context.
Since Yugoslavia is open to both Western and Eastern markets,
correctives also might be cast in the international setting, and this
chapter looks at three such initiatives. Section 6.1 focuses on
accelerated dinar depreciation. Section 6.2 turns to other means for
attracting hard currency, while Section 6.3 considers using the
additional foreign exchange to purchase more equipment and
improved technology from abroad. The three programs are
cumulative, as each builds upon its predecessor.

6.1 ACCELERATED DINAR DEPRECIATION

Consonant with the remarks in Section 3.7, two exchange rates can
be identified for Yugoslavia. One, ERSTAT, represents an official
measure that is used to convert export and import magnitudes into
dinar values for purposes of compiling the national accounts. The
other measure, DINDOAV, is the rate encountered in actual practice.
Both are denominated in dinars per dollar, both are nominal in the
sense that they do not adjust for domestic price changes, and—despite
frequent numerical disparities—both exhibit strong upward trends.
They both manifest dinar depreciation.

Depreciation of the dinar is documented in Table 1.1 and especially
in Table 1.2, where it is shown that the exchange rate soared in the
hope of preventing Yugoslav exports from suffocating under the
intense pressure of domestic inflation. Such depreciation, while rapid,
raises the question of whether it had been rapid enough, and two
reflections underscore the merit of the interrogatory. The first

thought centers on a common Yugoslav sentiment that devaluation was less a policy mechanism for managing trade and more a sign of government weakness, an admission of national defeat, and a plot for subsidizing certain republics. Sentiment of this sort would have encouraged depreciation reticence. The second reflection deals with a quantifiable fact. As Figure 6.1 illustrates, the real exchange rate, specified as PRELIND in equation (IA19) of Appendix A, fell along the baseline from 1984 to 1986 and remained below its 1984 level until 1988. In other words, the nominal exchange rate failed to keep pace with inflation, and exports suffered as a result. The remedy, of course, would have been faster depreciation.

To shape that corrective maneuver, the nominal exchange rate is adjusted by the rule $DINDOAV = (1 + \alpha) \cdot DINDOAV_{baseline}$, where the values of 100α are depicted by the dashed line in Figure 6.1. From 1980 to 1984 the exchange rate is imagined to lie 25 percent above its baseline mark. To eliminate the slump in the real rate, 100α rises to 35 percent in 1985 and to 75 percent in 1986. Afterward, it tails off to 55 percent and 20 percent. On balance, then, the new nominal rate is 32.3 percent greater than its baseline counterpart, and, as Figure 6.1 attests by the accelerated depreciation line, it prompts a continual increase in the real rate. The mid-1980s dip no longer occurs.

Consequences of accelerated dinar depreciation are presented in the first three columns of Table 6.1, which expands the format of the standard display employed in Chapter 5. Obviously, the domestic effects of the international endeavor are small. Output falls below baseline levels by 0.4 percent in the first triennium, years 1980-82, by 0.3 percent in the second, and by 0.1 percent in the third. Output's decline notwithstanding, employment rises relative to base, and correspondingly unemployment falls. Yet those movements are slight as well. More pronounced on the home front is the response of investment, which contracts by 3.2 percent, 2.7 percent, and 2.5 percent across trienniums. Its retrenchment follows from the drying up of real credit brought about by higher prices under depreciation. Equations (IN1) to (IN12), (PR1) to (PR6), and (PR8) to (PR11) of Appendix A provide the evidence.

Confirming intuition, the main impact of the international initiative happens in the foreign sector of the economy. Relative to baseline, goods exports to nonsocialist countries rise by 2.7 percent in triennium 1 and then by 4.7 percent and 6.5 percent. Exports to socialist countries fall, however. In interpreting this result, it must be recalled that socialist exports are driven not by exchange rates but rather by bilateral arrangements, and hence they need not behave like nonsocialist exports. A decline in industrial output together with a shrinkage in real credit helps to explain their reduction. Equation

Figure 6.1
Nominal and Real Exchange Rates: Accelerated Dinar Depreciation Versus Baseline Conditions

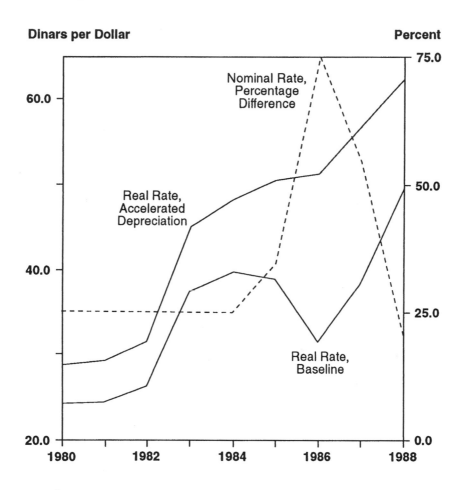

(IA2) makes the point.

Imports react to depreciation more strongly than do exports. For instance, total imports decline by 3.3 percent, 4.8 percent, and 6.7 percent over the trienniums, as opposed to the export gains of 0.5 percent, 1.4 percent, and 2.2 percent. Moreover, intermediate imports, which, as equation (YA1) indicates, are a critical part of industrial production, sag by 3.4 percent, 3.0 percent, and 4.9 percent. Equally troublesome are the forfeitures in capital goods imports: 4.6 percent, 7.6 percent, and 5.9 percent. Those losses echo the contraction in domestic investment and signal hard times for capital

Table 6.1
Economic Conditions under Various International Policy Maneuvers

Series	Accelerated Dinar Depreciation			Hard Currency Incentives			Equipment and Technology Transfers		
	1980–82	1983–85	1986–88	1980–82	1983–85	1986–88	1980–82	1983–85	1986–88
				Percentage Differences of Levels					
Output	-0.4	-0.3	-0.1	0.1	1.2	2.8	0.6	2.8	6.4
Employment	0	0.2	0.4	0.3	1.0	1.8	0.4	1.1	2.3
Real Wage	-1.4	-0.8	-1.0	-1.5	-0.4	-0.2	-1.3	0.2	1.1
Disposable Income	-0.8	0.1	0.3	0	2.1	3.7	0.2	3.0	5.6
Consumption	-0.7	-0.6	-0.7	-0.3	0.9	1.8	-0.2	1.4	3.2
Investment	-3.2	-2.7	-2.5	-2.5	0.1	3.1	-0.7	5.5	11.8
Exports:	0.5	1.4	2.2	2.7	4.9	5.6	3.7	4.8	6.3
Goods, Nonsocialist Nations	2.7	4.7	6.5	10.1	14.3	13.8	10.6	13.7	13.7
Goods, Socialist Nations	-1.7	-1.3	-2.1	-5.1	-7.4	-6.7	-4.2	-6.3	-3.4
Nonfactor Services	0.4	0.2	0.2	3.0	7.0	6.1	4.6	6.1	5.6
Imports:	-3.3	-4.8	-6.7	-1.4	0.4	-3.8	-0.1	1.0	-4.4
Intermediate Goods	-3.4	-3.0	-4.9	-1.3	2.6	-1.6	-0.7	1.0	-3.9
Capital Goods	-4.6	-7.6	-5.9	-2.3	-0.4	0.5	6.2	15.2	9.8
				Differences in Percentage Rates					
Output Growth	-0.1	0.1	0.2	0.1	0.4	0.8	0.4	0.8	1.6
Unemployment	0	-0.2	-0.3	-1.0	-1.8	-2.5	-1.0	-1.9	-3.0
Money-Wage Inflation	2.8	0.1	-5.2	2.9	-0.6	-6.7	2.7	-1.4	-8.4
CPI Inflation	3.3	0.1	-6.0	3.4	-0.8	-7.9	3.2	-1.8	-10.0

Notes: The symbolic names for most series appear in the notes to Table 5.1. Goods exports to nonsocialist nations are signified by EXPTNSR; those to socialist nations, by EXPTSR. Nonfactor service exports are EXNFSR, whereas the imports of intermediate goods and capital goods are IMPTIR and IMPTKR, respectively. As before, the percentage difference for X, a series expressed as a level, equals $100 \cdot (X - X_{\text{baseline}})/X_{\text{baseline}}$, while the difference in percentage rates equals $100 \cdot (X - X_{-1})/X_{-1} - 100 \cdot [(X - X_{-1})/X_{-1}]_{\text{baseline}}$. All entries are arithmetic averages. The three maneuvers here are cumulative, as each adds to the preceding one.

acquisitions under dinar depreciation policy.

Table 6.2 looks more closely at the consequences of that policy by turning attention to sectoral output and prices. As equations (YA1) to (YA10) of Appendix A reveal, sectoral outputs depend upon various trade series: intermediate imports, nonfactor service exports, and net exports, among others. The slippage in intermediate imports pulls down industry output, as already mentioned, whereas for construction output the devaluation-induced cutback in investment proves to be too great for the expansion in nonfactor service exports to overcome. Meanwhile, the improvement in social agriculture output can be traced to the price effect of dinar depreciation. Depreciation increases unit cost, which via equation (PR2) is passed forward in the form of a higher price that by formula (YA2) stimulates supply. According to Table 6.2, the price response to depreciation is strong across sectors; it is strongest in social agriculture and transportation.[1]

6.2 HARD CURRENCY INCENTIVES

Dubrovnik deserves recognition as a jewel in the crown of the Adriatic. This harbor city at the southern tip of Croatia meets the sea at a towering wall that extends around what might be called the central district. The centuries-old concern about protection from aggressors having yielded to more commercial notions, the wall draws attention to shops of all kinds and to restaurants that offer a wide selection of food from the native dish ćevapčići to standard Western fare. At night visitors might gather at Orlando's Pillar or dance down the cobblestone walks to the beat of music from the nearby inns. They even might try their luck at one of the casinos. During the day a swim in the crystal-clear bay or in the hotel pool would refresh, and for the more adventuresome a short boat trip to Lokrum Island would invigorate. For those seeking panoramic views, a ride to the mountaintop overlooking the Stari Grad, the sea, and the houses that dot the hillside would hardly disappoint.

Further north along the Adriatic lies Split, a scenic city whose harbor is outlined by gleaming cruise ships from seemingly every port and whose upper terrace affords a startling image of the water below. Still further north lies Primošten, its spectacular profile struck against the setting sun and its eager guests bathing and sailing in various degrees of attire. Next come the sister towns of Mali Lošinj and Veli Lošinj. Situated on an island that bears the same surname, they—like most sisters—have their similarities and their differences. Both have a peaceful charm that fills the streets and boat landings and that transports the imagination back to a simpler time. Mali, however, is

Table 6.2
Percentage Differences for Sectoral Output and Price Levels under Accelerated Dinar Depreciation

Sector	Output			Price		
	1980–82	1983–85	1986–88	1980–82	1983–85	1986–88
Industry	-0.5	-0.3	-0.2	5.4	4.1	2.5
Social Agriculture	0.7	1.1	2.0	9.8	10.9	14.1
Private Agriculture	-0.1	0	0.1	7.9	7.8	8.3
Catering	-0.6	-0.8	-1.2	7.7	6.1	8.6
Construction	-1.8	-1.9	-2.1	6.6	7.5	8.2
Forestry	-0.2	0	0.2	6.5	6.5	7.1
Handicraft	-0.3	-0.2	-0.2	5.2	5.8	6.1
Home Trade	-0.2	0	0.5	8.5	8.7	11.0
Residual	-0.4	-0.1	0.4	6.0	3.9	2.0
Transportation	-0.1	-0.2	-0.3	10.0	11.0	13.3

Note: Percentage differences are calculated relative to baseline levels in the manner described by Table 6.1.

the larger of the two (despite its name) and accordingly leaves the impression of offering a greater variety of activities.[2]

Turning inland, the traveler comes upon the Plitvice Lakes, whose beauty can only be described as breathtaking. Waterfalls, trails, boat rides, and homemade cheese, bread, and wine provide a fitting complement to this natural wonder. Lake Bled in Slovenia rests in the shadow of the Julian Alps and features an eleventh-century island church that, cradled by trees, serves as a manifestation of tranquillity. Samobor, southeast of Lake Bled, might be appropriately described as a village courtyard, and Medjugorje, on the distant outskirts of Dubrovnik, might be seen as the sacred destination of modern-day pilgrims who believe in a Higher Authority.

The point of this elliptical travelogue is that Yugoslavia is more than an Eastern European country that defied Stalin and that followed Tito into uncharted water. It is also a country that has much sun, shore, sea, sights, and sounds to export. Nonetheless, it failed to take full advantage of that richness and in effect passed up an immediate source of hard currency. Stimulating tourism necessarily would attract foreign exchange, but it also would boost the catering sector: Output, employment, and investment would rise there, prompting expansion elsewhere in the economy. Of course, ways other than tourism promotion might be used to generate hard currency. They include more vigorous marketing of Yugoslav products abroad and added incentives for Yugoslavs to pursue employment beyond the country's borders.

Formulating the hard currency initiative begins with the acceleration of dinar depreciation considered in the previous section. By stimulating exports, that action channels foreign money into the country. Advertising campaigns in Western Europe aimed at publicizing the Yugoslav coast are envisioned to bolster foreign tourists by 3 percent above the baseline level in 1980, by 6 percent of the 1980 level in 1981, and by 9 percent of that norm in each of the years from 1982 to 1988. Since a foreign tourist stays roughly 5.75 days per trip, the number of nights spent NIGHTF expands commensurately. By equations (CN4), (CN5), (CN11), and (IA3) in Appendix A, the new visitors stimulate the consumption of food, footwear, and transportation while raising the export of nonfactor services. Naturally, with more Westerners enjoying ćevapčići, output and employment in catering expand. The former schedule (YA4) shifts upward by the 3-6-9 rule, whereas the latter (LB3) drifts upward by 3 percent in 1980 but by smaller percentages afterward. Crowded cafes and overbooked hotels mean enlarged facilities or new establishments, and consequently the investment schedule (IN4) climbs as well. The movements of the three schedules are calibrated to keep the growth of the corresponding series balanced throughout the sequence.[3]

Intensified marketing of Yugoslav goods in Western nations, equation (IA1), quickens those exports by the 3-6-9 convention, ceteris paribus. Moreover, that new demand is presumed to have negative repercussions vis-à-vis socialist nations as some of the merchandise otherwise intended for the East is redirected to the West. More precisely, those exports, equation (IA2), decrease, ceteris paribus, by half the Western increase. Finally, the inducements for Yugoslavs to work outside the country expand exports of factor services EXFSR, augment foreign remittances FREMIT, and raise disposable income YDA72 in equation (CN14). Controlling those movements is the remittance variable BPXREMIT in the balance of payments; it conforms to the 3-6-9 hypothesis. To reflect the departure of Yugoslavs for employment on foreign soil, the labor-supply measure LSTOT declines by 0.50 percent relative to baseline in 1980, by 0.75 percent in 1981, and by 1.00 percent in each year afterward.

The results of the "selling Yugoslavia" strategy appear in the middle three columns of Table 6.1. Selling works. Output now exceeds baseline levels, and for triennium 3 it stands 2.8 percent above that reference path. Employment improves by 1.8 percent in that stanza, while disposable income gains 3.7 percent then. Investment, which declined by 2.5 percent in the years 1986-88 under accelerated dinar depreciation, now expands by 3.1 percent. Other favorable signs involve unemployment, whose rate in triennium 3 drops 2.5 percentage points below baseline, and CPI inflation, which declines by 7.9 points.

As anticipated, the big winners in this international game are exports. Total exports outstrip baseline levels by 2.7 percent, 4.9 percent, and 5.6 percent across trienniums, and Western goods exports soar by 10.1 percent, 14.3 percent, and 13.8 percent. The tourism factor shows up in nonfactor service exports, which swell by 3.0 percent, 7.0 percent, and 6.1 percent. Furthermore, because of the improvement in domestic demand and the increased availability of foreign exchange, capital goods imports, equation (IA5), behave more favorably than they did in the dinar depreciation sequence. However, they still shrink in the first two trienniums.

6.3 EQUIPMENT AND TECHNOLOGY TRANSFERS

One of the casualties in the efforts to accelerate dinar depreciation and to attract additional hard currency is the import of capital goods.

It generally declines. Yet turning aside foreign-made machinery may not be prudent for a country that craves equipment and the advanced technology which it may embody. Prudence therefore suggests that steps be taken to reverse the decline, and those initiatives may be presumed to raise capital goods imports IMPTKR by the 3-6-9 rule. Funding the acquisitions follows a 60-40 split, where 60 percent of the finance comes from the hard currency measures referenced in the previous section, while the remaining 40 percent comes from increased foreign credit FCREDIT.[4]

The newly arriving equipment is allocated across the ten sectors by their investment shares consonant with the distribution pattern invoked in Section 5.4 to convert government expenditures into investment spending. The technology being transferred stimulates output growth sectorally in a manner reminiscent of the surges posited in Section 5.2, although the degree of impact is much less (one-eighth) than before. The only exception to these allocation guidelines involves catering. By virtue of the hard currency inducements in place, catering already enjoys sizable investment and output gains, and consequently it experiences disproportionately smaller improvements under the equipment and technology transfers than do the other sectors.

How successful is the transfer campaign? The last three columns of Table 6.1 provide the answer. To be sure, the erosion of capital goods imports is reversed. Now those imports rise relative to baseline by 6.2 percent in triennium 1 and by 15.2 percent and 9.8 percent in trienniums 2 and 3. These numbers compare favorably with the -2.3, -0.4, and 0.5 postings for the hard currency sequence and the -4.6, -7.6, and -5.9 listings under accelerated depreciation alone. Similarly, total investment shows a healthy response to the point where it lies 11.8 percent above baseline in triennium 3. Fueled both by the new investment and by the technology transfer, output responds nicely as well. For instance, in triennium 3 it stands 6.4 percent above baseline. Correspondingly, disposable income is up by 5.6 percent; consumption, by 3.2 percent. Furthermore, unemployment and inflation finish 3.0 and 10.0 percentage points below base as opposed to 2.5 and 7.9 points below. The transfer program is not without its benefits.

This scenario builds upon the hard currency endeavor, which in turn builds upon the accelerated depreciation maneuver. It represents a cumulation of foreign policy strategies, but at the same time it appeals to domestic strategies in its investment and technology allocations. It both cumulates and blends. Such cumulating and blending of separate initiatives are fundamental to the preparation of a comprehensive package for treating the economic failure of Yugoslavia. That package, its outcomes, and an overall conclusion are subjects for the next chapter.

NOTES

1. The increases in sectoral price levels under dinar depreciation are not inconsistent with the decrease in the CPI inflation rate reported in Table 6.1 for triennium 3. Explained simply, a higher price level means a higher start value from which to calculate a rate of change, thereby implying a lower percentage, ceteris paribus. For the record, the CPI level exceeds its baseline counterpart by 6.7 percent, 7.0 percent, and 7.9 percent across the trienniums.

2. Speaking from personal experience, the present writer can confirm that Mali Lošinj is a delightful place to wait out the radioactive drift from a disintegrating nuclear reactor in Chernobyl.

3. In the end catering output exceeds baseline levels by 7.9 percent, 20.2 percent, and 23.9 percent across trienniums. The corresponding employment percentages are 7.4, 18.1, and 24.5, whereas the investment numbers are 9.5, 28.1, and 25.0.

4. Since capital goods imports are denominated in millions of dinars even though foreign credit is measured in millions of US dollars, the requisite amount of new credit is determined from the expression $\Delta FCREDIT = (\Delta IMPTKR) \cdot IMPTP / (ERSTAT / 17)$, where $\Delta IMPTKR$ equals 40 percent of the total increment in equipment imports.

7

Conclusions from a
Broader Perspective

Yugoslavia could have improved economic conditions during the 1980s by various means. Those policies include balanced wage-price controls, output or productivity stimulus, resource redistribution from government to investment, and hard currency incentives. By contrast, serious credit contraction along with its requisite workplace reorganization would have imposed hardship on the system. Nevertheless, a few favorable responses exhibit themselves even in that transition, leaving the impression that they might be enhanced and other gains might be made by combining policies along a broad front. Section 7.1 assumes that responsibility and discharges it by building upon the sequences discussed in Chapters 5 and 6. Section 7.2 extracts the sectoral and regional implications of the program, whereas Section 7.3 brings into play the ethnicity and nationalism ingrained in Eastern Europe. Section 7.4 then steps back to answer the question of whether, all things considered, the Yugoslav economic failure could have been prevented.

7.1 COMPREHENSIVE RESTRUCTURING

Credit contraction with workplace reorganization forms the basis of the comprehensive package. To that foundation is added a technical-progress initiative which extends disembodiment to private agriculture at a yearly rate of 0.25 percent from 1980 to 1982 and which increases the augmented rates of output growth to 0.50 percent for the other nine productive sectors.

Resource transfers from the government to investment take place much as before, with government expenditure being throttled down by 2,080 million dinars in 1980, by 4,160 million in 1981, and by 6,240 million in 1982 and beyond. Those dinars—which respectively represent 3 percent, 6 percent, and 9 percent of government spending in 1980—are first divided proportionately among the 11 investment lines, but then, in keeping with the investment reallocation scenarios, part of the industry "subsidy" is redirected proportionally to the remaining 10 lines. Specifically, 170 million industry dinars are spread elsewhere in 1980; 340 million in 1981; and 510 million in 1982 and afterward. Wage-price policy holds to the 2-3-2 rule for wages and to the 3-6-9 scheme for prices. Now, however, there is no separate restraint on nonproductive earnings since government wages and salaries are already bridled through the government-to-investment reallocation.[1] Another recalibration involves consumer credit, whose decline under the package is subject to a lower bound.

The measures aimed abroad cover, inter alia, tourism, the export of merchandise and factor services, and the import of capital goods. As earlier, foreign tourism in Yugoslavia expands by the 3-6-9 rule, while the number of tourist nights and the volume of tourist expenditure increase correspondingly. This boom in catering manifests itself in output, whose schedule rises further by the 3-6-9 criterion, and in employment and investment, whose schedules move together with output's. Merchandise exports to the West are bolstered in 3-6-9 fashion, partly at the expense of merchandise exports to the East, and factor service exports behave similarly. The import of capital goods also proceeds in a 3-6-9 manner, and again 40 percent of those acquisitions are financed by foreign debt. Their allocation across sectors follows the proportions inherent in the government-to-investment sequence; the technology that they embody boosts output growth by an extra 0.06 percentage point except for the already much-improved catering, where the new increment is capped at a token amount.

Two other international adjustments involve consumer goods imports and the nominal exchange rate. For the former, guidelines are imposed to control motion at the low end of the import scale, and for the latter, values are assigned to assure smooth and reasonable depreciation of the real dinar rate given the decided reduction in domestic inflation.

How successful would comprehensive restructuring be? Very, according to Table 7.1. Relative to baseline, comprehensive restructuring drives output upward by 2.3 percent in triennium 1, years 1980-82, and by 11.8 percent and 10.2 percent in trienniums 2 and 3. Employment too increases against baseline in both of those periods. The broad-based program not only offsets the output and employment losses prompted by the tightening of credit generally, by

Table 7.1
Consequences of a Comprehensive Program of Economic Restructuring

Series	1980-82	1983-85	1986-88
	Percentage Differences of Levels		
Output	2.3	11.8	10.2
Employment	-1.4	0.5	1.0
Real Wage	2.9	7.8	5.0
Disposable Income	2.1	8.6	8.0
Consumption	0.4	2.2	-0.4
Investment	10.3	45.3	10.1
Exports:	3.4	4.0	1.1
Goods, Nonsocialist Nations	7.1	8.4	11.3
Goods, Socialist Nations	-2.5	-2.6	-19.1
Nonfactor Services	5.4	6.4	5.6
Imports:	0.2	2.0	-0.3
Intermediate Goods	-1.6	1.0	-2.2
Capital Goods	8.5	15.7	9.3
	Differences in Percentage Rates		
Output Growth	1.8	2.7	-2.2
Unemployment	0.6	-1.4	-1.8
Money-Wage Inflation	-14.5	-16.9	-22.9
CPI Inflation	-15.3	-19.2	-21.6

Note: See Tables 5.1 and 6.1 for nomenclature and definitions.

the drying up of unintended credit particularly, and by the greater commitment to Western business principles. It also propels the economy to new heights. Comparing columns 4-6 of Table 5.6 with Table 7.1 indicates just how high the economy goes. Instead of output falling by 8.0 percent in triennium 3, it rises by more than 10 percent. Instead of employment sagging by 1.8 percent, it advances by 1.0 percent. Panels A and B of Figure 7.1 present those comparisons in bold relief.

The new-found output filters down to households as the real wage and disposable income swell and improve the standard of living.

Figure 7.1
Economic Performance under Different Reform Programs

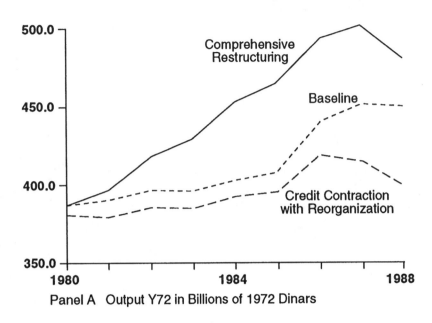

Panel A   Output Y72 in Billions of 1972 Dinars

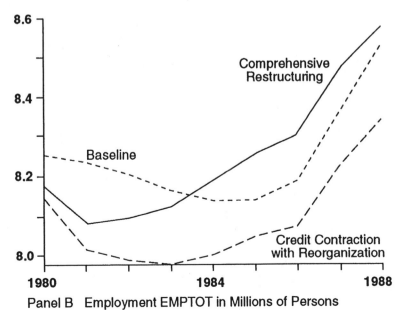

Panel B   Employment EMPTOT in Millions of Persons

Figure 7.1 (continued)

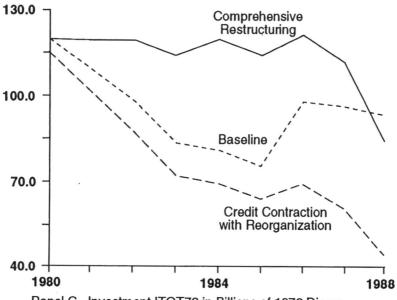

Panel C   Investment ITOT72 in Billions of 1972 Dinars

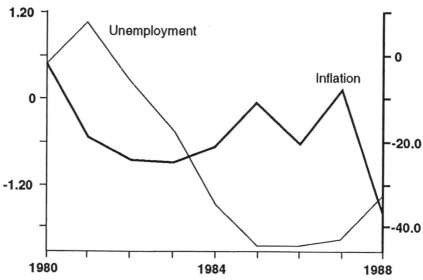

Panel D   Differences in Percentage Rates for Unemployment
and CPI Inflation under Comprehensive Restructuring

Especially striking is the response of investment. Since credit is a chief determinant there, sharp credit contraction with reorganization forces investment to dive by 40.0 percent in triennium 3 according to column 6 of Table 5.6. Yet under comprehensive restructuring, investment in that triennium actually grows by 10.1 percent—a difference of 50.1 percentage points. Moreover, in triennium 2 investment exhibits a 45.3 percent gain as opposed to a 14.9 percent loss under credit contraction. The reason for these big discrepancies is shown in Panel C of Figure 7.1: Comprehensive restructuring typically keeps investment at its 1980 level, whereas credit contraction with reorganization causes the bottom to fall out.

In its international ventures, too, Yugoslavia makes impressive strides. Merchandise exports to nonsocialist nations move ahead by 11.3 percent in triennium 3, and nonfactor service exports do likewise by 5.6 percent. Capital goods imports, a specific target of restructuring, advance nicely as well. Analogous conquests occur in the battles against unemployment and inflation. Although credit contraction with reorganization bumps the unemployment rate above baseline by 1.5 and 1.6 percentage points in trienniums 2 and 3, comprehensive restructuring tugs it below base by virtually equivalent amounts. Furthermore, it cuts CPI inflation by 15.3 points, 19.2 points, and 21.6 points across trienniums. Panel D of Figure 7.1 illustrates the good news regarding unemployment and inflation.

Judged from the standpoint of the economy as a whole, comprehensive restructuring must be regarded as successful. Besides toughening business canons, it has favorable effects on many aspects of economic life, and those effects are often substantial. In other words, it deserves high grades for breadth and depth.

7.2 SECTORAL AND REGIONAL IMPLICATIONS

Operating beneath the surface of the macro economy is an intricate network of sectoral transactions. Some sectors push while others pull, and in the process resources move from one endeavor to another. Those reallocations may cross territorial boundaries, and hence some regions may benefit whereas others may suffer. Still others may manage to remain unaffected on balance.

Table 7.2 looks at a few sectoral ramifications of comprehensive restructuring. Plainly, output expands in all sectors over virtually all trienniums. Catering leads the way by registering a 9.7 percent increase relative to baseline in triennium 1 and by posting figures of 25.1 percent and 26.8 percent in the next two epochs. Workplace reorganization takes its toll in triennium 1, as all sectors except private

Table 7.2
Percentage Differences for Sectoral Output, Employment, and Investment under Economic Restructuring

Sector	Output			Employment			Investment		
	1980-82	1983-85	1986-88	1980-82	1983-85	1986-88	1980-82	1983-85	1986-88
Industry	0.7	10.4	10.7	-2.8	-2.1	-1.4	7.4	41.7	-8.4
Social Agr.	1.3	4.2	-3.0	-4.5	-9.1	-8.4	9.5	36.1	31.0
Private Agr.	0.7	2.7	2.3	0	0	0	8.8	25.8	14.8
Catering	9.7	25.1	26.8	4.0	15.8	23.5	18.5	62.8	23.5
Construction	6.8	24.1	9.0	-0.3	9.6	3.7	15.4	63.9	13.4
Forestry	2.5	8.0	5.8	-1.4	0.5	0.1	5.7	18.0	-2.3
Handicraft	3.3	13.5	13.8	-3.8	-1.9	0.5	10.6	42.5	47.1
Home Trade	3.6	16.7	16.0	-2.9	0.8	3.2	17.1	91.6	47.6
Residual	2.9	15.8	11.1	-3.0	-1.2	0.2	11.4	55.8	14.5
Transportation	2.0	5.8	5.4	-3.0	0.9	3.7	12.7	45.1	14.7

Notes: Calculated relative to baseline levels, the percentage differences are formally defined in Tables 5.1 and 6.1. The employment entries for the residual sector refer to the only component undergoing workplace reorganization, namely, commercial and financial services.

agriculture and catering experience job losses. Still, in triennium 3
most sectors recover strongly enough to surpass their employment
record on the baseline. As for sectoral investment, the enormous
improvement that it displays in triennium 2 can be explained as in the
aggregate case: Comprehensive restructuring props up investment at
a time when capital acquisitions collapse along the baseline.

Perhaps more important than these sectoral similarities are the
sectoral differences that can be discerned from the table. Catering, for
instance, performs consistently well in terms of output, employment,
and investment; yet industry, contrary to the socialist mission recalled
by Goldman (1992, p. 46), performs less well. This disparity is rather
obvious. The subtler ones can be sharpened by establishing a ranking
system for the sectors. For any sector the percentage differences
pertinent to output are averaged across trienniums, and ranks are
assigned based on performance, a 1 being the most favorable mark.
The same procedure is also used for employment and investment. The
three numbers to arise for each sector are then summed to give an
overall rating. Those scores show catering to be the top performer,
followed by construction and home trade. At the bottom of the list
are private agriculture, forestry, industry, and—weakest of all—social
agriculture.

Another way to gauge the disparities across sectors involves the
sectoral shares of output, employment, and investment in their
respective totals. For each series the share in any triennium is
calculated under comprehensive restructuring and is expressed as a
percentage of the corresponding baseline share. Afterward, the three
triennium percentages are averaged, and the result finds its way into
Table 7.3. Patently, the output share for catering rises to 111.4
percent of the baseline norm, while that for industry dips slightly to
99.2 percent. More noticeably, social agriculture's share declines to
93.3 percent. The employment and investment statistics are
interpreted analogously.

Averaging the percentages in Table 7.3 by sector yields a second
rating scale, which gives an ordering much like that produced by
Table 7.2. As before, catering scores best, and construction and home
trade make up the second tier. Grouped at the bottom again are
forestry, industry, and the two agricultures.

What do these sectoral dissimilarities mean for the six republics and
two autonomous provinces? They mean that the gains and losses from
restructuring are not spread evenly among them. Indeed, some benefit
at the expense of others. Table 7.4 helps to explain the situation by
indicating how the sectoral activities are distributed geographically.
Industry is represented by capital stock; agriculture, by the production
of maize, wheat, and meat. Catering manifests itself by tourist nights,

Table 7.3
Indexed Changes in Sectoral Output, Employment, and Investment Shares Given Economic Restructuring

Sector	Output	Employment	Investment
Industry	99.2	97.8	93.0
Social Agriculture	93.3	92.6	104.0
Private Agriculture	94.3	100.0	96.6
Catering	111.4	114.4	110.7
Construction	104.6	104.3	106.4
Forestry	97.6	99.7	89.0
Handicraft	101.9	98.2	110.7
Home Trade	103.7	100.3	124.0
Residual	101.6	98.6	103.9
Transportation	96.6	100.4	101.8

Notes: Entries indicate whether a sector's share of the total changes relative to baseline and, if so, the extent of that change. For instance, an index of 95.0 means that the sector's share falls to 95.0 percent of its baseline value. Similarly, a value of 105.0 means an increase to 105.0 percent of the baseline mark. A 100.0 signals no change. All postings are averages for the entire 1980-88 period. Employment for the residual sector again refers to commercial and financial services alone.

and home trade translates into retail sales. To correct for regional size, the entries are expressed in per capita form, and to compensate for inflation, the currency magnitudes are calibrated in 1972 dinars.

Despite the fact that each region participates in every sectoral activity, the concentrations vary substantially from place to place. For example, industry can be found in the cities of sprawling Croatia and in the towns of tiny Kosovo, but it concentrates in Slovenia, where capital stock approximates 51,200 dinars per person. Similarly, agriculture dots the landscape of Bosnia-Herzegovina and the fields of Serbia Proper, but it centers itself in Vojvodina. On a per capita basis, that province annually yields about 2,050 kilograms of maize, 820 kilograms of wheat, and 115 kilograms of meat. Those volumes greatly exceed the harvests from any other area and earn Vojvodina recognition as the Breadbasket of Yugoslavia.

Table 7.4
Regional Breakdown of Sectoral Activity Measures Expressed in Per Capita Terms

Region	Industry Capital Stock in 1972 din.	Production of			Nights Spent by Tourists	Retail Sales in 1972 din.
		Maize in kg.	Wheat in kg.	Meat in kg.		
Bosnia–Herzegovina	22,971	169.9	87.3	32.8	1.0	4,869
Croatia	26,323	515.5	257.2	66.2	13.2	8,693
Macedonia	16,045	46.6	138.5	21.6	1.8	4,556
Montenegro	26,591	21.2	16.3	28.4	15.1	5,379
Slovenia	51,172	145.1	81.3	87.5	4.3	12,335
Serbia Proper	20,835	390.9	218.7	58.5	1.9	6,197
Kosovo	10,475	115.6	150.9	17.5	0.4	2,427
Vojvodina	23,416	2,048.7	822.0	115.7	0.6	7,004

Source: Statistički Godišnjak Jugoslavije.

Notes: Per capita values are derived by dividing the original series by the population of the region. Except for the capital-stock numbers, all entries represent annual flows; without exception all are averages for the period 1980–88. Serbia Proper refers to Serbia exclusive of its autonomous provinces.

The imagery behind the travelogue in Section 6.2 presumes that tourists in Yugoslavia head for the coast, and Table 7.4 validates that belief. Even though Kosovo and Vojvodina attract tourists, Montenegro and Croatia—the coastal republics sketched in Figure 1.1—draw the lion's share. Montenegro comes first with 15.1 annual nights per resident, but Croatia is close behind with 13.2. Actually, the low population count for Montenegro distorts the picture a bit, because when tourist nights are considered in levels rather than in per capita format, they show Croatia to be the top region by far. More precisely, Croatia averaged 61.1 million tourist nights yearly over the 1980s, while Montenegro averaged 9.2 million. Given Croatia's lengthy coastline, that contrast is hardly surprising. Finally, as regards home trade, Slovenia appears to be the focus of activity, at least when judged by retail sales per capita.

At this point the two lines of reasoning can be merged to complete the logical syllogism. Comprehensive restructuring favors catering and home trade at the expense of industry and agriculture. Croatia and Montenegro thrive on catering; Slovenia, on home trade and industry; and Vojvodina, on agriculture. Therefore restructuring favors Croatia and Montenegro, has mixed effects on Slovenia, and compromises Vojvodina. Naturally, this syllogism misses many of the hues that color the full interaction between sectors and regions, and in its efforts to convert limited data into simple sector-region pairings, it may stretch some of the relationships. Nonetheless, it does illustrate that restructuring requires a reallocation of resources within and across regions. The success of the program thus depends upon the extent to which resources can be reallocated.

7.3 A LESSON FROM EASTERN EUROPE

Western economic theory envisions the smooth movement of scarce resources in response to price signals from untrammeled markets. It further imagines that the invisible hand of competition diligently steers the economy toward a state that can be construed as optimal. Of course, practice seldom makes perfect theory, and many factors besides market structure can be singled out as impeding the flow of resources. Politics constitute one such factor. Driven by the need for votes and the hope of reelection, politicians may intentionally or unintentionally upset the economic process, lending credence to the adage that economics is good economics only if it is good politics. Moreover, bureaucracy, a stepchild of politics, may entangle the invisible hand, causing delays in individual or group responses. Still, the various participants in the functioning of a Western society lean in a roughly uniform direction, and even though ethnic and regional differences can be detected, they serve to add dimension to the same basic objectives.

Yugoslavia of the 1980s did not fit this conception. The ruling political party enjoyed monopoly status that distanced it from public opinion and that enabled it to turn a blind eye to economic distress. In the United States voter concern about poor economic performance ushered Ronald Reagan into the Oval Office and a dozen years later sent George Bush packing. Such episodes had little place in Yugoslavia. What did flourish there was bureaucratic inefficiency that wrapped business tightly enough in red tape to put a cramp in the allocative hand. Flourishing alongside the bureaucratic system was a legal framework which remained so complicated and capricious that firms offered premium pay to their senior accountants and legal advisors.

Politics, bureaucracy, and legalities generate their individual frictions that frustrate the kind of resource movements called for by comprehensive restructuring. Probably more important, however, are the ethnic concern and nationalistic spirit that characterized Yugoslavia from its very inception in 1918. As Chapter 1 asserted, the initial alliance among the separate peoples was an uneasy one, and the armed hostilities of the 1990s confirmed that ethnic and nationalistic sensitivities had not lost their virulence. But Yugoslavia is hardly a special case in this regard.

Ever since Stalin cast a pall over Eastern Europe, there have been expressions of ethnic pride and nationalistic zeal. Numerous examples leap to mind: Poland in 1956, Hungary also in 1956, Czechoslovakia in 1968, and Poland again in 1981. Ironically, though, some of the more dramatic expressions came from the Soviet Union itself. In March 1985 Mikhail Gorbachev succeeded Konstantin Chernenko as general secretary, and soon the words *glasnost* and *perestroika* became part of the English language. Beyond the words, however, the iron fist unclenched, the center of power crumbled, and the message spread into the countryside and throughout the Eastern bloc. Quite predictably, waves of ethnicity and nationalism hit the shore. In March 1990 Lithuania declared its independence, and a few months later Belorussia and Armenia issued proclamations of their own. The botched coup against Gorbachev on August 18, 1991, triggered even more defections. Within hours of that attempt, Estonia declared its independence, and within a week Latvia and the Ukraine did the same. By year's end Nobel Laureate Gorbachev had shouldered enough. On December 25, 1991, he resigned, and immediately after his farewell speech, the Soviet flag at the Kremlin was replaced by the flag of Russia. The Bear was dead.[2]

Blown by the winds of *glasnost*, the waves of nationalism continued to roll. Czechoslovakia again provided the setting, much as it had two decades earlier.[3] In January 1989 about 5,000 people demonstrated in Prague to demand more freedom and human rights. The ongoing protests reached their peak in November when for days Prague marchers numbering in the hundreds of thousands shouted for liberty and change. Before the month was over, the Czech Communist Party leadership, buckling under the pressure, resigned, and the Communist government pledged to give up its political monopoly. To many critics this Prague Fall of 1989 vindicated the Prague Spring of 1968, and almost as public apology laced with public approbation, the Soviet Union and its Warsaw Pact allies early in December denounced the Soviet-led invasion that had crushed the 1968 movement.

Waves are difficult to stop. With the Communist hold broken, nationalism turned inward, and within months tension between the Czechs and Slovaks surfaced. In April 1990 Slovaks, believing that they had been slighted at home and abroad, succeeded in changing the country's name to one having a coequal connotation. To them there was substance to symbolism. Some wanted to go even further—to full sovereignty. By the end of August, thousands of Slovaks were rallying for an independent state, and in December the Czechoslovak Parliament outlined the roles of the Czech and Slovak regional governments. Year 1991 witnessed a persistence of the separatist sentiment. In 1992 that force took sharper form, and during the summer leaders of the Czech and Slovak regions agreed to prepare for a division of the country into two nations. By then the nationalism among the Slovaks had been matched by equal resolve among the Czechs as the Velvet Revolution evolved toward what Western journalists called a Velvet Divorce. That split into the Czech Republic and Slovakia took place peacefully on January 1, 1993.

Nationalism and ethnicity are forces powerful enough to topple established governments, to change country names, and to alter territorial boundaries. It follows that they are easily powerful enough to undermine the resource reallocations of an economic restructuring program. That lesson from Eastern Europe is unmistakable.

7.4 A PREVENTABLE FAILURE?

With the death of Tito in 1980, Yugoslavia lost more than a head of state. It lost a leader who united the different peoples and who gave them a common sense of purpose and direction. The Presidency that succeeded him proved to be a weak replacement which, by rotating the spotlight of leadership from region to region, may have illuminated differences rather than muted them. Soon economic fortunes plummeted, nationalism swelled within regions, and ethnic stripe again became a basis for distinction.

As the analysis in this volume indicates, the economic failure could have been prevented by a comprehensive program of restructuring. That program, however, would have required a united effort in its implementation, a reallocation of resources during its operation, and a general acceptance of its results even though everyone would not have benefited equally. Being oriented toward the country as a whole, restructuring simply would have run counter to the intense nationalistic and ethnic mood that prevailed. Consequently, it can be concluded that although the economic failure of Yugoslavia in the post-Tito years could have been prevented on paper, it could not have been prevented in practice.

NOTES

1. Tightening fiscal and monetary operations when applying wage-price controls is the recommendation of various scholars, including Rockwood (1979, pp. 168, 175), Bresser Pereira and Nakano (1987, pp. 59, 103-4, 180-83), and Bruno (1989, pp. 281, 286).

2. Account of the events in Poland, Hungary, and Czechoslovakia was given by Tomaszewski (1989, pp. 237-45) and Simons (1991, pp. 94-101, 120-23, 175-78). Goldman (1992, pp. 80-84, 239-45) and the *New York Times* recounted the happenings in the Soviet Union.

3. The ensuing chronology was documented in the *New York Times*.

Appendix A

The EIZFSU Mark 4.0: Selected Equations and Glossary

Named after its sponsoring institutions, Ekonomski Institut Zagreb and Florida State University, the EIZFSU Mark 4.0 model contains 312 equations, 123 of which are behavioral and 189 of which are identities. Most of its equations, 241 by count, are simultaneous. To keep the exposition of such an involved system manageable, it seems prudent to set aside expressions that are conceptually tangential, econometrically basic, or definitionally obvious. This criterion, which affects both behavioral and identity relations, necessarily leads to an equation set that is not closed from a solution standpoint. Importantly, however, it preserves the thrust of the model and the degree of disaggregation on which the model rests.

The equations to survive the abbreviation rule fall into nine categories:

1. Consumption	6. International activity
2. Investment	7. Wages
3. Capacity output	8. Prices
4. Production	9. Other relationships
5. Labor	

Identities are included in the categories to which they fit most immediately. For instance, disposable income is referenced only by the consumption functions, and consequently its identity appears in the consumption block. Likewise, user cost is mentioned only by the investment equations, and thus its identities appear in the investment block.

Estimation takes place by ordinary least squares or by either the Beach-MacKinnon or the Cochrane-Orcutt method of autocorrelation correction.   Single-equation methods are used because of their convenience and because of their robustness to specification error, and in this regard the Mark 4.0 joins the precedents of the Duesenberry-Eckstein-Fromm model, the Suits model, the St. Louis model, the Chase Econometric model, and others surveyed by Intriligator (1978, pp. 454-56). Data supporting the estimation work are cited in Table 1.1. Notation is described in the glossary, which also gives the units of measurement; brackets below the coefficients contain the Student-t values.

	Equation	RBARSQ RHO DW Years
No.	Specification with Student-t Values	

1. CONSUMPTION

CN1 $CBEVER72 = 3798.6 - 1631.6\ DUM88 + .0252\ YDA72$
  $[7.160]\quad [-8.250]\qquad\quad [11.547]$

$\quad - 4538.8\ PIPDCBEV/PIPDC + .7291\ CBEVER72_{-1} - 1937.2\ STAXAER_{-1}$
  $[-7.383]\qquad\qquad\qquad [28.972]\qquad\qquad [-1.312]$

.9985
0
2.33
53-88

CN2 $CCLOTH72 = 7924.0 + .0343\ YDA72 + .0688\ CREDC/PIPDC$
  $[4.525]\quad [4.363]\qquad\quad [3.187]$

$\quad - 4186.6\ PIPDCCLO/PIPDC + .3045\ CCLOTH72_{-1}$
  $[-3.934]\qquad\qquad\qquad [2.444]$

.9865
.332
1.89
54-88

CN3 $CET72 = -262.00 + .0088\ YDA72 + .0043\ CREDC/PIPDC$
  $[-.328]\qquad [1.413]\qquad\quad [.272]$

$\quad - 589.51\ PIPDCET/PIPDC + .5925\ CET72_{-1} + .1408\ BOOKSPUB$
  $[-1.022]\qquad\qquad\qquad [3.866]\qquad\quad [2.094]$

$\quad + .0336\ NEWSCIRC$
  $[1.974]$

.9891
0
1.78
53-88

CN4 $CFOOD72 = 16365.0 + .0551\ YDA72 + .1508\ CREDC/PIPDC$
  $[5.257]\qquad [3.256]\qquad\quad [2.905]$

$\quad - 12302.0\ PIPDCFOD/PIPDC + .6527\ CFOOD72_{-1} + .4384\ TOURTOT$
  $[-3.527]\qquad\qquad\qquad [11.918]\qquad\quad [2.736]$

.9977
0
2.07
53-88

CN5 $CFOOTW72 = 1863.0 + .0065\ YDA72 + .0036\ CREDC/PIPDC$
  $[4.089]\quad [2.101]\qquad\quad [.457]$

$\quad - 813.40\ PIPDCFWR/PIPDC + .3030\ CFOOTW72_{-1} + .0397\ TOURTOT$
  $[-3.595]\qquad\qquad\qquad [1.590\qquad\qquad [1.818]$

.9881
.226
1.87
54-88

CN6 $CFURN72 = 2536.8 + .0544\ YDA72 + .0066\ CREDC/PIPDC$
  $[2.253]\quad [4.052]\qquad\quad [.239]$

$\quad - 2828.0\ PIPDCFUR/PIPDC + .3735\ CFURN72_{-1}$
  $[-3.068]\qquad\qquad\qquad [2.714]$

.9904
.216
1.88
54-88

	RBARSQ
Equation	RHO
	DW
No. Specification with Student-t Values	Years

CN7 CHEALT72 $= 1756.5 + .0338$ YDA72 $+ .0093$ CREDC/PIPDC
$\quad\quad$ [.854]$\quad$ [4.135]$\quad\quad\quad$ [.438]

$\quad$ $- 2824.5$ PIPDCHEL/PIPDC $+ .2847$ CHEALT72$_{-1}$
$\quad\quad$ [-2.426]$\quad\quad\quad\quad$ [2.915]

.8186
.866
1.90
54-88

CN8 CHELMA72 $= 2969.8 + .0062$ YDA72 $- 4674.4$ PIPDCHLM/PIPDC
$\quad\quad$ [2.629]$\quad$ [2.264]$\quad\quad$ [-6.283]

$\quad$ $+ .6932$ CHELMA72$_{-1}$ $+ .0142$ HOMEAREA
$\quad\quad$ [4.902]$\quad\quad\quad\quad$ [2.306]

.9956
.299
.204
54-88

CN9 COTHER72 $= 982.92 + .0052$ YDA72 $+ .0031$ CREDC/PIPDC
$\quad\quad$ [1.144]$\quad$ [1.051]$\quad\quad\quad$ [.090]

$\quad$ $- 1215.1$ PIPDCOTH/PIPDC $+ .9125$ COTHER72$_{-1}$
$\quad\quad$ [-1.025]$\quad\quad\quad\quad$ [7.369]

.9454
-.526
1.92
59-88

CN10 CTOBAC72 $= 2919.0 + .0207$ YDA72 $- 2842.8$ PIPDCTOB/PIPDC
$\quad\quad$ [5.016]$\quad$ [6.724]$\quad\quad$ [-4.775]

$\quad$ $+ .2817$ CTOBAC72$_{-1}$
$\quad\quad$ [2.729]

.9315
.645
1.46
54-88

CN11 CTRANS72 $= -171.79 + .0210$ YDA72 $+ .0638$ CREDC/PIPDC
$\quad\quad$ [-.107]$\quad$ [1.479]$\quad\quad$ [1.673]

$\quad$ $- 1236.3$ PIPDCTRA/PIPDC $+ .6860$ CTRANS72$_{-1}$ $+ .1955$ TOURTOT
$\quad\quad$ [-1.459]$\quad\quad\quad\quad$ [7.273]$\quad\quad\quad\quad$ [1.788]

.9916
.463
1.89
54-88

CN12 C72T $=$ CBEVER72 $+$ CCLOTH72 $+$ CET72 $+$ CFOOD72

$\quad$ $+$ CFOOTW72 $+$ CFURN72 $+$ CHEALT72 $+$ CHELMA72 $+$ COTHER72

$\quad$ $+$ CTOBAC72 $+$ CTRANS72

CN13 C72 $=$ C72T $-$ CFOREN72

CN14 YDA72 $=$ (WPROD $+$ GWS $+$ SSINC $+$ FREMIT $-$ HHTAX)/PIPDC

		RBARSQ
	Equation	RHO
		DW
No.	Specification with Student-t Values	Years

CN15 $d(CREDC/PIPDC)$ = -1525.1 + 1650.9 DUM5556 + 2206.4 DUM87   .5760
          [-3.384]   [1.521]   [1.443]   0
                                         1.62

         - 1322.2 DUM88 + .1357 KIZREAL + .1937 $d(M1/PZ)$ 55-88
          [-.888]   [3.409]   [5.324]

         + .2931 $[d(CREDC/PIPDC)]_{-1}$
          [2.379]

CN16 HOMEAREA = -1299.8 + .2472 IHOU72 + 1.0220 $HOMEAREA_{-1}$ .9994
                [-.942]   [3.193]   [197.830]   .591
                                         1.93
                                         54-88

2. INVESTMENT

IN1 IIND72 = 2231.0 + .3138 YIND72 - .0869 $KIND72_{-1}$ + .1502 ML1/PZ   .9444
            [1.762]   [2.259]   [-2.396]   [6.262]   0
                                         2.03
         - 3483.3 UCAZ   54-88
          [-1.438]

IN2 IAGR72S = 799.45 + .1335 dYAGR72S + .6524 $IAGR72S_{-1}$ + .0036 ML1/PZ   .7312
             [2.118]   [1.494]   [4.130]   [1.310]   .304
                                         1.87
         - 68.42 UCZ + 1.2853 $dLANDS_{-1}$ 55-88
         [-.149]   [1.093]

IN3 IAGR72P = 544.28 + 1024.1 SHIFT + .0070 dYAGR72P + .3977 $IAGR72P_{-1}$ .9113
            [2.606]   [2.947]   [.327]   [2.045]   .144
                                         1.84
         + .0039 ML1/PZ - 10.31 UCZ + .0085 dLANDP   54-88
         [1.310]   [-.026]   [.016]

IN4 ICAT72 = -1595.1 + .2938 YCAT72 - .0560 $KCAT72_{-1}$ + .0078 ML1/PZ   .3829
           [-1.800]   [1.364]   [-1.840]   [2.132]   .664
                                         1.47
         - 519.53 UCZ + 23.57 $OECDA_{-1}$ 53-88
         [-1.348]   [1.127]

		RBARSQ
	Equation	RHO
		DW
No.	Specification with Student-t Values	Years

IN5 $ICON72 = -36.03 + .1032\ dYCON72 + .7253\ ICON72_{-1} + .0043\ ML1/PZ$
         [-.395]   [4.251]   [5.387]   [1.825]

   - 7.1255 UCAZ
     [-.029]

.9576
-.319
2.03
55-88

IN6 $IFOR72 = 112.51 + .3732\ dYFOR72 + .4361\ IFOR72_{-1} + .0011\ ML1/PZ$
      [3.103]   [2.168]   [2.877]   [3.171]

   - 190.41 UCZ + .0085 $NEWSCIRC_{-1}$
    [-1.758]   [2.161]

.9348
-.347
2.04
54-88

IN7 $IHAN72 = 45.62 + .0914\ dYHAN72 + .8265\ IHAN72_{-1} + .0016\ ML1/PZ$
      [.655] [.872]   [7.599]   [1.247]

.9278
0
2.07
53-88

IN8 $IHTR72 = 14.56 + .1696\ dYHTR72 + .7091\ IHTR72_{-1} + .0041\ ML1/PZ$
      [.073] [4.998]   [6.113]   [1.862]

   - 58.59 DUM8488•UCZ
    [-.114]

.8620
.315
1.95
54-88

IN9 $IRES72 = 898.98 + .4782\ dYRES72 + .3930\ IRES72_{-1}$
      [1.304]   [1.563]   [2.037]

   + .0218 ML1/PZ - 236.51 UCZ
    [3.177]   [-.311]

.7818
.505
1.60
54-88

IN10 $ITRA72 = 455.61 + .8549\ dYTRA72 + .5194\ ITRA72_{-1} + .0238\ ML1/PZ$
       [.889] [2.661]   [3.700]   [2.739]

   - 284.40 UCAZ + .2767 OILUSSR/PZ
    [-.304]   [1.133]

.9308
0
1.93
54-88

	Equation	RBARSQ RHO DW
No.	Specification with Student-t Values	Years

IN11 $IHOU72 = 16088.7 + 1672.7\ DUM88 + 1.5427\ YRES72 - .0508\ KRES72_{-1}$
            [5.415]   [1.141]   [2.729]   [-1.654]

    $+ .0226\ ML1/PZ - .0511\ HOMEAREA_{-1} + .2006\ EXFSR_{-1}$
      [1.975]   [-2.077]   [2.375]

    $+ 1.7464\ [d(FCREDIT)/IMPTP]_{-1}$
    [1.685]

.6765
.572
1.65
60-88

IN12 $ITOT72 = IIND72 + IAGR72S + IAGR72P + ICAT72 + ICON72$

    $+ IFOR72 + IHAN72 + IHTR72 + ITRA72 + IRES72 + IHOU72$

IN13 $UCAZ = [(FTAX + PITAX + OTAX)/PZ]/KSUM72_{-1} + DRNBY - (dPZ/PZ_{-1})_{-1}$

IN14 $UCZ = [(FTAX + PITAX + OTAX)/PZ]/KSUM72_{-1} + DRNBY - dPZ/PZ_{-1}$

IN15 $KSUM72 = KIND72 + KAGR72S + KAGR72P + KCAT72 + KCON72$

    $+ KFOR72 + KHAN72 + KHTR72 + KRES72 + KTRA72$

IN16 $KIZREAL = Y72 - (C72 \cdot PIPDC)/PZ - (ITOT72 \cdot PIPDI)/PZ - G/PZ$

    $- NETEX72 - DISCY72$

3. CAPACITY OUTPUT

MX1 $\ln(MXIND72/EIND) = -4.3537 + .5943\ \ln(MXY72 - MXIND72)$
                [-14.908] [15.315]

    $+ .2377\ \ln(KIND72_{-1}/EIND)$
    [4.791]

.9952
.904
1.47
53-88

MX2 $\ln MXAGR72S = .0502 + .0148\ TIME + .2374\ \ln EAGRS$
             [.053] [2.355]   [2.041]

    $+ .3117\ \ln KAGR72S_{-1} + .6114\ \ln LANDS$
    [4.364]   [5.088]

.9852
.468
1.82
53-88

	Equation	RBARSQ RHO DW
No.	Specification with Student-t Values	Years

MX3 $\ln MXCAT72$ $= 5.1074 + .3941 \ln KCAT72_{-1}$
 [24.902] [18.308]

.9970
.925
1.26
53-88

MX4 $\ln MXCON72$ $= 4.9190 + .0209 [(IMPTKR/IMPTR) \cdot TIME]_{-1} + .5304 \ln KCON72_{-1}$
 [15.713] [1.091] [13.413]

.9831
.355
1.84
53-88

MX5 $\ln MXFOR72$ $= 5.6882 + 2.684 \ln KFOR72_{-1}$
 [14.930] [5.935]

.9877
.735
1.75
53-88

MX6 $\ln MXHAN72$ $= 4.7314 + .4865 \ln KHAN72_{-1}$
 [16.122] [14.503]

.9950
.939
1.04
53-88

MX7 $\ln MXHTR72$ $= 3.5016 + .7087 \ln KHTR72_{-1}$
 [7.625]   [15.089]

.9913
.904
1.94
53-88

MX8 $\ln MXRES72$ $= -5.5103 + 1.1131 \ln(MXY72 - MXRES72) + .0696 \ln KRES72_{-1}$
 [-7.872]   [14.154] [1.999]

.9946
.925
1.05
53-88

MX9 $MXTRA72$ $= 307.55 + 807.72 \, TIME + .0492 \, KTRA72_{-1}$
 [.646]   [11.722]   [4.120]

.9807
.801
1.38
53-88

MX10 $MXY72$ $= MXIND72 + MXAGR72S + MXAGR72P + MXCAT72 + MXCON72$

$ + MXFOR72 + MXHAN72 + MXHTR72 + MXRES72 + MXTRA72$

	Equation	RBARSQ RHO DW Years

No.	Specification with Student-t Values	

4. PRODUCTION

YA1 YIND72 = -1.5724 TIME•(MXIND72/100) + .8201 MXIND72
  [-7.787]   [8.721]

  + .0001 DEMD72•(MXIND72/100) + 8.5247 (PIND/PZ)•(MXIND72/100)
  [5.308]   [2.199]

  + 45.28 (IMPTIR/Y72)•(MXIND72/100)
  [1.841]

.9861
.745
1.76
53-88

YA2 YAGR72S = -15.23 DUM5357•(MXAGR72S/100) + .3926 MXAGR72S
  [-2.033]   [2.076]

  + .00005 DEMD72•(MXAGR72S/100)
  [3.545]

  + 23.01 (PIPDAGRS/PZ)•(MXAGR72S/100)
  [1.467]

  + 1640.4 (WHEAJUG + MAIZJUG)/(LANDS + LANDP)
  [4.021]

.9956
0
1.92
53-88

YA3 YAGR72P = 10.01 DUM55•(MXAGR72P/100) - 1.4978 TIME•(MXAGR72P/100)
  [2.649]   [-7.815]

  + .7092 MXAGR72P + .00005 DEMD72$_{-1}$•(MXAGR72P/100)
  [31.117]   [2.785]

  + 33.06 [(WHEAJUG + MAIZJUG)/(LANDS + LANDP)]•(MXAGR72P/100)
  [9.985]

.9736
0
1.79
53-88

YA4 YCAT72 = -1.8088 TIME•(MXCAT72/100) + .8105 MXCAT72
  [-4.763]   [10.871]

  + .0008 (CFOOD72 + CBEVER72)•(MXCAT72/100)
  [4.064]

.9383
.617
1.65
53-88

	RBARSQ
Equation	RHO
	DW
No. Specification with Student-t Values	Years

YA5 YCON72 = -.6069 TIME•(MXCON72/100) +.3635 MXCON72
             [-3.311]   [4.303]

+ 1.7774 (ITOT72/Y72)•MXCON72 +11.49 (PIPDCON/PZ)•(MXCON72/100)
  [8.088]   [1.302]

+.0003 EXNFSR•(MXCON72/100)
[2.295]

.9825
.469
2.09
53-88

YA6 YFOR72 = -.7727 TIME•(MXFOR72/100) +.8267 MXFOR72
             [-1.598]   [16.736]

+.0001 DEMD72•(MXFOR72/100)
[1.926]

.7614
.567
1.78
53-88

YA7 YHAN72 = -1.8410 TIME•(MXHAN72/100) + 1.0004 MXHAN72
             [-5.059]   [12.549]

+.0001 DEMD72•(MXHAN72/100)
[3.326]

.8994
.763
1.23
53-88

YA8 YHTR72 = -2.6609 TIME•(MXHTR72/100)
             [-12.095]

+.9200 MXHTR72 +.0002 DEMD72•(MXHTR72/100)
 [12.804]   [7.371]

+ 10.73 (PIPDHTR/PZ)•(MXHTR72/100)
  [1.332]

.9838
.542
1.67
53-88

YA9 YRES72 = -2.8994 TIME•(MXRES72/100) +.9875 MXRES72
             [-13.041]   [19.062]

+.0002 DEMD72•(MXRES72/100)
[8.228]

.9809
.564
1.73
53-88

YA10 YTRA72 = -1.4528 TIME•(MXTRA72/100) +.7762 MXTRA72
              [-4.912]   [14.546]

+.00004 DEMD72•(MXTRA72/100) +.4648 OECDA•(MXTRA72/100)
 [2.033]   [3.443]

.9919
.467
1.71
53-88

	RBARSQ
Equation	RHO
	DW
No. Specification with Student-t Values	Years

YA11 $Y72$ = $YIND72$ + $YAGR72S$ + $YAGR72P$ + $YCAT72$ + $YCON72$ + $YFOR72$

       + $YHAN72$ + $YHTR72$ + $YRES72$ + $YTRA72$

YA12 $YSTAR72$ = $Y72$ + $GWS72$ + $DNON/P$

YA13 Y = $PZ \cdot Y72$ + $KIFICT$

---

5. LABOR

LB1 $EIND$ = 71.88 - 75.15 $REFORMA_{-1}$ - $.0024$ $IIND72_{-1}$ + $.0007$ $DEMD72$ .9991
         [4.720] [-6.384]   [-2.003]   [2.281]   0
                                                       1.87
       + $.0006$ $(DEMD72_0$ - $DEMD72)$ + $.9215$ $EIND_{-1}$ 53-88
         [.625]   [21.485]

LB2 $EAGRS$ = 41.17 - $.0261$ $W12AGRS/PIPDC$ + $.0008$ $CFOOD72$ .8888
            [2.424] [-1.724]   [1.767]   .309
                                                       2.13
       + $.0004$ $(CFOOD72_0$ - $CFOOD72)$ + $.7744$ $EAGRS_{-1}$ 54-88
         [.147]   [7.320]

LB3 $EMPCAT$ = 8.2424 - $.0100$ $W12CAT/PIPDC$ + $.0002$ $(C72$ + $EXNFSR)$ .9980
              [1.938]   [-1.381]   [2.189]   .183
                                                       1.97
       + $.0001$ $[(C72$ + $EXNFSR)_0$ - $(C72$ + $EXNFSR)]$ + $.8646$ $EMPCAT_{-1}$ 54-88
         [.855]   [12.975]

LB4 $EMPCON$ = 205.52 - 25.79 $REFORMA$ - $.0758$ $W12CON/PIPDC$ .9809
              [5.533]   [-2.453]   [-2.936]   0
                                                       1.95
       + $.0031$ $ITOT72$ + $.0015$ $(ITOT72_0$ - $ITOT72)$ + $.2734$ $EMPCON_{-1}$ 53-88
         [5.194]   [3.302]   [2.085]

LB5 $EMPHAN$ = 23.26 - $.0131$ $W12HAN/PIPDC$ + $.0001$ $DEMD72$ + $.8250$ $EMPHAN_{-1}$ .9751
              [2.457] [-1.748]   [2.152]   [9.659]   .447
                                                       1.93
                                                      54-88

	Equation	RBARSQ RHO DW
No.	Specification with Student-t Values	Years

LB6 EMPHTR $= 11.18 + .0002$ DEMD72 $+ .8750$ EMPHTR$_{-1}$
        [2.561] [3.186]   [20.856]

.9967
.207
1.95
54-88

LB7 EMPTRA $= 39.42 - .0113$ W12TRA/PIPDC $+ .0003$ DEMD72
        [2.573] [-1.285]   [2.358]

$+ .0001$ (DEMD72$_0$- DEMD72) $+ .7582$ EMPTRA$_{-1}$
    [.337]   [6.424]

.9933
.354
2.09
54-88

LB8 ECOMFIN $= 15.71 - .0133$ [(W12COM $+$ W12FIN)/2]/PIPDC $+ .0002$ DEMD72
         [2.313] [-1.547]   [2.624]

$+ .000001$ (DEMD72$_0$- DEMD72) $+ .8222$ ECOMFIN$_{-1}$
    [.002]   [8.823]

.9946
.106
1.95
54-88

LB9 EMPEDU $= 19.39 + .0003$ GOVC72$_{-1}$ $+ .9265$ EMPEDU$_{-1}$
        [5.647] [1.822]   [32.081]

.9974
.536
2.25
55-88

LB10 EMPHEA $= 121.83 + 8.4779$ REFORMA$_{-1}$ $- .0257$ W12HEA/PIPDC
          [2.477]   [1.501]   [-1.745]

$+ .0260$ CHEALT72 $+ .0216$ (CHEALT72$_0$- CHEALT72)
    [7.304]   [3.786]

.0608
.988
.69
54-88

LB11 EMPSPC $= 59.30 - .0175$ W12SPC/PIPDC $+ .0011$ GOVC72$_{-1}$
          [1.447] [-1.340]   [-1.829]

$+ .0009$ (GOVC72$_0$- GOVC72)$_{-1}$ $+ .6071$ EMPSPC$_{-1}$
    [.697]   [2.381]

.9143
.487
2.00
55-88

LB12 EMPTOT $=$ EIND $+$ EAGRS $+$ EAGRP $+$ EMPCAT $+$ EMPCON $+$ EMPFOR

$+$ EMPHAN $+$ EMPHTR $+$ EMPTRA $+$ ECOMFIN $+$ EMPEDU $+$ EMPHEA

$+$ EMPSPC

LB13 ETOT $=$ EMPTOT $-$ EAGRS $-$ EAGRP $+$ EAGRSS

	Equation	RBARSQ RHO DW
No.	Specification with Student-t Values	Years

LB14 LSTOT = PARRATE•LFORCE

LB15 URATE = (LSTOT - EMPTOT)/LSTOT

LB16 URATEYU = (LSTOT - EMPTOT)/ETOT

---

6. INTERNATIONAL ACTIVITY

IA1 EXPTNSR = -3207.9 - 2030.8 DUM61 + 8490.8 DUM8788 - 86.10 KIND72/EIND
 [-2.956] [-1.932] [8.754] [-4.655]

  + 453.33 OECDA + 2.9407 (dFCREDIT)/IMPTP - .3716 dEXPTSR
  [11.916] [3.634] [-3.841]

  + 63.16 PRELIND + 42.11 PRELIND$_{-1}$ + 21.05 PRELIND$_{-2}$
  [2.535] [2.535] [2.535]

.9884
0
1.89
55-88

IA2 EXPTSR = -2452.6 - 2987.5 NOTRADE + 3157.6 DUM65 - 4389.3 DUM7778
 [-4.910] [-.834] [3.722] [-5.612]

  + 4891.1 DUM85 + .1693 dYIND72 + .0514 KIZREAL$_{-1}$ + .0226 ML1/PZ
  [5.291] [2.188] [2.306] [2.332]

  + (.2354 - .2079 DUM79)•EXNFSR + .4819 EXPTSR$_{-1}$ + 799.89 PML3REL
  [4.533] [-4.268] [7.933] [4.458]

  + 533.26 PML3REL$_{-1}$ + 266.63 PML3REL$_{-2}$
  [4.458] [4.458]

.9902
0
1.70
55-88

IA3 EXNFSR = 629.97 + .2113 NIGHTF + 3.98 (dFCREDIT)/IMPTP
 [1.572] [5.384] [5.228]

  + 44.95 {100•ln[(EXTRANS/TRASEA)/(EXTRANS/TRASEA)$_{-1}$]}
  [2.723]

  + .5210 EXNFSR$_{-1}$ - 10.51 [100•ln(PREXZ/PREXZ$_{-1}$)]
  [6.496] [-.708]

.9798
-.255
2.02
54-88

Equation	RBARSQ RHO DW Years
No. Specification with Student-t Values	

IA4 $\ln\text{IMPTIR}$ = 5.4213 + 1.2816 $\ln(\text{YIND72}_{-1}/\text{Y72}_{-1})$
     [3.757]   [4.273]

.9918
0
2.18
53-88

- .0240 $[\text{PRE65} \cdot \ln(\text{YAGR72S} + \text{YAGR72P})]_{-1}$
[-3.262]

- .5696 $\text{KIZREAL}_{-1}/\text{Y72}_{-1}$ - .2977 ITAXAER
[-1.187]   [-1.806]

+ .4250 $\ln(\text{FCREDIT}/\text{FCREDIT}_{-1})$ + .5185 $\ln\text{EXPTNSR}_{-1}$
[2.581]   [4.022]

- .0271 $\text{DUM8788} \cdot \ln\text{EXFSR}$ + .2143 $\ln\text{EXFSR}_{-1}$ - .2429 $\ln\text{PRELIND}$
[-4.061]   [6.526]   [-3.424]

IA5 IMPTKR = -1093.8 - 2644.2 DUM63 + 4172.1 DUM75 + .2513 dITOT72
        [-2.350]   [-3.264]   [4.530]   [7.088]

.9780
0
2.08
54-88

+ .0290 DEMD72_{-1} - 205.00 TIME$\cdot$ITAXAER + 5.8325 (dFCREDIT)/IMPTP
[3.810]   [-1.390]   [8.010]

+ .2279 EXPTNSR_{-1} - .2256 $(\text{dIMPTIR})_{-1}$ - 105.58 PRELIND
[4.382]   [-4.501]   [-3.049]

IA6 IMPTCR = -1807.1 + 1830.9 REFORMA - .0587 Y72
        [-2.158]   [4.649]   [-5.428]

.8519
0
1.91
54-88

- .0705 $[\text{d}(\text{YAGR72S} + \text{YAGR72P})]_{-1}$ + 103.36 KIND72/EIND
[-2.496]   [4.559]

- 535.00 ITAXAER + .0480 FB/[IMPTP$\cdot$(ERSTAT/17)]
[-.488]   [2.126]

+ .2460 EXPTNSR + .1841 IMPTCR_{-1} - 95.26 PRELC
[5.931]   [1.692]   [-2.648]

IA7 BPMTRAR = -3330.8 + 752.39 DUM76 + .4466 CET72
         [-3.803]   [3.611]   [5.022]

.9832
0
1.99
53-88

- 600.77 ITRA72/YTRA72 + 37.50 CUTRA72_{-1}
[-1.072]   [3.859]

+ .0116 (EXPTR + IMPTR) - 21.76 PRELIND
[2.143]   [-3.319]

	Equation	RBARSQ RHO DW
No.	Specification with Student-t Values	Years

IA8 BPMINTER $= [1.2847 - 1.7686$ DUM57 $+ 1.1662$ DUM6466 $\quad\quad\quad$ .9133
$\quad\quad\quad\quad\quad\quad$ $[2.798]$ $\quad$ $[-2.490]$ $\quad\quad\quad$ $[2.572]$ $\quad\quad\quad\quad\quad\quad\quad\quad$ 0
$\quad\quad\quad\quad\quad\quad\quad\quad\quad\quad\quad\quad\quad\quad\quad\quad\quad\quad\quad\quad\quad\quad\quad\quad\quad\quad$ 1.94

$\quad\quad + .4810$ $(100 \cdot$ BPMINTER$_{-1}$/FCREDIT$_{-2}) + .0337$ $(100 \cdot$ dEXPTNSR/EXPTNSR$_{-1})_{-1}$ $\quad$ 54-88
$\quad\quad\quad$ $[4.955]$ $\quad\quad\quad\quad\quad\quad\quad\quad\quad\quad\quad\quad\quad$ $[2.987]$

$\quad\quad + .1217$ DUM80S$\cdot$USTBILL $+ .2553$ USTBILL$_{-1}]\cdot$(FCREDIT$_{-1}$/100)
$\quad\quad\quad$ $[2.453]$ $\quad\quad\quad\quad\quad\quad\quad$ $[3.167]$

IA9 EXPTR $=$ EXPTNSR $+$ EXPTSR

IA10 EXGNFSR $=$ EXPTR $+$ EXNFSR

IA11 IMPTR $=$ IMPTIR $+$ IMPTKR $+$ IMPTCR

IA12 IMNFSR $=$ BPMTRAR $+$ BPMSROTR $+$ (BPMRMTOR $+$ DISCIMNF)

IA13 IMGNFSR $=$ IMPTR $+$ IMNFSR

IA14 NETEX72 $=$ EXGNFSR - IMGNFSR

IA15 FORTRAN $=$ [BPMINTER $+$ (BPMTROT - BPXINTER)]$\cdot$ERSTAT

IA16 FB $=$ -BPCABL $\cdot$ERSTAT $+$ DISCFB

IA17 PREXZ $= 17 \cdot$PZ/(DINDOAV$\cdot$EXPTP)

IA18 PRELC $=$ DINDOAV$\cdot$IMPTP/PIPDC

IA19 PRELIND $=$ DINDOAV$\cdot$IMPTP/PIND

IA20 PML3REL $=$ (PML3/100)/IMPTP

	RBARSQ
Equation	RHO
	DW
No. Specification with Student-t Values	Years

7. WAGES

WG1 $dW12IND/W12IND_{-1}$ = .0526 + .1614 REFORM + .2191 DUM54 - .1374 DUM56

                [3.995] [4.190]   [3.903]   [-2.497]

    + .2859 DUM59 + .2730 DUM86 + .8428 $dCPI/CPI_{-1}$

     [5.261]   [4.926]   [30.880]

    + .2407 $(dCPI/CPI_{-1} - dW12IND/W12IND_{-1})_{-1}$ + .0065 dCUIND72

     [2.553]   [1.683]

.9774 / 0 / 1.75 / 54-88

WG2 $dW12AGRS/W12AGRS_{-1}$ = -.2271 + .2159 REFORM + .0798 $dQAGRS/QAGRS_{-1}$

                 [-1.911] [4.843]   [.924]

    + .0160 ln$(KAGR72S_{-1} \cdot IMPTIR)$ + .0894 $dCUAGR72S/CUAGR72S_{-1}$

     [2.563]   [.640]

    + .5213 dPZ/PZ_{-1} + .2669 DUM8488$\cdot$$dML1/ML1_{-1}$

     [6.181]   [3.816]

.9720 / -.390 / 2.00 / 53-88

WG3 $dW12CAT/W12CAT_{-1}$ = .0680 + .2018 DUM54 - .1255 DUM56

               [3.697] [2.558]   [-1.573]

    - .2647 DUM60 + .2321 DUM86 + .8451 $dCPI/CPI_{-1}$

     [-3.381]   [2.821]   [22.776]

    + .1705 $(dCPI/CPI_{-1} - dW12CAT/W12CAT_{-1})_{-1}$

     [1.270]

.9538 / 0 / 1.53 / 54-88

WG4 $dW12CON/W12CON_{-1}$ = .0677 + .2004 DUM55 + .1078 DUM59

                [4.408] [2.826]   [1.552]

    + .3989 DUM86 + .8073 $dCPI/CPI_{-1}$ + .0372 $(dCPI/CPI_{-1}$

     [5.788]   [25.145]   [.337]

    - $dW12CON/W12CON_{-1})_{-1}$ + .0098 dCUCON72

                     [3.412]

.9624 / 0 / 1.95 / 54-88

	Equation	RBARSQ RHO DW Years
No.	Specification with Student-t Values	

WG5 $dW12FOR/W12FOR_{-1}$ = -.4300 +.2300 REFORM +.0686 $dQFOR/QFOR_{-1}$
$\qquad$ [-1.988] [3.851] $\qquad$ [.265]

$\qquad$ +.0222 $\ln(KFOR72_{-1} \cdot IMPTIR)$ +.0015 $CUFOR72_{-1}$ +.4241 dPZ/PZ_{-1}
$\qquad$ [1.873] $\qquad$ [.532] $\qquad$ [4.543]

$\qquad$ +.3585 $DUM8488 \cdot dML1/ML1_{-1}$
$\qquad$ [4.697]

.9615
-.320
2.27
53-88

WG6 $dW12HAN/W12HAN_{-1}$ = .0552 +.2978 REFORM - .2095 DUM61
$\qquad$ [3.137] [3.577] $\qquad$ [-2.513]

$\qquad$ +.3971 DUM86 +.8800 $dCPI/CPI_{-1}$ +.1756 $(dCPI/CPI_{-1}$
$\qquad$ [4.421] $\qquad$ [22.748] $\qquad$ [1.232]

$\qquad$ - $dW12HAN/W12HAN_{-1})_{-1}$ +.0191 dCUHAN72
$\qquad$ [3.574]

.9555
0
2.12
54-88

WG7 $dW12HTR/W12HTR$ = .0620 +.1328 REFORM +.2016 DUM54
$\qquad$ [3.254] [2.303] $\qquad$ [2.480]

$\qquad$ - .2617 DUM56 +.3215 DUM86 +.8624 $dCPI/CPI_{-1}$
$\qquad$ [-3.230] $\qquad$ [3.842] $\qquad$ [20.587]

$\qquad$ +.1195 $(dCPI/CPI_{-1}$ - $dW12HTR/W12HTR_{-1})_{-1}$ +.0094 dCUHTR72
$\qquad$ [1.000] $\qquad$ [2.418]

.9519
0
1.93
54-88

WG8 $dW12RES/W12RES_{-1}$ = -.4421 +.2859 REFORM +.0366 $dQRES/QRES_{-1}$
$\qquad$ [-2.509] [5.425] $\qquad$ [.195]

$\qquad$ +.0263 $\ln(KRES72_{-1} \cdot IMPTIR)$ +.3979 dPZ/PZ_{-1} +.3719 $DUM8488 \cdot dML1/ML1_{-1}$
$\qquad$ [3.025] $\qquad$ [5.553] $\qquad$ [6.499]

.9603
0
1.98
53-88

WG9 $dW12TRA/W12TRA_{-1}$ = .0552 +.1234 REFORM +.2784 DUM54 +.1881 DUM56
$\qquad$ [3.699] [2.565] $\qquad$ [4.120] $\qquad$ [2.799]

$\qquad$ - .0978 DUM80 +.2510 DUM86 +.8420 $dCPI/CPI_{-1}$
$\qquad$ [-1.462] $\qquad$ [3.612] $\qquad$ [27.463]

.9631
0
1.60
54-88

WG10 $\ln W12EDU$ = .8327 +.0480 DUM57 - .1461 DUM59 +1.0005 $\ln W12IND$
$\qquad$ [4.664] [1.527] $\qquad$ [-4.655] $\qquad$ [112.950]

$\qquad$ +.4536 $\ln (GWS/TOTTAX)$
$\qquad$ [3.623]

.9972
.737
1.86
55-88

	Equation	RBARSQ RHO DW
No.	Specification with Student-t Values	Years

WG11 ln W12HEA = .7207 + .0774 DUM57 - .0975 DUM59 + .9970 ln W12IND
$\qquad$ [4.835] [2.706] $\qquad$ [-3.412] $\qquad$ [152.330]

$\qquad$ + .4024 ln (GWS/TOTTAX)
$\qquad$ [3.685]

.9984
.646
1.65
55-88

WG12 ln W12SPC = .6412 - .1719 DUM59 + .9985 lnW12IND + .2937 ln(GWS/TOTTAX)
$\qquad$ [2.887] [-3.836] $\qquad$ [109.110] $\qquad$ [1.771]

.9972
.587
1.60
55-88

---

8. PRICES

PR1 dPIPDIND/PIPDIND$_{-1}$ = 1.2526 - .3022 REFORM - .5886 DUM86
$\qquad$ [2.180] [-3.852] $\qquad$ [-5.433]

$\qquad$ + .3995 (dW12IND/W12IND$_{-1}$ - dQIND/QIND$_{-1}$)
$\qquad$ [2.964]

$\qquad$ - .0141 CUIND72$_{-1}$ + 2.7885 (KIFICT/Y)$_{-1}$
$\qquad$ [-2.432] $\qquad$ [7.922]

$\qquad$ + .0892 d(DIND/YIND72)/(DIND/YIND72)$_{-1}$
$\qquad$ [1.472]

$\qquad$ + (.1456 - .2145 DUM8384) d[DINDOAV•IMPTP•(IMPTIR/YIND72)]
$\qquad$ [2.105] [-2.284]

/[DINDOAV•IMPTP•(IMPTIR/YIND72)]$_{-1}$

$\qquad$ + .1096 dML1/ML1$_{-1}$ + .0548 (dML1/ML1$_{-1}$)$_{-1}$
$\qquad$ [1.581] $\qquad$ [1.581]

.9769
0
1.95
55-88

PR2 dPIPDAGRS/PIPDAGRS$_{-1}$ = -.2979 - .2288 REFORM
$\qquad$ [-1.356] [-3.730]

$\qquad$ + .4393 (dW12AGRS/W12AGRS$_{-1}$ - dQAGRS/QAGRS$_{-1}$) + .0029 CUAGR72S
$\qquad$ [7.097] $\qquad$ [1.212]

$\qquad$ + .2845 d(DINDOAV•IMPTP)/(DINDOAV•IMPTP)$_{-1}$ + .3127 dML1/ML1$_{-1}$
$\qquad$ [6.519] $\qquad$ [5.852]

.9755
-.551
1.90
53-88

		RBARSQ RHO DW Years
No.	Equation — Specification with Student-t Values	

PR3 $dPIPDAGRP/PIPDAGRP_{-1}$ = .4348 + .3488 DUM86
                    [1.540] [3.221]

  + .2661 $[d(WINKIND/EAGRP)/(WINKIND/EAGRP)_{-1} - dQAGRP/QAGRP_{-1}]$
     [3.006]

  - .0075 CUAGR72P + .2515 $[CFOOD72/(YAGR72S + YAGR72P)]_{-1}$
     [-2.124]   [1.810]

  + .2430 $d(DINDOAV \cdot IMPTP)/(DINDOAV \cdot IMPTP)_{-1}$
     [4.801]

  + .1327 $dML1/ML1_{-1}$ + .0664 $(dML1/ML1_{-1})_{-1}$
     [2.260]   [2.260]

                                                          .9414 / 0 / 1.83 / 55-88

PR4 $dPIPDCAT/PIPDCAT_{-1}$ = -.1316 + .5896 DUM56 + .3119 DUM58
                    [-3.496] [4.636]   [2.422]

  + .2837 DUM61 + .7589 $(dW12CAT/W12CAT_{-1} - dQCAT/QCAT_{-1})$
     [1.962]   [5.600]

  + .0024 $(dCUCAT72)_{-1}$ + .1028 $(KIFICT/KI)_{-1}$ - .2453 $(KIZ/Y72)_{-1}$
     [.539]   [2.239]   [-3.389]

  + .1619 $d(DINDOAV \cdot IMPTP)/(DINDOAV \cdot IMPTP)_{-1}$
     [2.503]

  + .2880 $dML1/ML1_{-1}$ + .1440 $(dML1/ML1_{-1})_{-1}$
     [3.023]   [3.023]

                                                           .9320 / 0 / 2.19 / 55-88

PR5 $dPIPDCON/PIPDCON_{-1}$ = -.0444 - .0651 REFORM
                    [-.265]   [-.803]

  + .7494 $(dW12CON/W12CON_{-1} - dQCON/QCON_{-1})$ + .0005 CUCON72
     [5.930]   [.278]

  + .1014 $d(DINDOAV \cdot IMPTP)/(DINDOAV \cdot IMPTP)_{-1}$ + .1000 $dML1/ML1_{-1}$
     [1.857]   [1.164]

                                                           .9462 / -.611 / 1.98 / 53-88

	Equation	RBARSQ RHO DW
No.	Specification with Student-t Values	Years

PR6 $dPIPDFOR/PIPDFOR_{-1}$ = .0181 - .2109 REFORM
  [.817] [-2.760]

  +.8358 $(dW12FOR/W12FOR_{-1} - dQFOR/QFOR_{-1})$
  [8.055]

  +.1311 $d(DINDOAV \cdot IMPTP)/(DINDOAV \cdot IMPTP)_{-1}$ +.0367 $dML1/ML1_{-1}$
  [2.388]   [.575]

.9583
0
2.02
61-88

PR7 $dPIPDHAN/PIPDHAN_{-1}$ = -.0114 - .2871 REFORM
  [-.371] [-2.626]

  +.8173 $(dW12HAN/W12HAN_{-1} - dQHAN/QHAN_{-1})$ +.2119 $dML1/ML1_{-1}$
  [7.561]   [2.334]

.8824
0
2.07
53-88

PR8 $dPIPDHTR/PIPDHTR_{-1}$ = -.0680 + .7136 DUM56 - .2380 DUM57
  [-1.804]   [6.188]   [-1.891]

  +.5844 $(dW12HTR/W12HTR_{-1} - dQHTR/QHTR_{-1})$
  [3.767]

  +.1046 $(KIFICT/KI)_{-1}$ - .0464 $(KIZ/Y72)_{-1}$
  [2.411]   [-.725]

  +.2104 $d(DINDOAV \cdot IMPTP)/(DINDOAV \cdot IMPTP)_{-1}$
  [3.225]

  +.1223 $dML1/ML1_{-1}$ +.0816 $(dML1/ML1_{-1})_{-1}$ +.0408 $(dML1/ML1_{-1})_{-2}$
  [1.502]   [1.502]   [1.502]

.9329
0
1.91
55-88

PR9 PIPDRES = -.4587 +.1301 $(YIND72/YRES72) \cdot PIPDIND$
  [-2.416] [398.950]

.9998
-.626
2.16
61-88

	Equation	RBARSQ RHO
No.	Specification with Student-t Values	DW Years

PR10 $dPIPDTRA/PIPDTRA_{-1}$ = -.0091 - .3172 REFORM
    [-.440] [-3.794]

    + .6303 $(dW12TRA/W12TRA_{-1} - dQTRA/QTRA_{-1})$
    [6.185]

    + .9953 $dCUTRA72/CUTRA72_{-1}$
    [2.071]

    + .2073 $d(DINDOAV \bullet IMPTP)/(DINDOAV \bullet IMPTP)_{-1}$ + .1196 $dML1/ML1_{-1}$
    [3.711]   [1.859]

.9382
0
1.70
53-88

PR11 PZ = $(YIND72/Y72) \bullet PIPDIND$ + $(YAGR72S/Y72) \bullet PIPDAGRS$

    + $(YAGR72P/Y72) \bullet PIPDAGRP$ + $(YCAT72/Y72) \bullet PIPDCAT$

    + $(YCON72/Y72) \bullet PIPDCON$ + $(YFOR72/Y72) \bullet PIPDFOR$

    + $(YHAN72/Y72) \bullet PIPDHAN$ + $(YHTR72/Y72) \bullet PIPDHTR$

    + $(YRES72/Y72) \bullet PIPDRES$ + $(YTRA72/Y72) \bullet PIPDTRA$

PR12 PIPDC = .0021 + .9183 $(CBEVER72/C72T) \bullet PIPDCBEV$
    [1.388] [26.148]

    + .8714 $(CCLOTH72/C72T) \bullet PIPDCCLO$ + 1.0403 $(CET72/C72T) \bullet PIPDCET$
    [8.132]   [11.090]

    + 1.0031 $(CFOOD72/C72T) \bullet PIPDCFOD$ + .9840 $(CFOOTW72/C72T) \bullet PIPDCFWR$
    [78.840]   [14.262]

    + 1.1043 $(CFURN72/C72T) \bullet PIPDCFUR$ + .9305 $(CHEALT72/C72T) \bullet PIPDCHEL$
    [20.590]   [7.853]

    + 1.0634 $(CHELMA72/C72T) \bullet PIPDCHLM$ + 1.0281 $(COTHER72/C72T) \bullet PIPDCOTH$
    [14.038]   [26.769]

    + 1.2217 $(CTOBAC72/C72T) \bullet PIPDCTOB$ + .9593 $(CTRANS72/C72T) \bullet PIPDCTRA$
    [12.049]   [35.412]

1.0000
0
1.89
57-88

PR13 lnPIPDI = -.6307 + .0238 TIME + .7347 lnPIPDIND + .1329 lnPIPDCON
    [-3.689] [3.212]   [10.574]   [1.473]

    + .0800 $ln(DINDOAV \bullet IMPTP)$
    [2.166]

.9991
0
2.21
52-88

PR14 P = Y/Y72

	Equation	RBARSQ RHO DW
No.	Specification with Student-t Values	Years

PR15 lnPRETALL = 4.7807 + .6666 lnPZ + .1110 ln(STAX/C72) + .2678 lnPRETALL$_{-1}$
             [6.310]   [6.539]   [2.241]   [2.232]

.9985
.339
2.05
54-88

PR16 lnCPI = .7451 + .1069 lnPZ + .8950 lnPRETALL
         [2.561] [2.471]   [20.440]

.9967
.981
1.67
53-88

PR17 PIND = PIPDIND•DISCPIND

PR18 lnPAGR = -.1459 + .0068 TIME + 1.0248 ln[(PIPDAGRS•YAGR72S
         [-1.923]   [1.626]   [45.909]

    + PIPDAGRP•YAGR72P)/(YAGR72S + YAGR72P)]

.9976
.531
2.25
52-88

---

9. OTHER RELATIONSHIPS

OR1 DEMD72 = C72 + ITOT72 + G72 + GWS72 + NETEX72

OR2 G = P•G72

OR3 GWS = P•GWS72

OR4 GOVC72 = (G + GWS + DNON)/P

OR5 TOTTAX = PITAX + STAX + FTAX + ITAX + (HHTAX + OTAXNONH)

OR6 M1 = M1DOM + M1FOREN

OR7 M1FOREN = DINDOAV•DNBYRES + M1FOREN$_{-1}$

OR8 L1 = TOTTAX + dM1 + FB - G - GWS - DNON - GINTRAN - FORTRAN

OR9 ML1 = M1 + L1

Glossary

Variables are listed alphabetically, with each numeral being interpreted as the letter Z and with an ellipsis (...) being understood as the triple AAA. Accordingly, C72 lists as CZZ, and CU...72 orders as CUAAA72. A subscript 0 of a series name means peak value, whether present or previous.

BOOKSPUB: Newly published books. In units.

BPCABL: Balance of payments: current account balance. In millions of US dollars.

BPMINTER: Balance of payments: interest paid by Yugoslavia. In millions of US dollars.

BPMRMTOR: Balance of payments: travel expenditures and private transfers abroad. In millions of 1972 dinars.

BPMSROTR: Balance of payments: imports of services other than transportation. In millions of 1972 dinars.

BPMTRAR: Balance of payments: expenditures on shipping services. In millions of 1972 dinars.

BPMTROT: Balance of payments: other transfers abroad. In millions of US dollars.

BPXINTER: Balance of payments: interest paid to Yugoslavia. In millions of US dollars.

C...72:   Personal consumption expenditure by product type. Ellipsis refers to BEVER for beverages; CLOTH, clothing; ET, entertainment; FOOD, food; FOOTW, footwear; FURN, furniture; HEALT, health; HELMA, household operation; OTHER, other; TOBAC, tobacco; and TRANS, transportation. In millions of 1972 dinars.

CFOREN72:   Personal consumption expenditure by foreign tourists in Yugoslavia. In millions of 1972 dinars.

CPI: Consumer price index. 1955 = 100.0.

CREDC: Consumer credit at the end of year. In millions of dinars.

CU...72:   Capacity utilization by sector. Ellipsis reads AGR for agriculture (P, private; S, social); CON, construction; HAN, handicraft; HTR, home trade; IND, industry; and TRA, transportation. Measured as the percentage of actual output in capacity output.

C72:   Personal consumption expenditure excluding consumption expenditure by foreign tourists in Yugoslavia. In millions of 1972 dinars.

C72T: Personal consumption expenditure including consumption expenditure by foreign tourists in Yugoslavia. In millions of 1972 dinars.

d: First-difference operator. Thus $dx = x - x_{-1}$, and $(dx)_{-1} = x_{-1} - x_{-2}$.

DEMD72:   Aggregate demand for goods and services. In millions of 1972 dinars.

DIND: Financial depreciation of capital stock in industry. In millions of dinars.

DINDOAV: Exchange rate of the dinar against the US dollar. Annual average in dinars per dollar.

DISC... :   Statistical discrepancy for the series in ellipsis.

DNBYRES: Change in foreign exchange reserves. In millions of US dollars.

DNON: Financial depreciation of capital stock in the nonproductive part of the economy. In millions of dinars.

DRNBY: Discount rate set by the National Bank of Yugoslavia. Proportion.

DUM... :   Dummy variable with units in the inclusive period noted by ellipsis. Zeros otherwise. DUM61 equals one only in 1961. DUM80S has ones from 1980 to 1988 inclusive, whereas DUM8488 has them from 1984 to 1988 inclusive.

DW: Durbin-Watson statistic.

E... :   Employment by sector. Ellipsis signifies AGR for agriculture (P, private; S, social); COMFIN, municipal and financial services; and IND, industry. In thousands of persons.

EAGRSS: Employment in agriculture as officially recorded. In thousands of persons.

EMP... :   Employment by sector. Ellipsis covers CAT for catering; CON, construction; EDU, education; FOR, forestry; HAN, handicraft; HEA, health; HTR, home trade; SPC, sociopolitical communities; and TRA, transportation. In thousands of persons.

EMPTOT: Total employment. In thousands of persons.

ERSTAT: Statistical exchange rate of the dinar against the US dollar. In dinars per dollar.

ETOT: Total employment as officially recorded. In thousands of persons.

EXFSR: Exports of factor services. In millions of 1972 dinars.

EXGNFSR: Exports of goods and nonfactor services. In millions of 1972 dinars.

EXNFSR: Exports of nonfactor services. In millions of 1972 dinars.

EXPTNSR: Exports of goods to nonsocialist countries. In millions of 1972 dinars.

EXPTP: Dollar price of Yugoslav exports. Index with EXPTP = 1.0 in 1972.

EXPTR: Total goods (merchandise) exports. In millions of 1972 dinars.

EXPTSR: Exports of goods to socialist countries. In millions of 1972 dinars.

EXTRANS: Foreign-exchange revenue of sea transport firms. In millions of dinars.

FB: Foreign borrowing: deficit (+)or surplus (-) on the current account of the balance of payments. In millions of dinars.

FCREDIT: Foreign loans outstanding at end of year. In millions of US dollars.

FORTRAN: Net transfer payments of the government to foreigners. In millions of dinars.

FREMIT: Foreign remittances to Yugoslavia. In millions of dinars.

FTAX: Tax on firms. In millions of dinars.

G: Government purchases. In millions of dinars.

GINTRAN: Government internal transfers. In millions of dinars.

GOVC72: Government consumption. In millions of 1972 dinars.

GWS: Wages and salaries paid to government employees. In millions of dinars.

GWS72: Wages and salaries paid to government employees. In millions of 1972 dinars.

G72: Government purchases. In millions of 1972 dinars.

HHTAX: Tax on households. In millions of dinars.

HOMEAREA: Living space. In thousands of square meters.

I...72: Gross investment in plant and equipment by sector. Ellipsis covers AGR for agriculture (P, private; S, social); CAT, catering; CON, construction; FOR, forestry; HAN, handicraft; HTR, home trade; IND, industry; RES, residual; and TRA, transportation. In millions of 1972 dinars.

IHOU72: Gross investment in housing. In millions of 1972 dinars.

IMGNFSR: Imports of goods and nonfactor services. In millions of 1972 dinars.

IMNFSR: Imports of nonfactor services. In millions of 1972 dinars.

IMPTCR: Imports of consumer goods. In millions of 1972 dinars.

IMPTIR: Imports of intermediate goods. In millions of 1972 dinars.

IMPTKR: Imports of capital goods. In millions of 1972 dinars.

IMPTP: Dollar price of Yugoslav imports. Index with IMPTP = 1.0 in 1972.

IMPTR: Total goods (merchandise) imports. In millions of 1972 dinars.

ITAX: Tax on imports. In millions of dinars.

ITAXAER: Average effective tax rate on imports: import tax expressed in proportion to the value of total imports.

ITOT72: Total gross investment. In millions of 1972 dinars.

K...72: Capital stock by sector as listed for I...72. In millions of 1972 dinars.

KI: Inventory change as officially recorded. In millions of dinars.

KIFICT: Fictitious component of inventory change. In millions of dinars.

KIZ: Inventory change corrected for fictitious movements. In millions of dinars.

KIZREAL: Inventory change corrected for fictitious movements. In millions of 1972 dinars.

KSUM72: Total capital stock. In millions of 1972 dinars.

LANDP: Arable land in private-sector agriculture. In thousands of hectares.

LANDS: Arable land in social-sector agriculture. In thousands of hectares.

LFORCE: Males aged 15-64 and females aged 15-59. In thousands of persons.

LSTOT: Labor supply: employment-eligible individuals who are working or are actively seeking work. In thousands of persons.

L1: Volume of unintended (soft) credit. In millions of dinars.

MAIZJUG: Production of maize throughout Yugoslavia. In thousands of tons.

ML1: Volume of total credit (intended and unintended). In millions of dinars.

MX...72: Capacity (maximum) output by sector as listed for I...72. In millions of 1972 dinars.

MXY72: Total capacity output. In millions of 1972 dinars.

M1: Money supply. In millions of dinars.

M1DOM: Domestically induced portion of the money supply. In millions of dinars.

M1FOREN: Foreign-induced portion of the money supply. In millions of dinars.

NETEX72: Net exports of goods and nonfactor services. In millions of 1972 dinars.

NEWSCIRC: Average circulation of newspapers. In thousands.

NIGHTF: Nights spent in Yugoslavia by foreign tourists. In thousands.

NOTRADE: Dummy variable assuming units for the years of no trade with the Eastern bloc, 1952-55. Zeros otherwise.

OECDA: Industrial production in seven OECD countries. Index with OECDA = 100.0 in 1980.

OILUSSR: Imports of oil from the USSR. In millions of dinars.

OTAX: Other taxes. In millions of dinars.

OTAXNONH: Other taxes on nonhouseholds. In millions of dinars.

P: Official implicit price deflator for social product. P = 1.0 in 1972.

PAGR: Price index for agricultural products. PAGR = 1.0 in 1972.

PARRATE: Labor-force-participation rate. Proportion.

PIND: Price index for industrial products. PIND = 1.0 in 1972.

PIPD... : Implicit price deflator for output by sector as listed for I...72. Deflator PIPD... = 1.0 in 1972.

PIPDC: Implicit price deflator for consumption. PIPDC = 1.0 in 1972.

PIPDC... : Implicit price deflator for consumption by product type. Ellipsis signifies BEV for beverages; CLO, clothing; ET, entertainment; FOD, food; FUR, furniture; FWR, footwear; HEL, health; HLM, household operation; OTH, other; TOB, tobacco; and TRA, transportation. PIPDC... = 1.0 in 1972.

PIPDI: Implicit price deflator for investment in plant and equipment. PIPDI = 1.0 in 1972.

PITAX: Personal income tax. In millions of dinars.

PML3: Dollar price of Yugoslav imports in SITC 3. Index with PML3 = 100.0 in 1972.

PML3REL: Dollar price of SITC 3 imports to Yugoslavia relative to the dollar price of all imports. Proportion.

PRELC: Real exchange rate of the dinar against the US dollar based on the implicit price deflator for consumption, PIPDC.

PRELIND: Real exchange rate of the dinar against the US dollar based on the price index for industrial products, PIND.

PRETALL: Retail price index for all items. PRETALL = 100.0 in 1955.

PREXZ: Real exchange rate of the dinar against the US dollar from the perspective of foreign buyers of Yugoslav exports. Based on PZ.

PRE65: Dummy variable for the period of "less market, more plan." Units from 1952 to 1964; zeros afterward.

PZ: Implicit price deflator for social product corrected for fictitious inventory movements. PZ = 1.0 in 1972.

Q... :   Output per worker (labor productivity) by sector as listed for I...72. In 1972 dinars.

RBARSQ: Coefficient of determination adjusted for degrees of freedom.

REFORM: Dummy variable for the mid-1960s reforms. Units for 1965 and 1966; zeros otherwise.

REFORMA: Alternative dummy variable for the mid-1960s reforms. Units for 1965-67; zeros otherwise.

RHO: First-order autocorrelation coefficient.

SHIFT: Dummy variable for private-sector agricultural investment. Units for 1972-88; zeros otherwise.

SSINC: Social security income. In millions of dinars.

STAX: Sales tax. In millions of dinars.

STAXAER: Average effective tax rate on sales: sales tax expressed in proportion to sales.

TIME: Time, where year 1952 equals one.

TOTTAX: Total tax. In millions of dinars.

TOURTOT: Foreign and domestic tourists in Yugoslavia. In thousands of persons.

TRASEA: Physical volume of sea transport. Index with TRASEA = 100.0 in 1955.

UCAZ: User cost based on lagged inflation. Proportion.

UCZ: User cost based on current inflation. Proportion.

URATE: Unemployment rate based on labor supply. Proportion.

URATEYU: Unemployment rate according to the concept used in Yugoslavia. Proportion.

USTBILL: US Treasury bill rate. In percent.

WHEAJUG: Production of wheat throughout Yugoslavia. In thousands of tons.

WINKIND: In-kind wages of the productive sector. In millions of dinars.

WPROD: Wages in the productive sector. In millions of dinars.

W12... :   Monthly wage per worker by sector. Ellipsis signifies AGRS for social agriculture; CAT, catering; COM, municipal services; CON, construction; EDU, education; FIN, financial services; FOR, forestry; HAN, handicraft; HEA, health; HTR, home trade; IND, industry; RES, residual; SPC, sociopolitical communities; and TRA, transportation. In unit dinars.

Y: Social product excluding government services. In millions of dinars.

Y...72:   Social product by sector as listed for I...72. In millions of 1972 dinars.

YDA72:   Personal disposable income. In millions of 1972 dinars.

YSTAR72:   Social product including government services. In millions of 1972 dinars.

Y72:   Social product excluding government services. In millions of 1972 dinars.

Appendix B

Comparing the Marks

The EIZFSU Mark 4.0 model differs in numerous ways from the Mark 1.0, its chief precursor studied by Gapinski, Škegro, and Zuehlke (1989a, 1989b). Perhaps the major points of departure involve the quality of the underlying data, the sectoral emphasis on the domestic front, the financial indicators on the international front, and the linkages among the separate constructs.

Broadening the Mark 1.0 period of coverage 1952-84 to the period 1952-88, the Mark 4.0 does more than just add observations, because the years inserted were truly tumultuous as inflation broke from a trot into a gallop. Accordingly, the effects of that gallop now fall within the scope of the regression and simulation analyses. Moreover, the Mark 4.0, unlike its predecessor, purges the data of a substantial fiction that resides in the official inventory statistics and that necessarily contaminates the social accounts. To put a numerical face on matters, it might be noted that for the half decade 1984-88, the true inventory change averaged only 11.1 percent of the officially recorded change. The remaining 88.9 percent represented bogus information.

Not without its own sectoral divisions, the Mark 1.0 distinguished among industry, social agriculture, and private agriculture. However, it then grouped everything else into the category "other." By contrast, the Mark 4.0 decomposes this category into seven sectors: catering, construction, forestry, handicraft, home trade, residual, and transportation. But the Mark 4.0 has greater sectoral emphasis not only because it encompasses more sectors but also because it applies the sectoral framework to more facets of the economic order. In particular, it treats wage inflation and price inflation by sector, whereas the Mark 1.0 treated them aggregatively. Along similar lines, the Mark 4.0 divides consumption into 11 product types, a far cry from the single consumption measure of the Mark 1.0.

In its examination of foreign activity, the Mark 4.0 introduces expressions for international payments relating to transportation, debt service, and other services. These balance-of-payments items influence both the import of nonfactor services and the government's interest payments to foreigners. The Mark 1.0, on the other hand, made no reference to the balance of payments.

Formulating linkages among constructs proceeds more aggressively in the Mark 4.0. For instance, each consumption function contains a relative price variable, and relative prices also find their way into the output functions as the Mark 4.0 strengthens the bond between price and quantity. It likewise strengthens the bond between the domestic and international sides of the economy. For the first time, remittances from abroad shape disposable income, and borrowing from abroad governs domestic housing investment. Analogously, Yugoslav exports bear on the output level in construction and on the employment situation in catering. Furthermore, the dinar exchange rate now helps drive price inflation. Going the other way from the domestic setting to the international perspective, the Mark 4.0 uses capacity, consumption, investment, and output to determine the balance of payments. In addition, it draws upon the tax code to explain import flows.

Because the Mark 4.0 and the Mark 1.0 are part of an evolutionary process, they have features in common. Still, given the degree of difference in many of their characteristics, it should be clear that the two paradigms are generations apart.

Bibliography

"All the Party Chief's Men." *Time*, 28 September 1987, 40.

Alt, Christopher; Bopp, Anthony; and Lady, George. "Short Term Forecasts of Energy Supply and Demand." In *Econometric Dimensions of Energy Demand and Supply*, 81-90. Edited by A. Bradley Askin and John Kraft. Lexington, MA: Lexington Books, 1976.

Bailey, Martin J. *National Income and the Price Level.* New York: McGraw-Hill, 1962.

Ball, R. J., and Drake, Pamela S. "The Relationship Between Aggregate Consumption and Wealth." *International Economic Review* 5 (January 1964): 63-81.

Baltagi, Badi H., and Griffin, James M. "Gasoline Demand in the OECD: An Application of Pooling and Testing Procedures." *European Economic Review* 22 (July 1983): 117-37.

Barro, Robert J. "Are Government Bonds Net Wealth?" *Journal of Political Economy* 82 (November/December 1974): 1095-1117.

_____. "The Ricardian Approach to Budget Deficits." *Journal of Economic Perspectives* 3 (Spring 1989): 37-54.

Baumol, William J. "On Some Microeconomic Issues in Inflation Theory." In *Essays in Post-Keynesian Inflation*, 55-78. Edited by James H. Gapinski and Charles E. Rockwood. Cambridge, MA: Ballinger Publishing Company, 1979.

Behrman, Jere R. *Macroeconomic Policy in a Developing Country: The Chilean Experience.* Contributions to Economic Analysis, no. 109. Amsterdam: North-Holland Publishing Company, 1977.

Bennett, James T., and Johnson, Manuel H. *The Political Economy of Federal Government Growth, 1959-1978.* College Station: Texas A&M University, 1980.

Bernheim, B. Douglas. "Ricardian Equivalence: An Evaluation of Theory and Evidence." National Bureau of Economic Research Working Paper, no. 2330, July 1987.

————. "A Neoclassical Perspective on Budget Deficits." *Journal of Economic Perspectives* 3 (Spring 1989): 55-72.

Bonin, John P., and Putterman, Louis. *Economics of Cooperation and the Labor-Managed Economy.* Chur, Switzerland: Harwood Academic Publishers, 1987.

Boyd, Michael L. "The Performance of Private and Cooperative Socialist Organization: Postwar Yugoslav Agriculture." *Review of Economics and Statistics* 69 (May 1987): 205-14.

Bresser Pereira, Luiz. "The Perverse Logic of Stagnation: Debt, Deficit, and Inflation in Brazil." *Journal of Post Keynesian Economics* 12 (Summer 1990): 503-18.

Bresser Pereira, Luiz, and Nakano, Yoshiaki. *The Theory of Inertial Inflation: The Foundation of Economic Reform in Brazil and Argentina.* Boulder: Lynne Rienner Publishers, 1987.

Brewer, Anthony. "Technical Change in Illyria." *Journal of Comparative Economics* 12 (September 1988): 401-15.

Brown, T. M. "Habit Persistence and Lags in Consumer Behaviour." *Econometrica* 20 (July 1952): 355-71.

Bruno, Michael. "Econometrics and the Design of Economic Reform." *Econometrica* 57 (March 1989): 275-306.

Cagan, Phillip. "The Monetary Dynamics of Hyperinflation." In *Studies in the Quantity Theory of Money*, 23-117. Edited by Milton Friedman. Chicago: University of Chicago Press, 1956.

Canterbery, E. Ray. "Tax Reform and Incomes Policy: A VATIP Proposal." *Journal of Post Keynesian Economics* 5 (Spring 1983): 430-39.

Cardoso, Eliana A., and Dornbusch, Rudiger. "Brazil's Tropical Plan." *American Economic Review* 77 (May 1987): 288-92.

Chase Econometrics. "U.S. Macro Model: Structure and Methodology, Equations." Manuscript, Chase Econometrics, January 1983.

Chenery, Hollis B. "Overcapacity and the Acceleration Principle." *Econometrica* 20 (January 1952): 1-28.

Chirinko, Robert S., and Seidman, Laurence S. "The Impact of a Tax-Based Incomes Policy on U.S. Macroeconomic Performance: An Optimal Control Study." *Journal of Policy Modeling* 3 (Spring 1981): 93-105.

Chowdhury, Abdur R.; Grubaugh, Stephen G.; and Stollar, Andrew J. "Money in the Yugoslav Economy." *Journal of Post Keynesian Economics* 12 (Summer 1990): 636-46.

Christofides, L. N., and Wilton, D. A. "Incomes Policy Reconsidered." *Journal of Macroeconomics* 5 (Winter 1983): 119-34.

Colander, David. "Incomes Policies: MIP, WIPP, and TIP." *Journal of Post Keynesian Economics* 1 (Spring 1979a): 91-100.

_____. "Rationality, Expectations and Functional Finance." In *Essays in Post-Keynesian Inflation*, 197-215. Edited by James H. Gapinski and Charles E. Rockwood. Cambridge, MA: Ballinger Publishing Company, 1979b.

Data Resources, Inc. "Operations Overview: Levers, Equations, Program Examples, Retrieval Code Index." Manuscript, Data Resources, Inc., October 1976.

Dildine, Larry L., and Sunley, Emil M. "Administrative Problems of Tax-Based Incomes Policies." *Brookings Papers on Economic Activity*, no. 2 (1978): 363-89.

Domar, Evsey D. "The Soviet Collective Farm as a Producer Cooperative." *American Economic Review* 56 (September 1966): 734-57.

Dornbusch, Rudiger. Foreword to *The Theory of Inertial Inflation*, by Luiz Bresser Pereira and Yoshiaki Nakano. Boulder: Lynne Rienner Publishers, 1987.

Dornbusch, Rudiger, and Simonsen, Mario H. "Inflation Stabilization with Incomes Policy Support: A Review of the Experience in Argentina, Brazil, and Israel." National Bureau of Economic Research Working Paper, no. 2153, February 1987.

Drutter, Izak, and Lacković, Vjekoslav. "Price System and Policy." In *Essays on the Political Economy of Yugoslavia*, 107-19. Edited by Rikard Lang, George Macesich, and Dragomir Vojnić. Zagreb: Informator, 1982.

Dubravčić, Dinko. "Illyrian Theories in Quest of Application." Manuscript, Ekonomski Institut Zagreb, May 1988.

Duesenberry, James S. *Income, Saving and the Theory of Consumer Behavior*. Cambridge, MA: Harvard University Press, 1949.

_____. *Business Cycles and Economic Growth*. New York: McGraw-Hill, 1958.

Eckstein, Otto, and Girola, James A. "Long-Term Properties of the Price-Wage Mechanism in the United States, 1891 to 1977." *Review of Economics and Statistics* 60 (August 1978): 323-33.

Eisner, Robert, and Pieper, Paul J. "A New View of the Federal Debt and Budget Deficits." *American Economic Review* 74 (March 1984): 11-29.

Estrin, Saul. *Self-Management: Economic Theory and Yugoslav Practice*. Cambridge, England: Cambridge University Press, 1983.

Evans, Michael K. *Macroeconomic Activity: Theory, Forecasting, and Control*. New York: Harper and Row, 1969.

Fair, Ray C. "An Evaluation of a Short-Run Forecasting Model." *International Economic Review* 15 (June 1974): 285-303.

Figlewski, Stephen, and Wachtel, Paul. "The Formation of Inflation-
ary Expectations." *Review of Economics and Statistics* 63 (February
1981): 1-10.
Fischer, Stanley. "On Activist Monetary Policy with Rational
Expectations." In *Rational Expectations and Economic Policy*, 211-
35. Edited by Stanley Fischer. Chicago: University of Chicago
Press, 1980.
Ford Foundation. *The Finances of the Performing Arts*. Vol. 1. New
York: Ford Foundation, 1974.
Friedman, Milton. *Essays in Positive Economics*. Chicago: University
of Chicago Press, 1953.
_____. *A Theory of the Consumption Function*. Princeton: Princeton
University Press, 1957.
_____. "What Price Guideposts?" In *Guidelines, Informal Controls,
and the Market Place*, 17-39. Edited by George P. Shultz and Robert
Z. Aliber. Chicago: University of Chicago Press, 1966.
Gapinski, James H. "The Production of Culture." *Review of Econom-
ics and Statistics* 62 (November 1980): 578-86.
_____. "The Economics of Performing Shakespeare." *American
Economic Review* 74 (June 1984): 458-66.
_____. "TIP and Tradition as Tools Against Inflation." *Journal of
Post Keynesian Economics* 8 (Summer 1986): 591-606.
_____. "The Economic Right Triangle of Nonprofit Theatre."
Social Science Quarterly 69 (September 1988): 756-63.
_____. "Investment Fact and Fancy in Yugoslavia." *Applied
Economics* 22 (January 1990a): 45-58.
_____. "Inflation, Unemployment, and Optimal Credit Control:
Economic Reforms in Yugoslavia." *Economic Analysis and Workers'
Management* 24 (1990b): 395-409.
_____. "Inflation and the Real Wage in Yugoslavia." *Economic
Analysis and Workers' Management* 25 (1991): 37-50.
_____. "Output, Expectations, and Surprises." Manuscript, Florida
State University, June 1992a.
_____. "Sectoral Inflation in Yugoslavia." *Journal of Developing
Areas* 27 (October 1992b): 33-47.
_____. "Questions on the Economics of Saving." In *The Economics
of Saving*, 1-45. Edited by James H. Gapinski. Dordrecht: Kluwer
Academic Publishers, 1993.
Gapinski, James H., and Choudhary, Munir A. S. "Effects of Tax-
Based Incomes Policy: A Comparative Analysis." *Kentucky Journal
of Economics and Business* 7 (1986-87): 11-18.
Gapinski, James H.; Škegro, Borislav; and Zuehlke, Thomas W. "A
Model of Yugoslav Economic Performance." *Journal of Comparative
Economics* 13 (March 1989a): 15-46.

_____. *Modeling the Economic Performance of Yugoslavia.* New York: Praeger Publishers, 1989b.

Gedeon, Shirley J. "The Post Keynesian Theory of Money: A Summary and an Eastern European Example." *Journal of Post Keynesian Economics* 8 (Winter 1985-86): 208-21.

Glenny, Misha. "The Massacre of Yugoslavia." *New York Review*, 30 January 1992, 30-35.

Goldman, Marshall I. *What Went Wrong with Perestroika.* Updated ed. New York: W.W. Norton and Company, 1992.

Goodwin, Richard M. "Secular and Cyclical Aspects of the Multiplier and the Accelerator." In *Income, Employment and Public Policy: Essays in Honor of Alvin H. Hansen*, 108-32. New York: W. W. Norton and Company, 1948.

Gordon, David M. "Who Bosses Whom? The Intensity of Supervision and the Discipline of Labor." *American Economic Review* 80 (May 1990): 28-32.

Green, Francis, and Weisskopf, Thomas E. "The Worker Discipline Effect: A Disaggregative Analysis." *Review of Economics and Statistics* 72 (May 1990): 241-49.

Griliches, Zvi. "Productivity Puzzles and R&D: Another Nonexplanation." *Journal of Economic Perspectives* 2 (Fall 1988): 9-21.

Hamilton, F. E. Ian. *Yugoslavia: Patterns of Economic Activity.* New York: Frederick A. Praeger, 1968.

Heilbroner, Robert L. "On the Limited 'Relevance' of Economics." *Public Interest*, no. 21 (Fall 1970): 80-93.

Heller, Walter W. "Is Monetary Policy Being Oversold?" In *Monetary vs. Fiscal Policy*, 13-41. New York: W. W. Norton and Company, 1969.

Hollings, Ernest. "Gramm-Rudman Isn't Working; We Need a Better Alternative." *Tallahassee Democrat*, 3 April 1990, 11A.

Horvat, Branko. *Business Cycles in Yugoslavia.* White Plains: International Arts and Sciences Press, 1971.

_____. "The Theory of the Worker-Managed Firm Revisited." *Journal of Comparative Economics* 10 (March 1986): 9-25.

Houthakker, H. S., and Taylor, Lester D. *Consumer Demand in the United States: Analyses and Projections.* 2nd ed. Cambridge, MA: Harvard University Press, 1970.

Howitt, Peter. "Activist Monetary Policy under Rational Expectations." *Journal of Political Economy* 89 (April 1981): 249-69.

Intriligator, Michael D. *Econometric Models, Techniques, and Applications.* Englewood Cliffs, NJ: Prentice-Hall, 1978.

Ireland, Norman J., and Law, Peter J. *The Economics of Labor-Managed Enterprises.* New York: St. Martin's Press, 1982.

Jonung, Lars, and Laidler, David. "Are Perceptions of Inflation Rational? Some Evidence for Sweden." *American Economic Review* 78 (December 1988): 1080-87.

Kawasaki, Seiichi, and Zimmermann, Klaus F. "Testing the Rationality of Price Expectations for Manufacturing Firms." *Applied Economics* 18 (December 1986): 1335-47.

Kornai, J. "Resource-Constrained Versus Demand-Constrained Systems." *Econometrica* 47 (July 1979): 801-19.

_____. *Economics of Shortage.* Vol. A. Amsterdam: North-Holland Publishing Company, 1980.

_____. "The Soft Budget Constraint." *Kyklos* 39 (1986): 3-30.

Kraft, John; Kraft, Arthur; and Reiser, Eugene. "A National Energy Demand Simulation Model." In *Econometric Dimensions of Energy Demand and Supply*, 9-28. Edited by A. Bradley Askin and John Kraft. Lexington, MA: Lexington Books, 1976.

Leamer, Edward E., and Stern, Robert M. *Quantitative International Economics.* Boston: Allyn and Bacon, 1970.

Leonard, Jonathan S. "Wage Expectations in the Labor Market: Survey Evidence on Rationality." *Review of Economics and Statistics* 64 (February 1982): 157-61.

Lerner, Abba P. *Flation: Not Inflation of Prices, Not Deflation of Jobs.* New York: Quadrangle Books, 1972.

_____. "A Wage-Increase Permit Plan to Stop Inflation." *Brookings Papers on Economic Activity*, no. 2 (1978): 491-505.

_____. "The Market Antiinflation Plan: A Cure for Stagflation." In *Essays in Post-Keynesian Inflation*, 217-29. Edited by James H. Gapinski and Charles E. Rockwood. Cambridge, MA: Ballinger Publishing Company, 1979.

Lerner, Abba P., and Colander, David C. *MAP: A Market Anti-Inflation Plan.* New York: Harcourt Brace Jovanovich, 1980.

Lipsey, Richard G. "The Relation Between Unemployment and the Rate of Change of Money Wage Rates in the United Kingdom, 1862-1957: A Further Analysis." *Economica*, new series, 27 (February 1960): 1-31.

Liu, Ta-Chung, and Hwa, Erh-Cheng. "A Monthly Econometric Model of the U.S. Economy." *International Economic Review* 15 (June 1974): 328-65.

Lovell, Michael C. "Tests of the Rational Expectations Hypothesis." *American Economic Review* 76 (March 1986): 110-24.

Lucas, Robert E., Jr. *Studies in Business-Cycle Theory.* Cambridge, MA: MIT Press, 1981.

Lydall, Harold. *Yugoslav Socialism: Theory and Practice.* Oxford: Clarendon Press, 1984.

_____. *Yugoslavia in Crisis.* Oxford: Clarendon Press, 1989.

Maddison, Angus. "Growth and Slowdown in Advanced Capitalist Economies: Techniques of Quantitative Assessment." *Journal of Economic Literature* 25 (June 1987): 649-98.

March, James G. "Bounded Rationality, Ambiguity, and the Engineering of Choice." *Bell Journal of Economics* 9 (Autumn 1978): 587-608.

Matthews, R. C. O. *The Business Cycle.* Chicago: University of Chicago Press, 1959.

Meade, J. E. "The Theory of Labour-Managed Firms and of Profit Sharing." *Economic Journal,* supplement, 82 (March 1972): 402-29.

Mencinger, Jože. "A Quarterly Macroeconometric Model of the Yugoslav Economy." Ph.D. dissertation, University of Pennsylvania, 1975.

_____. "Acceleration of Inflation into Hyperinflation—The Yugoslav Experience in the 1980's." *Economic Analysis and Workers' Management* 21 (1987): 399-418.

Miyazaki, Hajime, and Neary, Hugh M. "The Illyrian Firm Revisited." *Bell Journal of Economics* 14 (Spring 1983): 259-70.

Modigliani, Franco. "Fluctuations in the Saving-Income Ratio: A Problem in Economic Forecasting." In *Studies in Income and Wealth.* Vol. 11, *Conference on Research in Income and Wealth,* 369-441. New York: National Bureau of Economic Research, 1949.

Muth, John F. "Rational Expectations and the Theory of Price Movements." *Econometrica* 29 (July 1961): 315-35.

O'Driscoll, Gerald P., Jr. "The Ricardian Nonequivalence Theorem." *Journal of Political Economy* 85 (February 1977): 207-11.

Okun, Arthur M. "The Great Stagflation Swamp." *Challenge* 20 (November-December 1977): 6-13.

_____. "Efficient Disinflationary Policies." *American Economic Review* 68 (May 1978): 348-52.

Olson, Mancur, and Clague, Christopher K. "Dissent in Economics: The Convergence of Extremes." *Social Research* 38 (Winter 1971): 751-76.

Orzechowski, William. "Economic Models of Bureaucracy." In *Budgets and Bureaucrats: The Sources of Government Growth,* 229-59. Edited by Thomas E. Borcherding. Durham: Duke University Press, 1977.

Patinkin, Don. *Money, Interest, and Prices.* 2nd ed. New York: Harper and Row, 1965.

Perry, George L. "Wages and the Guideposts." *American Economic Review* 57 (September 1967): 897-904.

Phelps, Edmund S., and Taylor, John B. "Stabilizing Powers of Monetary Policy under Rational Expectations." *Journal of Political Economy* 85 (February 1977): 163-90.

Phillips, A. W. "The Relation Between Unemployment and the Rate of Change of Money Wage Rates in the United Kingdom, 1861-1957." *Economica*, new series, 25 (November 1958): 283-99.

Phillips, Almarin. "An Appraisal of Measures of Capacity." *American Economic Review* 53 (May 1963): 275-92.

Pollock, Richard L., and Suyderhoud, Jack P. "An Empirical Window on Rational Expectations Formation." *Review of Economics and Statistics* 74 (May 1992): 320-24.

Prasnikar, Janez, and Pregl, Zivko. "Economic Development in Yugoslavia in 1990 and Prospects for the Future." *American Economic Review* 81 (May 1991): 191-95.

Ra'anan, Gavriel D. *Yugoslavia After Tito: Scenarios and Implications*. Boulder: Westview Press, 1977.

Rapping, Leonard A. *International Reorganization and American Economic Policy*. New York: New York University Press, 1988.

Rees, Albert. "New Policies to Fight Inflation: Sources of Skepticism." *Brookings Papers on Economic Activity*, no. 2 (1978): 453-77.

Robinson, Joan. "The Soviet Collective Farm as a Producer Cooperative: Comment." *American Economic Review* 57 (March 1967): 222-23.

Rockwood, Charles E. "The Antiinflation Value of Direct Controls." In *Essays in Post-Keynesian Inflation*, 161-77. Edited by James H. Gapinski and Charles E. Rockwood. Cambridge, MA: Ballinger Publishing Company, 1979.

Rusinow, Dennison. *The Yugoslav Experiment, 1948-1974*. Berkeley: University of California Press, 1977.

Sahota, Gian S. "Saving and Distribution." In *The Economics of Saving*, 193-231. Edited by James H. Gapinski. Dordrecht: Kluwer Academic Publishers, 1993.

Sapir, André. "Economic Reform and Migration in Yugoslavia: An Econometric Model." *Journal of Development Economics* 9 (1981): 149-87.

Sargent, Thomas J., and Wallace, Neil. "Rational Expectations and the Theory of Economic Policy." *Journal of Monetary Economics* 2 (1976): 169-83.

Seidman, Laurence S. "A New Approach to the Control of Inflation." *Challenge* 19 (July-August 1976): 39-43.

Shostak, E. "The Natural Rate Hypothesis: An Econometric Test for the South African Economy." *South African Journal of Economics* 49 (March 1981): 1-9.

Simon, Herbert A. *Models of Man*. New York: John Wiley and Sons, 1957.

————. "Rational Decision Making in Business Organizations." *American Economic Review* 69 (September 1979): 493-513.

Simons, Thomas W., Jr. *Eastern Europe in the Postwar World*. New York: St. Martin's Press, 1991.

Škegro, Borislav; Gapinski, James H.; and Anušić, Zoran. "Policy Initiatives for Improving Yugoslav Economic Performance." *International Economic Journal* 3 (Winter 1989): 95-107.

Sraffa, Piero, ed. *The Works and Correspondence of David Ricardo*. Vol. IV, *Pamphlets and Papers, 1815-1823*. Cambridge, England: Cambridge University Press, 1951.

Stanković, Slobodan. *The End of the Tito Era: Yugoslavia's Dilemmas*. Stanford: Hoover Institution Press, 1981.

Steinherr, A., and Thisse, J. F. "Are Labor-Managers Really Perverse?" *Economic Letters* 2 (1979a): 137-42.

_____. "Is There a Negatively-Sloped Supply Curve in the Labour-Managed Firm?" *Economic Analysis and Workers' Management* 13 (1979b): 23-34.

Stipetić, Vladimir. "Agriculture in Yugoslavia: Problems and Prospects." In *Essays on the Political Economy of Yugoslavia*, 327-48. Edited by Rikard Lang, George Macesich, and Dragomir Vojnić. Zagreb: Informator, 1982.

Stockton, David J., and Struckmeyer, Charles S. "Tests of the Specification and Predictive Accuracy of Nonnested Models of Inflation." *Review of Economics and Statistics* 71 (May 1989): 275-83.

Taylor, John B. "Monetary Policy During a Transition to Rational Expectations." *Journal of Political Economy* 83 (October 1975): 1009-21.

Tomaszewski, Jerzy. *The Socialist Regimes of East Central Europe: Their Establishment and Consolidation, 1944-67*. London: Routledge, 1989.

Ture, Norman B. "Tax-Based Incomes Policy: Pain or Pleasure in Pursuit of Price-Level Stability." *Tax Review* 39 (June 1978): 23-30.

Tyson, Laura D'Andrea. "The Yugoslav Inflation: Some Competing Hypotheses." *Journal of Comparative Economics* 1 (June 1977): 113-46.

United Nations. Economic Commission for Latin America and the Caribbean. *The Economic Crisis: Policies for Adjustment, Stabilization and Growth*. Santiago: United Nations, 1986.

van Bergeijk, Peter A. G., and Lensink, Robert. "Trade, Capital, and the Pace of Transition in Central Europe." Manuscript, University of Groningen, February 1990.

Vanek, Jaroslav. *The General Theory of Labor-Managed Market Economies*. Ithaca: Cornell University Press, 1970.

_____. "The Macroeconomic Theory and Policy of an Open Worker-Managed Economy." *Economic Analysis and Workers'*

Management 6 (1972): 255-69.

Wallich, Henry C., and Weintraub, Sidney. "A Tax-Based Incomes Policy." *Journal of Economic Issues* 5 (June 1971): 1-19.

Ward, Benjamin. "The Firm in Illyria: Market Syndicalism." *American Economic Review* 48 (September 1958): 566-89.

Wyzan, Michael L., and Utter, Andrew M. "The Yugoslav Inflation." *Journal of Comparative Economics* 6 (December 1982): 396-405.

Index

About the Author

JAMES H. GAPINSKI is Professor of Economics at Florida State University. He has authored and edited several books, including *Modeling the Economic Performance of Yugoslavia* (with B. Škegro and T. Zuehlke) (Praeger, 1989).